ONLINE TV

With growth in access to high-speed broadband and 4G, and increased ownership of smartphones, tablets and internet-connected television sets, the internet has simultaneously begun to compete with and transform television. *Online TV* argues that these changes create the conditions for an emergent internet era that challenges the language and concepts that we have to talk about television as a medium.

In a wide-ranging analysis, Catherine Johnson sets out a series of conceptual frameworks designed to provide a clearer language with which to analyse the changes to television in the internet era and to bring into focus the power dynamics of the online TV industry.

From providing definitions of online TV and the online TV industry, to examining the ways in which technology, rights, interfaces and algorithms are used to control and constrain access to audiovisual content, *Online TV* is a timely intervention into debates about contemporary internet and television cultures. A must-read for any students, scholars and practitioners who want to understand and analyse the ways in which television is intertwining with and being transformed by the internet.

Catherine Johnson is Professor of Media and Communications at the University of Huddersfield, UK. She is the author of *Promotional Screen Industries* (with Paul Grainge, 2015), *Branding Television* (2012) and *Telefantasy* (2005), and the co-editor of *Transnational Television History* (with Andreas Fickers, 2012) and *ITV Cultures* (with Rob Turnock, 2005).

ONLINE TV

Catherine Johnson

Routledge
Taylor & Francis Group

LONDON AND NEW YORK

First published 2019
by Routledge
2 Park Square, Milton Park, Abingdon, Oxon OX14 4RN

and by Routledge
52 Vanderbilt Avenue, New York, NY 10017

Routledge is an imprint of the Taylor & Francis Group, an informa business

British Library Cataloguing-in-Publication Data
A catalogue record for this book is available from the British Library

Library of Congress Cataloging-in-Publication Data
Names: Johnson, Catherine, 1973- author.
Title: Online TV / Catherine Johnson.
Description: London ; New York : Routledge, 2019. | Includes bibliographical references and index.
Identifiers: LCCN 2018042741 (print) | LCCN 2018053707 (ebook) | ISBN 9781315396828 (ebook) | ISBN 9781138226876 | ISBN 9781138226876 (hardback :alk. paper) | ISBN 9781138226883(paperback :alk. paper) | ISBN 9781315396828(ebk)
Subjects: LCSH: Internet television.
Classification: LCC PN1992.923 (ebook) | LCC PN1992.923 .J64 2019 (print) | DDC 384.550285/4678--dc23
LC record available at https://lccn.loc.gov/2018042741

ISBN: 978-1-138-22687-6 (hbk)
ISBN: 978-1-138-22688-3 (pbk)
ISBN: 978-1-315-39682-8 (ebk)

Typeset in Bembo
by Taylor & Francis Books

MIX
Paper from
responsible sources
FSC
www.fsc.org   FSC® C013056

Printed and bound in Great Britain by
TJ International Ltd, Padstow, Cornwall

For Bruno Johnson

CONTENTS

ILLUSTRATIONS

Figures

Tables

ACKNOWLEDGEMENTS

The original idea for this book came from in-depth discussions with Paul Grainge about potential collaborative research projects. Those conversations helped me to frame the questions that I wanted to ask in this book, and I am deeply grateful to Paul for his generosity in supporting me in taking the project forward as a single-authored monograph. The book was researched and written over a number of years while I was working as an Associate Professor in the Department of Cultural, Media and Visual Studies at the University of Nottingham. I count myself very lucky to have had the opportunity to work in a department with such a fantastic group of colleagues. In particular, Roberta Pearson has been not only a wonderful Head of Department but also a trusted friend who has listened with unending patience to my moans and groans, and has always been there when I needed support. I'd also like to express particular thanks to the members of the Institute for Screen Industries Research at the University of Nottingham (Hongwei Bao, Ian Brookes, Liz Evans, Mark Gallagher, Paul Grainge, Leora Hadas, Daniel Mutibwa, Jack Newsinger, Roberta Pearson, Gianluca Sergi, Alex Simcock, Julian Stringer, Jan-Noel Thon) for their incredibly helpful feedback on the first iteration of this book's definition of online TV. Emily Rees also offered useful comments on an early version of Chapter 1. Finally, the members of the 2017 'sabbatical club' (Liz Evans, Gillian Roberts, Maria Ryan and Katherine Shingler) helped me realise how important the communal eating of cake is to the overall writing process. As I move on to pastures new, I'm going to miss all of you – it is hard to imagine a better bunch of colleagues. Thanks for creating such a warm and supportive environment to work in.

I would not have been able to write this book without a 12-month sabbatical from the University of Nottingham, including six months funded by a Pro-Vice Chancellor's Award. Both my department and the School of Cultures, Languages and Area Studies have also provided me with financial assistance to present work in progress at conferences, where I have received insightful feedback that has helped refine and improve my ideas. Beyond my department, Ansgar Koene and Filippo

Gilardi gave generously of their time to help me understand algorithms and Chinese online TV services respectively. I was also fortunate enough to be invited by Jonathan Gray to a three-day workshop on the future of television at the University of Wisconsin, Madison, where I had the opportunity to discuss all things 'online TV' with a veritable who's who of TV and media studies scholars: Tim Havens, Eric Hoyt, Derek Johnson, Lori Lopez, Jason Lopez, Jeremy Morris, Amanda Lotz and Serra Tinic. Beyond the pleasures of sipping beer in good company on the shores of Lake Mendota, the in-depth discussions over the course of the workshop helped me clarify just what this book was about. Closer to home, Kim Akass and Sian Barber have been hugely supportive in getting me over the finishing line – thanks for your warmth and friendship, and for consistently being able to make me laugh until I cry.

This is the fourth book that I have published with Routledge and I would like to extend my deepest thanks to Natalie Foster, Sheni Kruger, James Askew, Jennifer Vennall and Ruth Berry for their support of the project and for making the whole publishing process so seamless and stress free.

It's hard to write a book without it encroaching into everyday life from time to time, and I'm eternally grateful to my friends and family (you know who you are) for their love, patience and forbearance. Special thanks must go to Rob Turnock, not only for putting up with the multitude of occasions when my mind has been preoccupied with book-writing, but also for reading drafts of the entire manuscript not once, but twice! Rob has the uncanny ability of being able to identify exactly where a chapter or argument is going off the rails, and this would not be the book it is without him.

This book is dedicated to my brother, Bruno Johnson, who has always been somewhat of a trailblazer in our family in exploring the links between television and computing. For many years the television set in his living room has been hooked up to a computer and operated by a wireless mouse and keyboard, exemplifying the integration of television and the internet analysed in this book. Just over a week into the sabbatical dedicated to writing this book, my brother fell ill with a serious and life-threatening illness. As I put the finishing touches to the book, he is coming towards the end of almost 18 months of treatment, thankfully with a positive prognosis. In so many ways, then, this book feels intricately connected with my brother, who has been an inspiration both in terms of his early adoption of online TV and in terms of the incredible bravery and resilience he has shown over the course of his illness. If I can carry just an ounce of that bravery with me going forward, I will be a stronger and better person.

ABBREVIATIONS

3D	3-dimensional
4OD	4 On Demand
ABC	Australian Broadcasting Corporation
AMC	American Movie Classics
AMPTP	Association of Motion Picture and Television Producers
AT&T	American Telephone and Telegraph
ATP	The Association of Tennis Professionals
AVOD	advertising video on demand
AWS	Amazon Web Services
BARB	Broadcasters' Audience Research Board
BAT	Baidu, Alibaba, Tencent
BBC	British Broadcasting Corporation
BIDI	BBC Internet Distribution Infrastructure
BT	British Telecom
CBBC	Children's BBC
CBS	Columbia Broadcasting System
CDN	content distribution network
DRM	digital rights management
DTO	download to own
DVD	digital versatile disc
DVR	digital video recorder
EPG	electronic programme guide
EST	electronic sell through
EU	European Union
FANG	Facebook, Amazon, Netflix, Google
FTSE	Financial Times Stock Exchange
GAFA	Google, Apple, Facebook, Amazon

GUI	graphical user interface
HBO	Home Box Office
HD	high-definition
ID	identification
IMDb	The Internet Movie Database
IP	intellectual property
IPTV	internet protocol television
ISP	internet service provider
IT	information technology
MCN	multichannel network
MVPD	multichannel video programming distributor
NBC	National Broadcasting Company
NFL	National Football League
NRK	Norsk rikskringkasting AS
OS	operating system
OTT	over-the-top
P2P	peer-to-peer
PC	personal computer
PPV	pay-per-view
PVR	personal video recorder
SAPPRFT	State Administration of Press, Publication, Radio, Film and Television
SDK	software development kit
SVD	singular value decomposition
SVOD	subscription video on demand
TVOD	transactional video on demand
UGC	user-generated content
URL	uniform resource locator
USB	universal serial bus
VCR	videocassette recorder
VHS	video home system
VOD	video on demand
VPN	virtual private network
VR	virtual reality
WGA	Writers Guild of America

1

FROM BROADCAST TO ONLINE TV

Introduction

In 2015 the UK media regulator, Ofcom, stated that the 'key enablers of on-demand television are now mass-market' (Ofcom 2015, p.18). Coming almost a decade after the first on-demand player, Channel 4's 4 On Demand (4OD), was launched by a UK broadcaster, this statement spoke to a series of changes to the media landscape in the early 2010s that, this book will argue, demand a reconceptualisation of television as a medium. For Ofcom, the key enablers of on-demand television were threefold: broadband access, ownership of smartphones and tablets, and the roll-out of internet-connected television sets. Although Ofcom was writing specifically about the UK context, this book will argue that these three factors can be understood as the conditions for an emergent **'internet era'** in which television and the internet become indelibly intertwined. This era is characterised by the development of the internet into a medium for accessing audiovisual content at the same time that the technologies for accessing television are connected to the internet. Taken together, this book will argue, these changes are not only driving the development of on-demand services (as Ofcom claims) but are also transforming television into **online TV**: *services that facilitate the viewing of editorially selected audiovisual content through internet-enabled devices.*[1]

Increased broadband access, ownership of smartphones and tablets, and roll-out of internet-connected television sets create the conditions for the development of online TV in a number of ways. Higher levels of broadband access enable the internet to become a ubiquitous part of everyday life. However, for online TV it is the development and uptake of superfast broadband, as well as 4G for out-of-home access, that is particularly significant because it facilitates the streaming and down-loading of audiovisual content that takes up large amounts of bandwidth. Broadband access (and superfast broadband and 4G in particular) is, therefore, a crucial driver in the development of online TV. Meanwhile, rises in smartphone and tablet ownership enable flexible and individualised access to internet-delivered audiovisual content beyond the television set and outside of the home. Smartphones and tablets have effectively become what Peter Rice (Chairman of Walt Disney Television) referred to in 2016 as television sets in your pocket.[2] Smartphones and tablets not only make access to television ubiquitous, they also situate television viewing alongside other forms of mediated activity, such as reading, writing and communicating, enabling users to switch between different applications and tasks all within one device.

If smartphones and tablets turn television into something you can carry with you in your pocket and easily interact with, then internet-connected televisions further blur the boundaries between television and computing technologies, potentially transforming the 'goggle box' in the corner of the living room into a multifaceted site of media entertainment. Darcy Gerbarg and Eli Noam describe internet-connected television as 'the quintessential digital convergence medium, putting together television, telecommunications, the Internet, computer applications, games, and more' (2011, p.xxi). Through internet-connected televisions it is possible to access television programmes and movies on demand, watch an array of content on YouTube, play games, look at photos, chat with friends through social networks and conduct any of the other myriad activities associated with contemporary convergent internet-connected devices.[3]

This book will argue that the internet era represents a distinct phase in the development of television that differs from the earlier broadcast, cable/satellite and digital eras of television. Media periodisations are always contested and depend on the focus of a given study. I have written elsewhere about the value of different models of media periodisation and my own preference for technologically based periodisations for television (Johnson 2012, pp.6–10). There I argued that changes to the technologies used to deliver television provide a useful focus for assessing changes to television as a medium. Television's origins in broadcasting are fundamental to the ways in which television has been studied, regulated, produced and consumed. The growth of cable/satellite technologies in the 1980s and digital technologies in the 1990s challenged foundational assumptions about television as a medium of broadcasting – that it cannot be paid for at the point of reception, that it is a medium of the masses, that it is a national medium. The internet era that emerged in the 2010s represents a further shift in the way that **television services** are delivered to audiences that, once again, challenges normative definitions of television as a medium.

My concern here in particular with the technologies used to *deliver* television is important, because it is only since the early 2010s that the internet has started to have a significant impact on the delivery of television programming. As I shall examine in more detail below, from the 1990s television companies began developing and using websites to engage their audiences beyond the television set. In this period, the internet was largely understood as a separate medium to television; a medium that required its own distinct forms of content, from websites and blogs to experiments in interactive, multiplatform and transmedia storytelling. What changed around 2010, however, was *the increased ubiquity of the internet as a means of delivering television programming and other audiovisual content to audiences*, facilitated by the rise of superfast broadband and 4G, adoption of tablets and smartphones, and increased ownership of internet-connected television sets. It is the consequences of this emergence of the internet as a mainstream means of distributing audiovisual content that is the focus of this book. As the internet simultaneously intertwines with and competes with television as a means of providing viewing experiences, it becomes harder to conceptualise television as a medium distinct from the internet. Therefore, this book asks: how do we conceptualise television as a medium in a period in which the internet and television compete and converge in the delivery of audiovisual content?[4]

It is worth stating at the outset that while widespread, such changes are not uniform around the world. As Jinna Tay and Graeme Turner (2008, p.72) have argued, we need to pay attention to the uneven nature of television's development in different national and regional contexts as the media landscape has become more complex. Elizabeth Evans et al. point to a series of factors that shape the (uneven) development of online viewing in different geographic contexts, arguing that 'Differences in network coverage, broadband access and speed, levels of device ownership, corporate strategies and IT Internet policy or media regulation all contribute towards setting the contextual parameters of online viewing' (2016, pp.410–1). In countries where internet and/or television infrastructure is less developed or only accessible to those with disposable income in urban centres, the development of television plays out differently from the Western contexts of Europe, Australasia and Northern America that have dominated television studies. Evans et al. and Tay and Turner caution against making generalised claims about television when the changes to television infrastructure, technology, industry and policy are so variable around the globe. Indeed, Tay and Turner argue that 'We can no longer talk about "television" as if it were a singular entity if we are to adequately understand the social, cultural and political functions of the media today' (2008, p.72).

Therefore, it is important to remember that while the rise of online TV can be traced around the globe it is not universal and emerges primarily in economies with developed **technological infrastructures** and/or amongst segments of the population with access to the disposable income and technologies required to access internet-connected television services. The primary examples throughout this book are drawn from the UK context in which, as the quote from Ofcom that opened this book indicates, fulfils the three conditions that characterise the internet era.[5] The focus on the UK in this book stems partly from the time constraints of writing a book about such a fast-moving media landscape and partly in order to rebalance the US-centrism of current scholarship about online TV (Landau 2016; Lotz 2016; Robinson 2017; Wolk 2015). However, in researching this book my aim has been to draw on as wide a range of secondary literature as possible, including work from scholars in Asia and Latin America, as well as in Europe, Australasia and North America. This book also works to develop theorisations that can be adapted to any regional or national context, beginning, in this chapter, with a conceptual framework for tracing change and continuity to television as a medium over time. Although the book draws primarily on the Western context, this conceptual framework is designed to be flexible enough to be adapted to different regional or national contexts and, specifically, to facilitate comparative analysis in order to enhance understanding of the varied and uneven ways in which changes to television are enacted around the world.

The work of scholars such as Tay and Turner speaks to a broader difficulty in conceptualising television, a medium that Joshua Green describes as a 'leaky object that both aspires to, or borrows from, other media' (2008, p.96). Although there has been much academic attention on the transformation of television by digital technologies (see, for example, Bennett & Strange 2011; Jenner 2016; Meikle & Young 2008; McDonald & Smith-Rowsey 2016; Spigel & Olsson 2004), over its long history television has undergone seemingly continuous technological and cultural transformation. William Uricchio has written that,

> Television's ongoing change seems endless – from tubes, to transistors, to chips; from cathode ray displays, to plasma, to projection; from broadcast, to cable, to Internet streaming; from dial-up, to remote control, to algorithmic recommendation; from mass audiences, to niche audiences, to individuals.
>
> (2014, p.275)

When attempting to theorise television as a medium, therefore, it is important that we avoid essentialist claims. At the same time, however, it is possible to identify the core components that make up any given medium. Amanda Lotz speaks to this point when she writes that 'A "medium" derives not only from technological capabilities, but also from textual characteristics, industrial practices, audience behaviors, and cultural understanding' (2016, p.3). In this sense, television needs to be understood as a cultural construct or, as Mike Van Esler puts it, a 'concept rather than an object or technology' (2016, p.133). However, taking a conceptual approach to television need not involve erecting binary oppositions between television as concept and as object/technology. As I shall go on to argue, we can conceptualise television as a medium made up of different technological, cultural, industrial, organisational and experiential components.

Adopting a conceptual, rather than empirical, approach to television in this book is a deliberate choice designed, in part, to deal with the difficulty of researching such a fast-moving ecosystem as the world of internet-connected television. This is a media environment characterised by rapid change, where new initiatives rise and fall in the blink of an eye and scholarship can date with startling speed. Empirical studies play an important role in providing a snapshot of these changes as they happen. However, this book starts from the contention that the transformations we are witnessing challenge the usefulness of the terminology and concepts that we have at hand to talk about television. Therefore, we need to take a step back from tracing the details of change in individual contexts and spend some time thinking about what language and concepts we need to make sense of these changes. M.J. Robinson writes that 'What we call things creates meanings that affect how they are perceived' (2017, p.5). For example, if I were to ask you 'Did you watch television yesterday?' I can no longer be sure that we would both be operating from the same conceptual understanding of what 'watching television' constituted. Perhaps you watched an episode of *Game of Thrones* (HBO, 2011–) on an online streaming service on your laptop while travelling home from work or college on the bus. For some, this would count as watching television, regardless of the service and technology used to access the content. For others, this would not count as watching television because it bears little resemblance to the experience of viewing **linear television** channels on a set in the living room.

These questions of terminology are important not just for academics, but also for industry and regulators. How we conceptualise television as a medium shapes how we understand its role and function in society. For example, early conceptualisations of broadcast television as a domestic mass medium for the delivery of audiovisual content from a central point to dispersed viewers within a specific nation led to the regulation of UK television as a public service. When VHS and DVD emerged as alternative ways of delivering television, a different mode of regulation was adopted, with VHS tapes and DVDs being subjected to a ratings system borrowed from that used for movies. In this sense, VHS tapes and DVDs of television programmes were not seen as TV-like, but rather understood as consumer products (Kompare 2006) that should be regulated through mechanisms adopted from cinema ratings that were designed to increase consumer knowledge. In the internet era, one service can combine both means of accessing television, allowing viewers to watch an aggregated stream of linear content (akin to broadcasting) or to purchase an individual programme for download (akin to buying a DVD). As former distinctions collapse it becomes important to ask what we mean by television: what are the characteristics that make something TV-like?

One of the dangers of a conceptual approach, however, is that the terminology, models and frameworks developed can be understood as rigid, classifying concepts that could be seen to close down, rather than open up, explorations of difference and change. By contrast, this book understands the conceptual frameworks that it develops as *tools for thinking with*, rather than as rigid models. Specifically, my adoption of a conceptual approach stems from my own sense that as television as a medium has become more fragmented, complex and convergent, we need new tools that help us think through and analyse these changes. The conceptual models and frameworks outlined in this book should not, therefore, be approached as rigid categorisations, but rather as tools to be adapted, challenged and played with through different lenses and in divergent contexts. Specifically, they are designed to help us think through what is happening to television, rather than to be seen as immutable models of what television is or was.[6]

This first chapter approaches the problem of conceptualising television in the internet era by examining the historical development of television from a broadcast to an internet-connected medium. There are many ways in which one could approach the task of tracing the history of television, given its multifaceted nature as a medium. This book is particularly interested in interrogating the changing conceptualisations of television *as a medium for delivering audiovisual content to viewers.*[7] The primary reason for this is that the internet era is the first time in which television has faced significant competition to its dominant sociocultural position as the primary medium for delivering video content. This is not to argue that television has never faced competition from other media, such as print, cinema, radio and gaming, over its history. However, each of these media offered distinctly different experiences to that of television. For example, even though cinema also delivered audiovisual content to viewers, the cinema-going experience has remained a public one that has been developed precisely to distinguish itself from the domestic, small-screen viewing experience of television. Although television has arguably become more 'cinematic,' with larger screens, better-quality sound and changing aesthetics, watching television remains a fundamentally different experience to that of going to the cinema. What has changed since the late-2000s, however, is that the internet has begun to offer viewing experiences that are arguably indistinguishable from those offered by television, while at the same time converging with television in ways that change how it delivers audiovisual content to viewers. It is this process of change that this chapter aims to trace.

By charting change over time this chapter teases out the core components that could be said to make up television as a medium for delivering video content to audiences, expanding Raymond Williams' (1990) theorisation of television as technology and cultural form. Although this book adopts a technological periodisation, by understanding television as a medium composed of technology, culture, user experiences, funding and organisational structures, the book resists a technologically determinist approach and regards the technologies of television as a part of wider social, political, economic and cultural processes. Specifically, this book adopts the approach taken by Raymond Williams in understanding that all technologies are developed 'with certain purposes and practices already in mind' (1990, p.14). These intentions typically arise from multiple conflicting parties and cannot be understood to determine the use to which people put the technology at hand. However, they do play a powerful role in shaping how media are constructed, developed and changed. At the heart of this book is the assumption that the changes that are taking place to television are not driven by technology or in some way inevitable, but stem from the direct interventions of industrial (and other) actors. In particular, this book is interested in how the industry works to construct television as a medium and as a particular kind of cultural experience, and how this has changed as the internet has developed as a medium for delivering audiovisual content.[8]

Conceptualising television as a medium: a framework

This section approaches the question of how to conceptualise online TV by tracing the development of television as a medium for delivering audiovisual content from its origins in broadcasting to the contemporary media landscape of the internet era. The aims of this section are twofold: first, to draw up a framework of the components that make up television as a medium for the delivery of audiovisual content to viewers; second, to map these components over time in order to make visible the continuities and changes to television as it transforms from a broadcast to an online medium. In doing so, this section reveals how online TV is as much shaped by television's historical origins as it differs from them, challenging arguments that we are entering a 'post-TV' era in which the structures of broadcast, cable and satellite television are no longer relevant (see, for example, Strangelove 2015). Through this method, it is possible to identify a set of characteristics that are shared by broadcast, cable/satellite, digital and a specific segment of online audiovisual services, and these form the foundation of the book's working model of online TV that will be outlined in more detail in Chapter 2.

To trace the development of television over its history, this chapter builds on Raymond Williams' theorisation of television as a technology and cultural form, identifying the different components that make up television as a medium. In the broadcast era when Williams was writing, the technology of television consisted of a network of transmitters capable of conveying images and sounds through the electromagnetic spectrum, whose signals could be picked up by aerials positioned on the top of buildings and converted into programmes displayed on television sets.[9] Williams argued that the cultural form of television consisted of more than just programmes. Rather, he claimed that television as a cultural form needed to be understood as a continuous flow in which different types of communication (drama, news, comedy, trailers, adverts and so on) are organised into a schedule according to perceived understandings of the rhythms of everyday life (Ellis 2000; Scannell 1996). As Williams and others have demonstrated, the structure and cultural form of the scheduled flow contributed to the meanings of individual programmes and channels, and of television overall as a medium (Barra 2015; Bruun 2016; Ellis 2011; Johnson 2013; Johnson & Weissmann 2017; Van Den Bulck & Enli 2014; Ytreberg 2002).

Williams was writing in the mid-1970s at a moment in which television was on the brink of technological change, with cable, satellite and videotape all poised to introduce new forms of television and upset old ones. This emergent cable/satellite era expanded the technologies of television and introduced new cultural forms. To understand these changes, it is necessary to unpack the different components that make up television as a technology and a cultural form (see Table 1.1).[10] In terms of technology, it is helpful to distinguish between the **technological *infrastructures*** for delivering television and the technological *devices* through which television programming is accessed. From the late-1970s to the mid-1990s, the cable/satellite era expanded the infrastructure of television beyond the transmitters and aerials of broadcasting by using the alternative technologies of coaxial cable and satellites.[11] The television set remained the primary **viewing device** for television as a medium, although there was a shift from black and white to colour. More significantly for the technological devices of television was the introduction of a number of **add-on devices** that could be attached to the viewing device of the television set to bring extra features to the experience of television. Set-top boxes aggregated programmes in new ways; VHS players enabled television programmes to be recorded, sold and/or rented as products; games consoles turned the television set into a screen for playing as well as viewing; and remote controls enabled viewers to change channel from the comfort of their sofas.

TABLE 1.1 The components of television as a medium for delivering audiovisual content in the broadcast, cable/satellite, digital and internet eras

	Technology	Device		Cultural form			Funding	Organisational structures	User experience
	Infrastructure	Viewing	Add-on	Service	Frame	Content			
Broadcast era 1930s–70s	Broadcasting	TV set		Mass channels	Linear schedule	Professional programmes, ads, interstitials	State/licence fee Advertising	National/regional/ local broadcasters Regulated	Viewing
Cable/satellite era 1970s–90s	Broadcasting Cable Satellite	TV set	Remote control VHS player Set-top box	Mass and niche channels Channel bundles	Linear schedule EPG	Professional programmes, ads, interstitials	State/licence fee Advertising Subscription Transaction	National/regional/ local broadcasters Global conglomerates Deregulated	Viewing Surfing Buying
Digital era 1990s–2000s	Broadcasting Cable Satellite Digital (terrestrial, satellite, cable)	TV set	Remote control VHS/DVD player Set-top box/ PVR	Mass and niche channels Channel bundles PPV	Linear schedule EPG Interfaces	Professional programmes, ads, interstitials Transmedia	State/licence fee Advertising Subscription Transaction	National/regional/ local broadcasters Global conglomerates Deregulated	Viewing Surfing Buying Playing
Internet era 2010s+	Digital (terrestrial, satellite, cable) Broadband/4G/ wifi Cloud computing	TV set Smart TV Desktop Laptop Tablet Smartphone	Remote control DVD player Set-top box/ PVR Digital media player Games console	Mass and niche channels Channel bundles PPV VOD P2P	Linear schedule EPG Interfaces Algorithms	Professional programmes, ads, interstitials Transmedia Semi-professional Pro-amateur Amateur	State/licence fee Advertising Subscription Transaction	National/regional/ local broadcasters Global conglomerates Deregulated	Viewing Surfing Buying Playing Curating Sharing Uploading Downloading Liking Commenting Rating

These technological shifts were accompanied by changes to the cultural form of television. I want to argue that to understand these changes it is necessary to distinguish between three interrelated components of television as a cultural form: *content, services* and *frames*. **Television content** refers to the programmes, adverts, idents, interstitials and other forms of audiovisual material distributed through television's technological infrastructures and devices. In both the broadcast and the cable/satellite eras television showed professionally produced programmes from a range of genres alongside advertising and other interstitial content (such as idents, promos, continuity announcements and so on). However, the new add-on devices enabled the use of the television set for different forms of content and experiences. VHS players allowed viewers to record and purchase individual programmes separated from the broadcast flow, so that television programmes could be watched and re-watched at the convenience of the viewer. The games console transformed the television set into a site for experiencing the emerging cultural form of the videogame.

The cable/satellite era also introduced new *services* through which television content was delivered to viewers. **Television services** function as the cultural entry point through which viewers encounter the content of television as a medium.[12] In the broadcast era, viewers encountered television programmes through the service of the television channel, which typically targeted mass audiences with a mixed schedule of programmes. Alongside the continuing availability of the free-to-air channels from the broadcast era, the cable/satellite era introduced new types of channel that addressed niche audiences through more narrowly focused schedules of programming. Cable and satellite providers introduced a new kind of service, the 'cable/satellite bundle,' in which viewers subscribed to an aggregated range of channels according to the amount paid. These services require **frames** that organise content within services and devices and shape how it is experienced. In the broadcast era, the experience of television was framed by the linear schedule that communicated ideas about what kinds of programmes were appropriate for specific times of day (light news in the morning, serious drama in the evening) and combined with continuity materials to convey the 'communicative ethos' of a particular channel (Scannell 1996, pp.19–20; see also Johnson 2012, pp.116–9). Such frames are a crucial but often overlooked component of television as a cultural form that perform a paratextual function in constructing the experience of watching television.[13] With the expansion of channels in the cable/satellite era and the introduction of new add-on devices, such as the set-top box and remote control, the frame of the electronic programme guide (EPG) emerged as an important component of television's cultural form, playing a crucial role in navigating viewers through a landscape of increased choice (Ward 2015).

With these developments came changes to the ways in which television could be funded. In the early years of television broadcasting it was not possible to prevent viewers from picking up television signals once they had been broadcast. As such, in the broadcast era television could not be charged for at the point of reception. This led to two dominant ways in which television was funded: through public funding (state, taxation or licence fee payments) or through advertising.[14] Cable and satellite infrastructure introduced the possibility of paying for television by subscription as the signals could be encrypted, although many of the channels available as part of cable and satellite bundles remained funded by advertising or state/licence fee payments. These technologies also introduced new transactions between cable/satellite operators and channel owners in the form of retransmission payments and carriage fees paid to ensure that cable/satellite bundles carried certain channels (Wolk 2015, p.5). Meanwhile, the introduction of domestic VHS players and the availability of pay-per-view (PPV) through some cable/satellite services introduced payment through direct transaction as a further way in which television could be funded, although this practice was relatively limited in this period.[15]

The cable and satellite era also introduced new organisations and industrial structures to television. In the broadcast era, regulated national, regional and/or local broadcasters and networks generally provided television services. Tay and Turner argue that the broadcast era of free-to-air television was defined by its public function, where all broadcasters (even advertiser-funded ones) had certain national and civic responsibilities in exchange for access to the public resource of the airwaves (2008, pp.72–3). The development of cable and satellite was accompanied by a deregulatory turn, which allowed large global (often US) conglomerates to provide cable/satellite services and channels around the world and undermined (but did not erode) the concept of television as a public utility.

Thus far, I have argued that to understand the changes that emerged over the cable/satellite era from the mid-1970s to the mid-1990s it is necessary to distinguish between the different components of television as a technology and cultural form. The technology of television can be understood to be made up of the *infrastructures* for delivering television and the tangible *devices* through which television is accessed, which can be categorised as *viewing devices* (through which television content can be directly watched) and *add-on devices* (that attach to the viewing device to facilitate or expand the television experience). The cultural form of television consists of three elements: the *services* through which television *content* is provided to viewers and the *frames* that shape how the content and service are experienced. Although materially different, infrastructures, devices, services, frames and content are fundamentally dependent on each other. Infrastructures and devices have no value if they are not delivering services, frames and content of some kind, and services, frames and content cannot exist without the infrastructures and devices to deliver them.

In the broadcast era the technology and cultural form of television worked to offer a relatively coherent experience. The experience of television consisted of turning on the television set (viewing device), selecting a channel (service) delivered through transmitters and aerials (infrastructure) and watching the scheduled flow (frame) of programmes and interstitials (content). All elements of television's technology and cultural form intertwined: television's *content* could not be experienced outside of the technological *infrastructure* of broadcasting, beyond the *device* of the television set or outside of the *service* of the television channel and the *frame* of the scheduled flow. However, in the cable/satellite era the act of watching television became more multi-faceted. New technologies introduced additional layers to the experience of television, from the add-on devices of set-top boxes, VHS players and games consoles, to the frames of EPGs. The cable and satellite era also introduced subscription and direct payment as new means through which access to television content could be paid for. In addition, for the first time, viewers could step out of the linear flow and watch individually selected programmes on PPV or VHS, although the choice of programmes available in these forms was limited and channels remained the primary organising structure for television as a medium. However, despite these changes *television remained primarily a medium associated with viewing professionally produced audiovisual content through a television set.*[16]

It was the digital era, beginning in the second half of the 1990s, in which normative assumptions about television as a medium began to be more broadly challenged. Lucy Küng, Robert G. Picard and Ruth Towse argue that digitalisation differs from earlier developments in media and communications because 'it allows the development of fundamentally new products, services and processes' (2008, pp.15–6). In many ways, however, digitalisation extended changes that had begun in the cable and satellite era (see Table 1.1). In terms of *infrastructure*, the 2000s witnessed a gradual move away from analogue towards digital delivery systems with many countries around the globe switching off their analogue signal in the late 2000s and early 2010s (Sparks 2007). Digital terrestrial, cable and satellite infrastructure enabled further expansion in the number of channels and services. New *add-on devices*, in particular the DVD player and the personal video recorder (PVR), extended the changes introduced by the VHS and set-top box in the cable and satellite era. Many PVRs, such as TiVo which was introduced in 1999, had automated functions that recorded programmes that viewers might be interested in based on their previous usage, and enabled pausing, rewinding and replaying of live television broadcasts. The DVD had a significant impact on the television industry from the late-1990s as its increased capacity made it far more suited than VHS to the expansive texts of television series. At the same time, the availability of PPV through set-top boxes became more prevalent. As such, it was in this period that the television programme as a consumer product came to the fore (Kompare 2006).

These changes to television's technological infrastructures and devices had an impact on television as a cultural form. With the vast expansion in the number of channels and services available, the cultural *frame* of the EPG became increasingly important as a means of guiding and shaping user experience, and PVRs began to adopt more complex **interfaces** to navigate viewers through the wider range of viewing options. This included experiments with new on-demand services, such as the red button in the UK (Bennett 2008). PVRs, DVDs and red button services functioned to separate individual programmes from the linear stream of the broadcast flow and provide viewers with more control over when and how they watched television (Lotz 2014, p.66).

At the same time, the internet began to be positioned by the television industry as a site for new forms of transmedia and multiplatform *content* that extended beyond the bounds of the television set. In the late 1990s and early 2000s multiplatform production and commissioning emerged as a dominant industrial strategy as television services attempted to respond to the challenges of the digital era.[17] This is a period in which 360-degree commissioning took hold within many television organisations (Doyle 2010, p.432; Grainge & Johnson 2018, p.24). In the context of the BBC, 360-degree commissioning signalled a move from the development of single programmes to a range of linked content extended across multiple media (Strange 2011, p.136). In its objective to produce content that utilised the affordances of different media, 360-degree commissioning tied the idea of multiplatform to transmedia story-telling (Evans 2011; Jenkins 2006). Jennifer Gillan (2011, pp.3–4) describes how developments in multiplatform television in the USA invited viewers to immerse themselves in the world of shows that they had first experienced on television, with websites, online shorts, games and social media content turning programmes into franchises that offered viewers a number of different ways of participating in an extended storyworld. However, Gillan argues that the emergence of multiplatform content did not replace traditional programming strategies. Rather, she describes a context in which transmedia extensions sat alongside traditional linear flow strategies through which networks attempted to keep viewers tied to their channels.[18] Indeed, one of the features of multiplatform and transmedia strategies is that the internet is conceptualised as a separate medium from television, one with its own distinct affordances. In this sense, implicit in these strategies was an understanding that the internet offered something that television could not provide and needed to be treated as a different medium with its own specific opportunities and demands.

As I have argued elsewhere (Grainge & Johnson 2018, pp.24–5), a number of academics have noted a gradual retreat from multiplatform and transmedia strategies by the television industry in the late-2000s and early-2010s. Denise Mann claims that by the 2010s the US networks had stepped back from transmedia storytelling strategies to focus on using new media in ways that align with traditional programming, marketing and licensing practices (2014, p.10). In a similar vein, James Bennett and Niki Strange trace a move away from the experimentation of 360-degree commissioning at the BBC in the same period, towards a strategy focused on using the internet as a site for delivering the same content as broadcast on linear television channels (2014, pp.75–83).[19] Central to this shift in industrial strategy is developments in video on demand (VOD).

YouTube's success as an online video **platform** in 2005 was a catalyst in encouraging television providers to experiment with online delivery of television programmes. However, the move of the television industry into the provision of VOD services in the mid- to late-2000s was uneven. In some contexts, particularly those where regulatory structures encouraged broadcasters to innovate with new digital services, this period saw the launch of a swathe of VOD television services.[20] In other contexts, the television industry was hesitant to embrace a new means of delivering television that might cannibalise existing linear business models.[21] However, in this period there was a clear distinction between YouTube and the on-demand services of television providers. Between 2005 and 2008, YouTube positioned itself explicitly as 'a platform for sharing self-made amateur video, an "alternative" to watching television' (van Dijck 2013, p.110). By contrast, in the same period television VOD services were largely described as 'catch-up' players that enabled viewers to watch programmes that they had missed when first broadcast on television.

José van Dijck argues that between 2008 and 2012, YouTube shifted its strategy and began to collaborate, rather than compete, with the television industry (2013, pp.110–1). Meanwhile, in 2007, the online DVD rental service Netflix launched its first streaming service, enabling subscribers to watch television shows and movies on their computers on demand. These developments point to a significant shift in the relationship between television and the internet that took place towards the end of the 2000s and into the first half of the 2010s. In this emergent internet era, the internet began to be positioned as a means of delivering and experiencing television, rather than as an alternative to, or extension of, television.

Crucial to the internet era, as we saw at the opening of this chapter, were developments in broadband *infrastructure*, including superfast broadband, 4G and wifi, which enabled the internet to emerge as a site for the delivery of audiovisual content. New forms of physical and digital infrastructure, such as mobile phone masts, fibre optic cables, servers, cloud computing and **content delivery networks** (CDNs), facilitated the streaming and downloading of audiovisual content to internet-connected devices (Holt & Vonderau 2014). Maria Michalis and Paul Smith (2016, pp.667–8) argue that broadband developed in this period into a fourth distribution platform (or what I would term infrastructure) for television alongside terrestrial, cable and satellite. Broadband underlines two different forms of online delivery for audiovisual content: **internet protocol television** (IPTV) and **over-the-top** (OTT) television. IPTV refers to content and services delivered on a private dedicated internet protocol network managed by a service provider, usually one of the telecoms, cable and/or satellite providers offering combined internet and television services. It is this technological infrastructure that has enabled telecoms companies, such as BT and AT&T, to compete with cable/satellite companies for television viewers

(Strangelove 2015, p.9). OTT refers to content and services delivered via an internet browser or application over the public internet.

Most of the recent academic work on internet television has focused on OTT television, often with a specific focus on Netflix (Jenner 2016; Jenner 2017; Lobato 2018; Lobato 2019). For example, both Michael Strangelove (2015) and Amanda Lotz (2016) argue that OTT television is the primary site through which the internet's transformation of television is being enacted. However, to overlook IPTV, or to position broadband as separate from cable, satellite and digital television, fails to recognise that broadband is deeply intertwined with older forms of television's infrastructure. As shall be explored in more detail in Chapter 3, the industrial landscape of television infrastructure is one in which telecoms, cable and satellite providers are frequently also responsible for providing the internet access that enables the delivery of IPTV and OTT services. Beyond this, rather than operating as an alternative to cable or satellite, broadband is frequently integrated with cable and satellite infrastructure, with, for example, fibre optic cable operating as a technological infrastructure for delivering broadband and cable TV. Furthermore, many OTT services such as Netflix are also offered through IPTV, particularly when delivered through a cable subscription service. As such, we can understand broadband not so much as an alternative to broadcasting, cable and satellite, but as integrating with these earlier forms of technological infrastructure in potentially transformative ways.

While television's technological infrastructure has been undergoing a series of changes since the broadcast era, the television set has remained as the primary viewing device for television over the broadcast, cable/satellite and digital eras. It is arguable, then, that the most significant technological change in the internet era has been the development of alternative *viewing devices* to the television set for watching television content. High-quality access to television programmes and services is provided in the internet era through desktops, laptops, tablets and smartphones. At the same time, the television set itself has been transformed. No longer reliant on the cathode ray tube, in the digital era new plasma and LCD screens flattened the television set and increased the screen size and quality (alongside developments in HD and home cinema), while in the internet era smart televisions that connect to the internet transform television sets into 'giant computer screens (or more likely, Netflix, Amazon Instant Video, YouTube, or Hulu viewers)' (Robinson 2017, p.37).[22] Robinson argues that smart TVs change 'the viewer experience of online content since it makes the "switch" between traditional forms of television (channels and networks delivered through broadcast, cable or satellite) and online video seamless' (ibid.). This ability to switch within a single viewing device between different forms of video service, as well as to other forms of mediated activity (such as social networking, gaming or emailing), is also facilitated by the new viewing devices of the tablet, desktop, laptop and smartphone. In this sense, television viewing now takes place on devices that facilitate far more than just viewing experiences.

New *add-on devices* contribute to the development of new means of, and environments for, viewing television. In particular, digital media players such as Slingbox, Apple TV, Roku, Amazon Fire TV Stick and Google Chromecast enable content to be streamed to a range of viewing devices.[23] These add-on devices vary in terms of their features and capabilities. For example, Slingbox streams the signal from a cable/satellite set-top box to viewing devices beyond the TV set, such as a smartphone or tablet. Many of the other devices, such as Apple TV, Google Chromecast and Amazon Fire TV Stick, are designed to stream content to a television set. In so doing they transform the television set into a device for viewing a range of web content and often also enable the streaming of other digital content, such as photos, music, games, apps and podcasts, or the use of the television set as a second monitor for computer devices.[24] At the same time, existing add-on devices have developed in ways that change the experience of television. By the mid-2010s, it had become commonplace for set-top boxes to be connected to the internet, enabling access to internet-delivered content and interactive services. Games consoles, such as Microsoft's Xbox and Sony's PlayStation, also developed into entertainment hubs that enable the streaming of audiovisual content and television services.

Alongside the expansion and increased complexity of television as a technology in the internet era there has been a transformation in the cultural form of television. Channels and cable/satellite bundles remain as important *services* for delivering content to viewers. However, access to channels and cable/satellite bundles is now provided online alongside a range of other internet-enabled services that provide access to audiovisual (and other forms of) content. VOD services offer a different way of constructing and organising the viewing experience by providing viewers with a menu of audiovisual content from which they can select what to watch. Many VOD services continue to provide access to linear streams of television channels or use the channel as an organising structure (Johnson 2017). However, these linear streams typically sit within nonlinear services that provide 'personalized delivery of content independent of a [linear] schedule' (Lotz 2016, p.2). Viewers are no longer bound by the linear schedules of the television channel.

Beyond specific VOD services that focus on providing access to audiovisual content, video has become a more integral and quotidian component of the web. Social media sites, such as Facebook and Twitter, now position video as central to their offer, online newspapers place video reports alongside written text and still images, and video advertising punctures the internet browsing experience. Internet technology enables greater two-way communication between provider and user. In addition to increased emphasis on searching for and selecting content, online services enable viewers to curate content and personalise access. The networked landscape of internet infrastructure also places greater emphasis on sharing and participation, including producing, uploading and downloading content, interacting, commenting and liking.

With these different kinds of online video services often offering a range of user activities, the *frame* of the interface has come to play an increasingly important role in constructing the experience of engaging with audiovisual content online. Interfaces shape, and are shaped by, the data and **algorithms** that drive much of the internet. Internet infrastructures enable detailed monitoring of user behaviour online and online video services are frequently driven by such user data, with algorithms that shape their interfaces and determine what content is made available to individual users at any given time. The range of audiovisual *content* offered by these diverse services is plentiful. Many VOD services ape the broadcast model of offering a wide range of content aggregated from a number of genres (for example, BBC iPlayer, CBS All Access, Hulu and HBO). These can be differentiated from services offered around a singular genre and reminiscent of the niche channels of cable and satellite providers (such as Vevo and Mubi), as well as highly specialised services focused on very narrowly defined forms of content such as a specific football team (Chelsea football's Chelsea TV Online) or theatre company (Globe Player, provided by Shakespeare's Globe theatre in London). In addition, many online audiovisual services include amateur and 'pro-am' content (Cunningham & Silver 2013, p.10).[25] Michael Strangelove refers to this as a 'post-television' phenomenon in which television is transformed into 'a complex mix of professional, semi-professional, and amateur content that competes for attention across all screens' (2015, p.164). It is notable, however, that despite all of these changes, the means of paying for television remain largely unchanged, although over the digital and internet eras subscription has emerged as a significant growth area in revenues for the television industry. In addition, increasingly services are combining different funding mechanisms, offering free content supported by advertising, alongside a subscription service without adverts, with premium content available to rent or buy for a one-off fee.

In the internet era, then, television and the internet have become increasingly intertwined as technologies and cultural forms. Table 1.1 demonstrates how the internet era has led to an expansion of television at all levels, across infrastructure, devices, services, frames and content. It is no wonder that it has become harder and harder to pin down what television as a medium might be. However, at the same time as recognising the ways in which the internet era transforms television it is also important to note the continuities amidst all of this change. It is striking to see that many of the changes to television over its history have been additive rather than substitutive. VOD, for example, has transformed the services and frames of television as a medium, yet it has not replaced the earlier forms of the channel and cable/satellite bundle. Indeed, although there is widespread evidence that consumption of online content is growing, in some contexts it seems to be complementary to, rather than substituting for, linear television (Michalis & Smith 2016, p.668).[26]

Yet even thinking about linear and nonlinear viewing as in some ways separate or different is problematic. The development of online services that provide access to streams of linear television represents a collapse in the boundaries between linear and nonlinear TV (Johnson 2017).[27] It is for this reason that, like Van Esler (2016, pp.132–3), I am wary of proclamations that we are entering into a post-TV era. For example, Mareike Jenner, in an insightful article about Netflix, argues that we are moving into a new era of TVIV in which 'viewing patterns, branding strategies, industrial strategies, the way different media forms interact with each other or the various ways content is made available shift completely away from the television set' (2016, p.260). Yet, as we have seen, rather than constituting a move away from the television set, the internet era can be better understood as a period in which the television set is transformed into an internet-connected device that carries simultaneously its earlier associations with viewing linear television schedules and newer associations with on-demand and interactive engagement.

It is in recognition of these continuities with older forms of television that this book adopts the term 'online TV' to describe television as a delivery mechanism for audiovisual content in the internet era. This term comes from a talk given by Tony Hall in October 2013, six months after his appointment as the new Director General of the BBC (see Grainge & Johnson 2018, p.21). In the speech Hall outlined his vision for the BBC on its hundredth birthday in 2022. Central to this vision was a transformation of BBC iPlayer from 'catch-up TV to online TV' (Hall 2013). The term online TV here expressed a future in which the internet is not a secondary and separate site from television, a place where viewers go to catch up on content missed on the TV set or for additional and different multiplatform and transmedia content. Rather, online TV becomes the BBC's service, or, in Hall's words, 'the front door to many people to the whole BBC' (ibid.).

In this book, the term 'online TV' speaks to a shifting understanding of the relationship between television and the internet, one in which the internet is conceptualised as a medium and technology that intertwines with television in the provision of audiovisual content. Where Hall used the term to speak directly to the role of the BBC's on-demand service, BBC iPlayer, in this book I am expanding and extending the term beyond the new kinds of video services that have emerged in the internet era to encompass the ways in which the internet is transforming forms of television founded in the broadcast, cable/satellite and digital eras. As such, although VOD is central to online TV, this book uses the term online TV to refer to any television service delivered through internet-connected devices and infrastructure.

Thus far this chapter has traced the core changes to television as a medium for the delivery of audiovisual content to viewers from the broadcast to the internet era. From this it is possible to identify two key challenges that the internet era presents to any attempt to conceptualise television as a medium. First, the internet expands and disrupts television as a technology and a cultural form at every level, from infrastructure and devices to content, frames and services. Second, in the internet era television is situated within a media ecosystem in which the boundaries that have existed for many decades between different forms of media (such as print, television and radio) are no longer secure.[28] In the media ecosystem of the internet era, video content becomes a constitutive and quotidian part of a wide range of activities and services enacted through internet-connected infrastructure and devices, from online newspapers interspersing video content within written text to social media sites encouraging users to upload video as part of their routine interpersonal communications.

To conceptualise online TV in the internet era, we therefore need to consider how the infrastructure of the internet differs from analogue and digital broadcast, cable and satellite infrastructures. Lucy Küng et al. caution against seeing the internet and digital as interchangeable terms. They argue that digital refers to a technology that stores data in binary form, whereas the internet refers to a 'system that links computers and computer networks worldwide to permit distribution of data, e-mail, messages and visual and audio materials to individuals, groups of individuals and the public' (2008, p.15). The internet is a worldwide network, compared to the more geographically bounded services of broadcasting, cable and satellite television.[29] The network of the internet can be used by individuals and organisations to distribute a wide range of content from previously distinct media industries (print, telephone, television, radio etc.). In doing so, the internet also operates simultaneously as a medium of two-way communication and as a one-way medium for the delivery of content for users' consumption. Particularly since the development of Web 2.0, the services offered through the internet have become interactive, two-way vehicles for networked sociality (van Dijck 2013, p.5). The internet situates audiovisual content and services within an ecosystem characterised by fluid geographical boundaries in which peer-production, collaboration and sociability rubs up against consumerism. If broadcasting had its origins in a world of mass media with concomitant ideals of universality and nation-building (Tay & Turner 2008, pp.72–3), online TV emerges in a context in which the dividing lines between public, private and corporate space emerge as a new battleground (van Dijck 2013, p.17).

The internet, therefore, needs to be understood as a network of connective media that enables a range of different kinds of content and activities to exist alongside each other. One of the difficulties of conceptualising television in the internet era is the sheer complexity and volatility of this media ecosystem. In 2013, John Thornton Caldwell pointed to the 'messiness' of the contemporary cultural industries in describing the collapsing boundaries between film, television and marketing with the development of multiplatform production (2013, p.163). This sense of mess is arguably even more applicable to the media landscape of the internet era in the 2010s. This is an ecosystem characterised by convergence, where different forms of media are intertwined within services that facilitate a wide variety of experiences and are provided by a range of industry players operating with divergent business models. It is also an ecosystem characterised by the possibility, and often the reality, of rapid change. It is a media landscape characterised, therefore, by volatility. A central aim of this book is to bring some order to this volatile and messy media landscape by providing a language that helps us identify the shared characteristics across and between different components of this ecosystem. The conceptual framework outlined in this chapter is a crucial starting point by enabling us to identify and describe the different components that make up television as a medium for delivering audiovisual content. It is then possible to interrogate the ways in which these components operate and interact in the contemporary media ecosystem and to look for sites of commonality and difference that can help us make sense of the messiness and volatility of the internet era. Rather than attempting to account for all of the different kinds of infrastructure, device, service, frame and content that could be associated with television in the internet era (see Table 1.1), therefore, this book puts forward a definition of online TV that focuses on a particular subset of online audiovisual services that share characteristics with earlier forms of television, but are delivered through internet-connected infrastructures and devices. This definition of online TV will be elaborated in Chapter 2.

Identifying and analysing the components that make up online TV as a subset of a broader set of online audiovisual service also enables examination of the ways in which industry players are attempting to exert control over television and the internet in the face of the volatility of the contemporary media ecosystem. The explosion in availability of video across the internet has led to what Mark Stewart refers to as the 'myth of televisual ubiquity,' which describes the 'touted ability to watch any television content we want, anywhere, anytime' (2016, p.692). As Stewart argues, this myth of ubiquity overlooks issues of geographic boundaries, perpetuates assumptions about taste and quality, and fails to account for the ongoing industrial strategies at work to constrain access to television. The changes to television in the internet era, therefore, speak to broader questions of agency and power (Curtin et al. 2014, p.16). As Michael Strangelove states, 'The fight over the future of television is in essence a fight for control of culture' (2015, p.199). This book will demonstrate how industrial control is exerted at the level of infrastructure, device, content, frame and service as the industry responds to the volatility of the internet era.

How to read this book

The conceptual framework outlined in this opening chapter shapes the structure of this book. Chapter 2 elaborates on this book's definition of online TV by examining the different kinds of online video services that have emerged since the mid–late 2000s. It argues that it is possible to distinguish between online video and online TV services. In doing so, it unpacks the key stakes that are driving these different segments on the online video ecosystem and draws attention to the sites and strategies through which the online TV industry is attempting to limit user choice and control. Chapter 3 turns its attention to defining the industry that provides online TV services. It demonstrates that this is a highly varied industry composed of multiple kinds of business operating in a range of sectors with divergent business models. The chapter offers two approaches to help navigate this 'mess.' The first approach categorises the industry according to business origins, which makes it possible to identify the competencies and dependencies at work within different segments of the industry. The second approach dissects the industry according to core business focus, which reveals the controlling points through which different segments of the industry attempt to exert competitive advantage. The chapter ends by focusing on industrial control over technological infrastructures and devices to demonstrate how these approaches can be used to examine the power dynamics within the online TV industry. The subsequent chapters each take a further area of industrial control as their focus.

Chapter 4 concentrates attention on the ways in which content functions as a site of competition and co-dependence in the online TV industry. Examining the impact of online TV on industrial practices for the production and distribution of content, it argues that intellectual property rights are a central battleground in the online TV industry in which new and old strategies for constructing artificial scarcity compete in the attempt to control user access to content. Chapter 5 turns attention to the role of frames in constructing viewing experiences for online TV users. It argues for the centrality of interfaces as the frame that structures the experience of online TV and acts as a significant mechanism of control in the delivery of online TV services. By unpacking the ways in which online TV interfaces construct user experiences, it argues that interfaces create an illusion of content abundance and user agency that belies the ways in which online TV services offer highly structured viewing experiences for users.

Chapter 6 examines a more hidden frame in contemporary television, that of data and algorithms. It examines the ways in which online TV services use data and algorithms, and asks how this differs from earlier uses of data in the production and distribution of television. Drawing on literature from software and computer studies, the chapter unpacks how algorithms work in online TV services, and asks whether data and algorithms have the potential to upset traditional power hierarchies in the television industry by reducing editorial control, enabling greater understanding of user behaviour and opening up the potential for content and viewers to be valued in new ways. Ultimately, the chapter argues that the ways in which algorithms are used by the online TV industry tend to replicate the strategies of traditional 'push' media in which the service exerts significant control over the user's media experience.

The book's Conclusion returns to the concept of volatility, and draws on the analysis laid out over the preceding chapters to argue that online TV can be characterised by volatility. The Conclusion demonstrates how the conceptual models developed across the book can help us examine online TV in ways that enable us to unpack, rather than close down, the volatility that is, arguably, its key feature. These conceptual models provide tools to think with that enable us to challenge the myth of ubiquity and reveal the strategies and sites through which the industry variously attempts to control access to culture. In bringing these strands together, the Conclusion returns to the questions raised in this chapter of how the changes to television in the internet era might disrupt some of the fundamental assumptions that have shaped our understanding of television as a medium. Specifically, the Conclusion examines how online TV can be understood as indicative of a shift in the meanings of the word 'service' as it is applied to television, and speaks of a broader context in which public service television as a concept has been undermined. In doing so, it demonstrates how the questions of agency and control examined across the book might play out in relation to one of the foundational concepts of television – that it is a medium with the ability to exert significant power for, or against, the public interest.

In an ideal world, I would hope that every reader would read the entire book in the order in which it has been written. However, I understand that in the contemporary academic and media landscape many of us struggle to find the time to read books in their entirety. If you are unable to read the whole book I have included a brief recap of the key ideas from earlier chapters at the start of each chapter to facilitate understanding. I would, however, urge you to read Chapters 1 and 2, as they provide the conceptual frameworks that inform the analysis developed over the rest of the book. While the subsequent chapters can be read on their own, Chapters 5 and 6 inform each other, offering insight into the visible (Chapter 5) and invisible (Chapter 6) frames that construct the experience of using online TV services.

As with any book, there are significant aspects of television in the internet era that are not examined in detail, specifically changing production practices, the texts of television (from the programmes to the paratexts that circulate around them) and audience practices. Rather, the focus of this book is on conceptualising the changing ways in which the experience of television is constructed by industry, through television's technology and cultural form. As such, at the heart of this book is an interest in the services that producers make content for and through which audiences encounter television. Despite the centrality of the service as the cultural entry point through which viewers encounter the content of television as a medium, television studies has paid relatively little attention to services (such as channels or VOD players) in comparison to other aspects of television, such as studies of programmes, production, institutions and fans/audiences.[31] Part of the aim of this book is to place the service more firmly on the agenda of television studies and to demonstrate its crucial role in structuring the experience of television as a medium. The next chapter, then, turns to the television service and unpacks this book's definition of online TV.

Notes

1 Chapter 2 will unpack this book's definition of online TV in detail.
2 Peter Rice made this comment at a lecture on 20 July 2016 following his award of an honorary doctorate at the University of Nottingham, UK.
3 A number of academic studies have pointed to the importance of broadband speeds, mobile devices and internet-connected sets in driving on-demand television. See, for example, Jock

Given et al. (2015) in relation to Australia, Junghwan Kim et al. (2016) in relation to South Korea, Mercedes Medina et al. (2015) in relation to Spain, Elaine Jing Zhao (2017) in relation to China and Amanda Lotz (2014; 2016) in relation to the USA.

4 Convergence, however, does not mean that television and the internet are seamlessly integrated. As will become apparent across this book, the intertwining of television and the internet is uneven and determined by social, cultural, industrial, political, economic and technological factors.

5 Although access to high-speed broadband, 4G, tablets, smartphones and internet-connected television sets is widespread across the UK, it is not universal. Geographic and social factors (including age and income) continue to have an impact on the accessibility of online TV even in developed economies like the UK.

6 Indeed, a key experience of writing this book is that it has invited me to challenge my own historical assumptions about what television is as an object. As such, I hope that this book might also provide some inspiration for new historical studies that examine overlooked aspects of the history of this complex medium.

7 As a consequence, this book places less focus on certain aspects of television as a medium, such as changing production practices, or the wider cultures that surround television viewing, such as fan communities or forms of audience interaction.

8 Chapter 3 will unpack in more detail what I mean by the 'online TV industry.'

9 Television as a medium is also shaped by changing technologies of production, such as cameras, editing equipment, lights and so on. The changing technologies of production are outside of the scope of this book, but future studies could use this method to analyse the changes and continuities to production technologies and their impact on television as a medium. Indeed, as cloud services offering integrated end-to-end production, distribution and delivery systems for television become more ubiquitous it will be important to include production technologies in such a mapping exercise.

10 Table 1.1 focuses on those aspects of television associated with the delivery of audiovisual content to viewers. It also includes all of the ways in which the internet could be understood to expand television in the internet era. In doing so, it includes aspects of contemporary online video culture that would fall outside of this book's definition of online TV. The relationship between online TV and other forms of online audiovisual services will be examined in Chapter 2.

11 Cable technology has a longer history, particularly in the US, but began to be adopted more broadly as an alternative to broadcasting from the 1980s onwards in a number of countries around the world (Banet-Weiser et al. 2007).

12 Chapter 2 will unpack the concept of the television service in more detail. The Conclusion will explore how the concept of online TV as a service differs from that of television as a public service.

13 In this book I am particularly interested in the frames that emerge *within* the services and devices used to watch television. However, the concept of a frame could be usefully broadened to include other paratextual content encountered outside of the service that shapes the experience of watching television, such as marketing, websites, social media content, fan sites and so on (see Gray 2010).

14 The technology and cultural form of television was shaped by nationally specific social, cultural and political factors. For example, the scarcity of the electromagnetic spectrum through which television was broadcast led to the development of television as a public service in much of Western Europe and as an arm of the state in more authoritarian countries. Countries structured their television services differently, with some placing more emphasis on regional broadcasters and others focusing on the development of national services. In some developing countries television only emerged as a significant cultural force in the cable/satellite era.

15 There had been earlier experiments with pay-TV but these did not take off. Thanks to Emily Rees for this observation.

16 This is not to deny that there were developments in the cable and satellite era that challenged the conceptualisation of television as a medium for watching audiovisual content on a television set. Cable allowed community television channels to emerge in some contexts,

yet the majority of the content shown on television in the cable/satellite era was professionally produced. The expansion of channels and the frames of EPGs did introduce the cultural experience of channel surfing, although this can be understood as a viewing-related activity. The development of games consoles and interactive services (such as Teletext in the UK) did offer new experiences on television sets (Gazzard 2015), but these did not undermine television's central position as a medium for viewing audiovisual content.

17 Definitions of multiplatform over this period are not fixed. Gillian Doyle argues that the term tends to refer to the production of content and services to be delivered and distributed across multiple platforms (2015, p.51). It can be used to refer to the reuse of existing content across additional digital platforms, as well as the extension of single storyworlds across multiple media and services (Doyle 2010, p.433). Doyle argues that one consequence of the shift to multiplatform is that companies began to think about their work as building and sustaining relationships with audiences, rather than just creating and distributing content (2015, p.52). In this sense, multiplatform chimes with broader developments in the branding and marketing of television at this time (Johnson 2012).

18 See also Ross (2008) and Holt & Sanson (2014).

19 See also Doyle (2016) and Evans et al. (2017).

20 In the UK and in the Nordic contexts, for example, public service broadcasters were early and proactive developers of VOD services (see, for example, Ofcom 2014, p.143; Andersson Schwarz 2016, p.130). Elaine Zhao argues that in China the broadcast regulator has been active in attempting to protect broadcasters from the competition of internet video services and to establish control over the VOD streaming market (2017, pp.34–6).

21 In some national contexts, television broadcasters and networks have been far slower to launch on-demand television services (see, for example, Lotz 2014 on the USA). Michael Strangelove argues that many US broadcast, cable and satellite providers only offered VOD services once they began to face the threat of piracy facilitated by developments in peer-to-peer sharing services on the internet (2015, p.10).

22 There have also been attempts to revive 3D television technology in the early 2010s, alongside experiments in virtual reality.

23 There is a lack of consistency in the terminology used to describe these devices. At the time of writing in early 2018, Wikipedia listed 31 different terms used to describe digital media players (Anon. 2018).

24 For example, Apple TV allows users to extend the display of Mac devices to the television set as a second monitor.

25 Cunningham and Silver (2013, p.105) use the term 'pro-am' to refer to a blurring of the boundaries between amateur and professional content initiated largely by YouTube. It encompasses content produced by amateurs whose practice becomes increasingly professionalised through investment from industry initiatives, such as YouTube's Partnership programme.

26 Michalis and Smith are writing specifically about the UK context, but Graeme Turner notes the resilience of free-to-air television even in countries such as South Korea and Hong Kong, where take-up of subscription television is near universal (Turner 2016, p.19).

27 This argument will be explored in more detail in Chapter 5.

28 This blurring of boundaries between media forms has its origins in the digital era but is exacerbated and extended in the internet era.

29 Although the cable/satellite era saw a rise in global conglomerates offering cable/satellite services and channels, these services and channels were largely regionally or nationally specific. By contrast, the internet offers the promise of truly global services that are not differentiated by region. In practice, however, it is still common for online video services to differ according to the region from which the service is being accessed.

30 There are a few notable exceptions. Julie Light's (2004) excellent PhD thesis on the television channel in the UK offered a sustained conceptualisation and examination of the channel in the digital era. Derek Johnson's (2018) edited collection convincingly

argues for the continued significance of channels and channel logics to the internet era of television. My own work has argued for channels and services as central structuring devices for both the industry and viewers (Johnson 2012; Johnson 2013).

Bibliography

Andersson Schwarz, J., 2016. Public Service Broadcasting and Data-Driven Personalization: A View from Sweden. *Television & New Media*, 17(2), pp.124–141.

Anon., 2018. Digital Media Player. *Wikipedia*. Available at: https://en.wikipedia.org/wiki/Digital_media_player [Accessed August 13, 2018].

Banet-Weiser, S., Chris, C. & Freitas, A. eds., 2007. *Cable Visions: Television beyond Broadcasting*, New York: New York University Press.

Barra, L., 2015. *Palinsesto: Storia e Tecnica Della Programmazione Televisiva*, Bari: Laterza.

Bennett, J., 2008. 'Your Window-on-the-World': The Emergence of Red-Button Interactive Television in the UK. *Convergence: The International Journal of Research into New Media Technologies*, 14(2), pp.161–182.

Bennett, J. & Strange, N., 2014. Linear Legacies: Managing the Multiplatform Production Process. In D. Johnson, D. Kompare & A. Santo, eds. *Making Media Work: Cultures of Management in the Entertainment Industries*. New York: New York University Press, pp. 63–89.

Bennett, J. & Strange, N. eds., 2011. *Television as Digital Media*, Durham, NC: Duke University Press.

Bruun, H., 2016. The Prism of Change: 'Continuity' in Public Service Television in the Digital Era. *Nordicom Review*, 37(2), pp.33–49.

van Den Bulck, H. & Enli, G.S., 2014. Bye Bye 'Hello Ladies?' In-Vision Announcers as Continuity Technique in a European Postlinear Television Landscape: The Case of Flanders and Norway. *Television & New Media*, 15(5), pp.453–469.

Caldwell, J.T., 2013. Para-Industry: Researching Hollywood's Blackwaters. *Cinema Journal*, 52(3), pp.157–165.

Cunningham, S. & Silver, J., 2013. *Screen Distribution and the New King Kongs of the Online World*, Basingstoke: Palgrave Macmillan.

Curtin, M., Holt, J. & Sanson, K., 2014. Introduction: Making of a Revolution. In M. Curtin, J. Holt & K. Sanson, eds. *Distribution Revolution: Conversations about the Digital Future of Film and Television*. Berkeley: University of California Press, pp. 12–31.

van Dijck, J., 2013. *The Culture of Connectivity: A Critical History of Social Media*, Oxford and New York: Oxford University Press.

Doyle, G., 2010. From Television to Multi-Platform: Less from More or More for Less? *Convergence: The International Journal of Research into New Media Technologies*, 16(4), pp.431–449.

Doyle, G., 2015. Multi-Platform Media and the Miracle of the Loaves and Fishes. *Journal of Media Business Studies*, 12(1), pp.49–65.

Ellis, J., 2000. *Seeing Things: Television in the Age of Uncertainty*, London and New York: I.B. Tauris.

Ellis, J., 2011. Interstitials: How the 'Bits in Between' Define the Programmes. In P. Grainge, ed. *Ephemeral Media: Transitory Screen Culture from Television to YouTube*. London: British Film Institute, pp.59–69.

Evans, E., 2011. *Transmedia Television*, Abingdon and New York: Routledge.

Evans, E., Coughlan, T. & Coughlan, V. 2017. Building Digital Estates: Multiscreening, Technology Management and Ephemeral Television. *Critical Studies in Television: The International Journal of Television Studies*, 12(2), pp.191–205.

Evans, E., McDonald, P., Bae, J., Ray, S. & Santos, E., 2016. Universal Ideals in Local Realities: Online Viewing in South Korea, Brazil and India. *Convergence: The International Journal of Research into New Media Technologies*, 22(4), pp.408–425.

Gazzard, A., 2015. Extending the Aerial: Uncovering Histories of Teletext and Telesoftware in Britain. *VIEW Journal of European Television History and Culture*, 4(7), pp.90–98. Available at: http://viewjournal.eu/index.php/view/article/view/JETHC083/182.

Gerbarg, D. & Noam, E., 2011. Introduction. In E. Noam, J. Groebel & D. Gerbarg, eds. *Internet Television*. New York: Routledge, pp.xxi–xxvii.

Gillan, J., 2011. *Television and New Media: Must-Click TV*, New York: Routledge.

Given, J., Brealey, M. & Gray, C., 2015. *Television 2025: Rethinking Small-Screen Media in Australia*. Hawthorne: Swinburne University of Technology. Available at: http://apo.org.au/node/54739.

Grainge, P. & Johnson, C., 2018. From Catch-Up TV to Online TV: Digital Broadcasting and the Case of BBC iPlayer. *Screen*, 59(1), pp.21–40.

Gray, J., 2010. *Show Sold Separately: Promos, Spoilers, and Other Media Paratexts*, New York: New York University Press.

Green, J., 2008. Why Do They Call It TV When It's Not on the Box? 'New' Television Services and Old Television Functions. *Media International Australia*, 126, pp.95–105.

Hall, T., 2013. Director-General Tony Hall Unveils His Vision for the BBC. BBC Media Centre. Available at: https://www.bbc.co.uk/mediacentre/speeches/2013/tony-hall-vision.html [Accessed August 7, 2018].

Holt, J. & Sanson, K. eds., 2014. *Connected Viewing: Selling, Streaming, and Sharing Media in the Digital Era*, New York: Routledge.

Holt, J. & Vonderau, P., 2014. 'Where the Internet Lives': Data Centres as Cloud Infrastructure. In L. Parks & N. Starosielski, eds. *Signal Traffic: Critical Studies of Media Infrastructures*. Urbana: University of Illinois Press, pp. 88–114.

Jenkins, H., 2006. *Convergence Culture: Where Old and New Media Collide*, New York and London: New York University Press.

Jenner, M., 2016. Is this TVIV? On Netflix, TVIII and Binge-Watching. *New Media & Society*, 18(2), pp.257–273.

Jenner, M., 2017. Binge-Watching: Video-On-Demand, Quality TV and Mainstreaming Fandom. *International Journal of Cultural Studies*, 20(3), pp.304–320.

Johnson, C., 2012. *Branding Television*, London: Routledge.

Johnson, C., 2013. The Continuity of 'Continuity': Flow and the Changing Experience of Watching Broadcast Television. *Key Words: A Journal of Cultural Materialism*, 11, pp.23–39.

Johnson, C., 2017. Beyond Catch-Up: VoD Interfaces, ITV Hub and the Repositioning of Television Online. *Critical Studies in Television: The International Journal of Television Studies*, 12(2), pp.121–138.

Johnson, C. & Weissmann, E., 2017. Ephemeral TV – Special Edition. *Critical Studies in Television: The International Journal of Television Studies*, 12(2), pp.97–101.

Johnson, D. ed., 2018. *From Networks to Netflix: A Guide to Changing Channels*, New York: Routledge.

Kim, J., Kim, S. & Nam, C., 2016. Competitive Dynamics in the Korean Video Platform Market: Traditional Pay TV Platforms vs. OTT Platforms. *Telematics and Informatics*, 33(2), pp.711–721.

Kompare, D., 2006. Publishing Flow: DVD Box Sets and the Reconception of Television. *Television & New Media*, 7(4), pp.335–360.

Küng, L., Picard, R.G. & Towse, R., 2008. Introduction. In L. Küng, R.G. Picard & R. Towse, eds. *The Internet and Mass Media*. London: Sage, pp.13–26.

Landau, N., 2016. *TV Outside the Box: Trailblazing in the Digital Television Revolution*, New York: Focal Press.

Light, J.J., 2004. *Television Channel Identity: The Role of Channels in the Delivery of Public Service Television in Britain, 1996–2002*. PhD Thesis. University of Glasgow.

Lobato, R., 2018. Rethinking International TV Flows Research in the Age of Netflix. *Television and New Media*, 19(3), pp.241–256.

Lobato, R., 2019. *Netflix Nations: The Geography of Digital Distribution*, New York: New York University Press.

Lotz, A.D., 2014. *The Television Will Be Revolutionized*, 2nd ed., New York: New York University Press.

Lotz, A.D., 2016. *Portals: A Treatise on Internet-Distributed Television*, Ann Arbor, MI: Maize Books.

McDonald, K. & Smith-Rowsey, D. eds., 2016. *The Netflix Effect: Technology and Entertainment in the 21st Century*, New York: Bloomsbury.

Mann, D., 2014. Introduction: When Television and New Media Work Worlds Collide. In D. Mann, ed. *Wired TV: Laboring Over an Interactive Future*. New Brunswick, NJ: Rutgers University Press.

Medina, M., Herrero, M. & Guerrero, E., 2015. Audience Behaviour and Multiplatform Strategies: The Path towards Connected TV in Spain. *Austral Communicacion*, 4(1), pp.153–172.

Meikle, G. & Young, S., 2008. Beyond Broadcasting? TV for the Twenty-First Century. *Media International Australia*, 126, pp.67–70.

Michalis, M. & Smith, P., 2016. The Relation between Content Providers and Distributors: Lessons from the Regulation of Television Distribution in the United Kingdom. *Telematics and Informatics*, 33(2), pp.665–673.

Ofcom, 2014. *The Communications Market Report 2014*, London: Ofcom. Available at: http://stakeholders.ofcom.org.uk/binaries/research/cmr/cmr14/2014_UK_CMR.pdf.

Ofcom, 2015. *Public Service Broadcasting in the Internet Age*, London: Ofcom. Available at: https://www.ofcom.org.uk/__data/assets/pdf_file/0025/63475/PSB-statement.pdf.

Robinson, M.J., 2017. *Television on Demand: Curatorial Culture and the Transformation of TV*, New York and London: Bloomsbury.

Ross, S.M., 2008. *Beyond the Box: Television and the Internet*, Malden, MA and Oxford: Blackwell.

Scannell, P., 1996. *Radio, Television and Modern Life: A Phenomenological Approach*, Oxford: Blackwell.

Sparks, M., 2007. *Switching to Digital: UK Public Policy and the Market*, Bristol and Chicago: Intellect.

Spigel, L. & Olsson, J. eds., 2004. *Television after TV: Essays on a Medium in Transition*, Durham, NC: Duke University Press.

Stewart, M., 2016. The Myth of Televisual Ubiquity. *Television & New Media*, 17(8), pp.691–705.

Strange, N., 2011. Multiplatforming Public Service: The BBC's Bundled Project. In J. Bennett & N. Strange, eds. *Television as Digital Media*. Durham, NC: Duke University Press, pp.132–157.

Strangelove, M., 2015. *Post-TV: Piracy, Cord-Cutting, and the Future of Television*, Toronto: University of Toronto Press.

Tay, J. & Turner, G., 2008. What is Television? Comparing Media Systems in the Post-Broadcast Era. *Media International Australia*, 126, pp.71–81.

Turner, G., 2016. Surviving the Post-Broadcast Era: The International Context for Australia's ABC. *Media International Australia*, 158(1), pp.17–25.

Uricchio, W., 2014. Film, Cinema, Television … Media? *New Review of Film and Television Studies*, 12(3), pp.266–279.

Van Esler, M., 2016. Not Yet the Post-TV Era: Network and MVPD Adaptation to Emergent Distribution Technologies. *Media and Communication*, 4(3), pp.131–141.

Ward, S.J., 2015. *Branding Bridges: Imported Drama and Discourses of Value in the British Digital Television Industry*. PhD Thesis. University of Nottingham.

Williams, R., 1990. *Television: Technology and Cultural Form,* 2nd ed., London: Routledge.

Wolk, A., 2015. *Over the Top: How the Internet Is (Slowly But Surely) Changing the Television Industry*, CreateSpace Independent Publishing Platform.

Ytreberg, E., 2002. Continuity in Environments: The Evolution of Basic Practices and Dilemmas in Nordic Television Scheduling. *European Journal of Communication*, 17(3), pp.283–304.

Zhao, E.J., 2017. The Bumpy Road towards Network Convergence in China: The Case of Over-the-Top Streaming Services. *Global Media and China*, 2(1), pp.28–42.

2

DEFINING ONLINE TV

RECAP

- Since the late-2000s, the penetration of fast broadband speeds, tablets, smartphones and internet-connected televisions has heralded a new '**internet era**' for television. The internet era challenges television in two ways:

  1 The internet emerges as a mainstream medium for viewing audio-visual content and is able to offer viewing experiences akin to those that previously only television could provide.
  2 Television is delivered through internet-connected devices, such as smart TVs, digital media players, tablets and smartphones.

- Chapter 1 outlined a conceptual framework for analysing changes to television as a medium over time. It argued that television is made up of five components:

  1 *Technological infrastructures* that deliver television services to people (e.g. cable or broadband).
  2 *Technological devices* through which people directly experience television. These can be divided into *viewing devices* for watching television programming (e.g. TV set or tablet) and *add-on devices* that attach to the viewing device (e.g. personal video recorder or digital media player).
  3 *Services* that are the entry point for viewers to television content (e.g. TV channels, subscription TV services offered by cable and satellite operators or on-demand services like Netflix).
  4 *Content* such as the programmes, adverts and interstitials delivered through television services.

5   *Frames* that organise television content and shape how it is experienced (e.g. the linear schedule, electronic programme guide or interface).

• Over time, each component of television has multiplied. However, these changes have been largely additive rather than substitutive. Newer iterations of television's technology and cultural form frequently sit alongside older ones.

Introduction

In the summer of 2015 my father proudly announced that he had 'got a Roku.' Not being an early adopter of technology or a particularly avid television viewer, I was surprised by this announcement and intrigued as he proudly showed me how his Roku allowed him to access the BBC's on-demand service, iPlayer, through his television set. For my father, Roku mattered because it attached to the traditional device of the TV set and therefore made on-demand television accessible and worth watching for the first time. I start with this personal anecdote because of the ways in which it speaks to the changes wrought in the internet era (examined in Chapter 1) in which television and the internet are increasingly intertwined. My father's Roku transformed his television set from a medium of (digital) broadcasting into a medium that also depended on broadband, and from a medium that provided access to linear TV to one that also enabled him to access content on demand. In doing so, this small anecdote reveals the interconnections between different elements of the conceptual model of television laid out in Chapter 1 – between infrastructures, devices, services, frames and content – and the dynamic relationship between older and newer forms of television in the internet era. It speaks to the ways in which the newer forms of **nonlinear** and on-demand content and the devices that deliver them are not separate from older broadcast technologies and cultural forms. Rather, the internet era is characterised by the interdependence of television and the internet, and continuities, as well as changes, to television as a medium.

These changes to television, the internet and the relationship between them take place within what Chapter 1 defined as an internet era characterised by the penetration of high broadband speeds, tablets, smartphones and internet-connected televisions. Although these changes are not felt everywhere across the globe, around the world these conditions are altering the relationship between television and the internet (Ofcom 2017). Since 2010 the internet has begun to provide viewing experiences that are largely indistinguishable from those offered by television, while simultaneously transforming how television delivers audiovisual content to viewers. These changes present a particular challenge to normative understandings of television as an audiovisual medium. Should the internet now be considered a form of television? Does the definition of television need to be extended to include all internet-enabled video services? This chapter asks how we make sense of television as an audiovisual medium once the internet begins to compete and converge with television in the delivery of audiovisual content. In doing so, it sets out a definition of online TV that frames the rest of this book

The chapter will begin by asking what is at stake in defining television in the internet era. It argues that the converged and volatile media ecosystem of the internet era has undermined normative assumptions about television as a medium. As television has fragmented, the potential definitions of television have multiplied. This requires academics to be more overt in outlining their conceptual approach to television. The chapter then goes on to unpack this book's definition of online TV as *services that facilitate the viewing of editorially selected audiovisual content through internet-connected devices and infrastructure*. This definition recognises the continuities (as well as the differences) between contemporary internet-connected television and earlier forms of television that emerged in the broadcast, cable/satellite and digital eras. However, it also distinguishes online TV from other forms of online video service, such as YouTube. In unpacking this definition of online TV, this chapter explores how online TV differs from the concept of platforms, particularly as it relates to the major tech platforms provided by Google, Apple, Facebook and Amazon that have come to dominate the internet. Through exploring the boundaries of the book's definition of online TV, the chapter also asks how online TV services can be situated in relation to sites that use video as a supplement to other forms of activity, such as news websites and pages dedicated to television programmes that privilege reading or interacting over viewing. The chapter ends by examining how the definition of online TV draws attention to the key stakes for the online TV industry, providing an agenda for academic studies that wish to examine how this industry is responding to the volatile changes wrought by the internet era. As such, the aim of this chapter is to provide a definition of online TV that can be utilised by scholars (and industry/policy-makers) to understand the ways in which television is being transformed as a consequence of the penetration of high broadband speeds, tablets, smartphones and internet-connected televisions.

Approaching television in the internet era

As discussed in Chapter 1, television is a hybrid medium that has been subject to seemingly endless change (see, for example, Uricchio 2014) and whose definition has never been stable. Yet the internet era that has emerged since the late 2000s has been particularly disruptive to accepted definitions of television as a medium. Not only has television become increasingly internet-connected, changing and expanding at the level of infrastructure, device, service, frame and content (see Chapter 1), but also the internet era situates television within a fundamentally different media ecosystem. This is a media ecosystem that is geographically expansive, characterised by increased storage capacity, networked and participative. In this ecosystem multiple different forms of audiovisual content are delivered through a dizzying array of technological infrastructures and devices by services that often combine viewing with other forms of user experience (such as playing, reading, interacting and participating). One consequence of this is that previously normative assumptions about what counts as television come under threat.

It is, therefore, perhaps unsurprising that there is little consistency in the academic attempts to conceptualise television in the internet era. Amanda Lotz, for example, defines a new form of television that emerges in the internet era that she terms 'portals.' For Lotz (2016, p.9), portals are internet-distributed television services that are delivered on the open web (rather than through **internet protocol television** (IPTV)), are nonlinear in organisation, distribute 'long-form content most similar to that recognizable as "television"' and are funded by subscription. In developing this definition, Lotz usefully identifies a group of services, such as Hulu, Netflix and HBO Go, that share much of cable television's content and funding mechanisms, but, Lotz argues, are distributed and organised in new ways. One difficulty with Lotz's understanding of online television as portals, however, is that these characteristics are specific to the US context within which she is working. In much of Europe, for example, there are a number of internet-distributed television services provided by television broadcasters that would fit Lotz's model, but which are funded by advertising rather than by subscription, such as ITV Hub and All 4 in the UK. This speaks to a different industrial and cultural context in which the free-to-air television market is more robust, and the penetration of subscription cable and satellite services is less strong. Similarly, it is commonplace for these services to include linear streams of their broadcast channels, effectively combining the linear and nonlinear within one service (Johnson 2017).[1]

Where Lotz explicitly focuses her study on the US, Jorge Abreu et al. develop a taxonomy of contemporary television services that is designed to transcend geographical and national boundaries. Their model divides the landscape of television in the internet era into four quadrants determined by whether the service offered is linear or nonlinear and delivered over a managed or unmanaged operator network (2017, pp.56–62). A managed operator network is one in which the provider of the service controls the infrastructure through which that service is delivered, such as a cable provider's control of the fibre optic cable network. An unmanaged operator network is an 'over-the-top' (OTT) service provided on the open web, such as Netflix. The distinction here between managed and unmanaged operator networks draws attention to the ways in which the control of technological infrastructure can be used to dominate specific markets.[2] Lotz excludes internet-distributed television services offered by cable, arguing that they are shaped by different practices based on cable's linear delivery of channels. By contrast, Abreu et al. incorporate these services, enabling them to examine how control over cable and internet infrastructure can shape the development of internet-connected TV.

Although Abreu et al.'s model is more inclusive than Lotz's it does retain a distinction between linear and **nonlinear television**, making it difficult to account for services that combine linear and nonlinear provision. Abreu et al. do acknowledge that certain services could be placed within more than one of their categories. BBC iPlayer, for example, could be placed in three of their categories. It functions as 'catch-up TV' (nonlinear content over managed operator networks); it streams BBC's broadcast channels (linear content via OTT); and it provides access to nonlinear content (non-linear content via OTT). The convergent nature of the online video ecosystem, in which one service like BBC iPlayer can deliver multiple forms of content in a range of different ways, makes segmentation into hard and fast categories a difficult task.

In addition, in focusing specifically on streaming services neither Lotz's nor Abreu et al.'s models account for downloading and other forms of electronic sell through (EST), interactive services and peer-to-peer (P2P) services providing informal/illegal access to content. Both of these studies also overlook sites that provide streamed video as part of a wider set of services (such as social media sites like Periscope) and fail to account for online video services like YouTube. For Michael Strangelove the presence of television content on YouTube invalidates claims for the taxonomic distinction between YouTube and television. He writes, 'The argument that YouTube is categorically different from television falls apart when I can turn on my television and watch a complete episode of *I Dream of Jeannie* streaming in from YouTube or, conversely, turn on my computer and watch television shows on YouTube' (2015, p.165).

A key difference between the more expansive definitional approach taken by Strangelove and the narrower definitions of Lotz and Abreu et al. lies in how they deal with social media sites and P2P streaming services where video content increasingly appears.[3] This choice appears to be determined in part by whether television as an object is being studied from the top down or from the bottom up. Both Lotz and Abreu et al.'s primary intention is to examine changes to the industrialised production and provision of television. By contrast, central to Strangelove's book is the question of how online piracy has challenged understandings of television as a medium (2015, p.15). As a consequence of this, he is more broadly concerned with television as it has developed within and outside of industrial modes of production.[4] This distinction is an important one in the internet era because historically television has been a medium largely confined to industrial modes of production. Due to the expense involved in the production of television programmes and the restrictions developed around the infrastructures of television broadcasting (such as the decision by governments in the broadcast era to allocate the limited electromagnetic spectrum to a small number of largely national companies), there have been few opportunities for television to develop outside of industrial structures. Digitalisation and the development of the internet into a medium for the delivery of video have reduced the barriers to the production and distribution of audiovisual content, making it significantly easier for non-industrial forms of 'television' to emerge. Today, arguably anyone with access to a computer can create and distribute user-generated audiovisual content through online services like YouTube and Facebook. As we shall go on to see, this distinction between professional and user-generated forms of internet video is crucial to understanding the place of television in the contemporary media ecosystem.

Defining online TV

Much of the academic literature on online TV has focused on the difference of internet-enabled television from the cultural forms of linear, broadcast television (Lotz 2016; Jenner 2016; McDonald & Smith-Rowsey 2016). Strangelove, for example, argues that with the convergence of television and the internet, older definitions of television need to be radically overhauled. In particular, he is critical of approaches to contemporary television that draw from the characteristics of television's historical origins in broadcasting, writing that 'The argument that online television is not really television because it lacks some essential character of twentieth-century television is misguided. Television is not a fixed experience defined by a particular industry structure, ontological status, or technological context' (2015, p.164). Strangelove's insistence on the 'complex, heterogeneous, and rapidly changing' (2015, p.166) nature of television is to be welcomed, as is his emphasis on avoiding essentialist definitions of television and video. Yet his argument assumes that 21st-century definitions of television should disregard television's 20th-century origins, that television should not be defined by what it *was* but rather by what it *is* in the mid-2010s. The problem with this argument is that it overlooks the ways in which historical social, cultural, political and institutional forces continue to shape the development, and definitions, of television in the present. Chapter 1 demonstrated that the changes to television over its history have been additive rather than substitutive. New devices like tablets, nonlinear video-on-demand (VOD) services and user-generated content (UGC) have not replaced older forms of television, such as the television set, linear schedule or professionally produced programming. Indeed, increasingly these older and newer technologies and cultural forms intertwine and coexist.

To understand this phenomenon, we need a definition of television that is able to account for the continuities between television in its broadcast/cable/satellite/digital eras and its contemporary formation, as well as the differences. Identifying the *shared* characteristics between older forms of television and contemporary online audiovisual services helps reveal the ways in which definitions of what television was are continuing to shape how television is imagined and constructed in the future. At the same time, identifying these shared characteristics also allows us to distinguish between the different kinds of video service that coexist in the internet era. Video has come to be an increasingly important component of the internet since 2010, making up 73 percent of all consumer internet traffic globally in 2016 (Cisco 2017). By the mid-2010s, video had become a quotidian component of the internet browsing experience, featuring on many websites, whether as produced, acquired, user-generated and/or advertising content. At the same time, there has been an explosion in the number of services dedicated specifically to online video. Strangelove argues that YouTube should be understood as television because it provides access to television programmes and can be viewed on a television set. Yet such an argument overlooks the differences between the sites and services offering access to video content through internet-connected devices.

This book, therefore, argues that it is possible to identify *online TV* as a subset of internet-connected video services that shares core characteristics with earlier forms of television. These online TV services provide access to editorially selected audiovisual content through internet-connected devices within a closed infrastructure, and privilege viewing over other forms of activity. As we shall go on to see, this definition differentiates online TV from the other forms of online video services that provide access to audiovisual content through internet-connected devices and infrastructure, such as social media, online news and TV-related websites (see Table 2.1).

TABLE 2.1 Online TV vs online video

Online TV	Online video		
	Social media	News websites	TV-related websites
Provide access to audiovisual content through internet-connected devices and infrastructure			
Video as primary content	Video as primary or supplementary content	Video as supplementary content	Video as supplementary content
Viewing	Viewing and communicating	Reading	Reading and participating
Editorially selected content	Passively acquired content	Editorially selected content	Passively acquired and/or editorially selected content
Closed	Open	Closed	Closed or open

In addition, this definition of online TV draws attention to the ways in which historically dominant constructs of television as a medium are both continued and challenged in the internet era. Adopting this approach is not to 'risk reinforcing the ideological strategy of the television industry' (Strangelove 2015, p.165), as Strangelove argues of scholars who 'insist on rigid distinctions between television and online hybrid forms such as YouTube' (ibid.). Rather it is to reveal for scrutiny the ways in which historically dominant definitions in which the television industry is particularly embedded are operative at a moment of rapid change, and to ask what might be at stake for those segments of the industry as the contemporary ecosystem subjects those definitional boundaries to the threat of transformation.

There are five components to this book's definition of online TV:

1. Online TV can be understood as services.
2. Online TV services are oriented towards the creation of viewing experiences.
3. Online TV services provide access to editorially selected content.
4. Online TV services are closed.
5. Online TV services are delivered through internet-connected devices and infrastructure.

These components differentiate online TV services from the many other websites, apps and social networks that provide access to audiovisual content online.

Online TV as service

Chapter 1 defined the television service as a cultural form that acts as the entry point for viewers to television content. In the broadcast era there was no significant distinction between the technology of television and its cultural form (see Figure 2.1). Television consisted of content organised into the flow of channels that was delivered to the device of the television set through broadcast infrastructure.

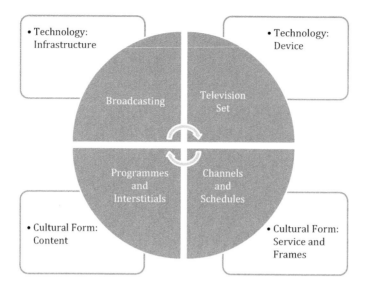

FIGURE 2.1 Broadcast television as technology and cultural form

'Watching television' effectively referred to the experience of turning on the television set and viewing video content delivered through broadcast infrastructure, organised into channels and framed by scheduling. It was not possible to watch television outside of broadcast infrastructure, beyond the TV set or removed from the structures of channels and schedules.

In the internet era, as the technologies of television have become more dispersed, it is the cultural form of the service that has emerged as the central site that mediates our experience of watching television (see Figure 2.2). As television viewing has gradually become decoupled from its links to a single infrastructure (broadcasting) and a single device (the television set), the service acts as a vital entry point for viewers regardless of the technology that they are using. For example, I am watching the service of Netflix or BBC One regardless of whether I watch it through a set-top box or an app, on a television set or a tablet. Although infrastructure and device may shape the form and nature of television services, *it is through the service that we experience television in the internet era*. It is for this reason that the 'service' is at the centre of the definition of online TV outlined in this book.[5]

In the internet era a wide range of different kinds of video services coexist and combine, multiplying the ways in which audiovisual content can be experienced. Some of these are dedicated to video, such as YouTube. Others include video as a component of a broader service, such as the use of video content in online news sites or the presence of video on social media sites like Facebook. Oftentimes, the same content appears across multiple video services. Not all of these can be understood as online TV services. Specifically, online TV services can be distinguished from other forms of internet-connected video service because they share three core features with

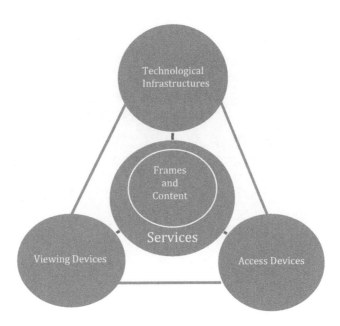

FIGURE 2.2 Online TV as technology and cultural form

earlier forms of broadcast, cable/satellite and digital television: they construct viewing experiences; they provide access to editorially selected content; and they are closed.

Online TV as viewing services

As explored in Chapter 1, the dominant television services in the broadcast and cable/satellite eras were focused primarily on the user experience of viewing, even if engagement with television involved a wide range of different social and cultural activities, from reading about television to writing in to broadcasters or talking back to the television set (Wood 2009). The affordances of the services that provided television were oriented around constructing viewing experiences rather than providing platforms for other forms of activity and participation.[6] One of the key characteristics of the online video ecosystem, however, is that the affordances of the internet facilitate different kinds of social and cultural activity within one device and service, from reading and playing to communicating, participating and interacting. Many services that offer access to online video do so to support a broader aim of facilitating interaction and participation. For example, Facebook and Twitter both enable viewers to upload, share and view video content. However, video operates on these sites primarily as a support to the broader communicative aims of a social networking site.[7] Similarly, video forms a central component of numerous news websites, such as *BBC News*, *The Guardian* and *Vice*. However, here video sits as an accompaniment to written news, and these sites are not constructed primarily around the experience of viewing.

Online TV services can be differentiated from these other sites where video content appears online because they explicitly and specifically focus on offering a viewing experience to their users. A fundamental difference between BBC iPlayer, for example, and the BBC News website is the former's construction as a site for the viewing of audiovisual content. Indeed, this emphasis on viewing is so explicit that the BBC has a separate on-demand service (iPlayer Radio) for the audio content from its radio stations. Online TV services from broadcasters and cable networks (such as Hulu, CBS All Access and Disney Life), OTT providers (such as Netflix and Amazon Prime Video) and smaller niche providers (such as Globe Player, a dedicated site for on-demand video content from Shakespeare's Globe theatre), all share this central focus on constructing viewing experiences. While the key to a social media site, such as Facebook, is the provision of an interface and **protocols** that enable social connectivity, central to online TV is the construction of a service focused on facilitating the viewing of audiovisual content.

Online TV as editorial services

A further distinction between online TV and social media sites is that online TV services acquire (through producing or licensing) the content that they use to construct their viewing experiences. Here my definition of online TV accords with Stuart Cunningham and Jon Silver's (2013) distinction between the 'passive' acquisition of content on social media platforms and the active sourcing of content for television services. For example, the service offered by YouTube depends on users uploading content to the platform. In this sense, YouTube passively acquires content by creating a service that facilitates the provision of content by its users. By contrast, central to the work of online TV services, such as Netflix, Hulu, Amazon Prime Video and HBO Now, is the production and/or acquisition of the audiovisual content that they provide access to, making the control (and sale) of intellectual property rights a core component of online TV businesses, as will be examined in Chapter 4. The *service* of online TV is providing the frictionless experience of watching a range of editorially selected audiovisual content across multiple devices, while the service of social media sites, such as YouTube and Facebook, is providing a networked space for the contributions of users.

Online TV as closed services

The distinction between content that is actively, rather than passively, acquired points to a further characteristic of online TV, which is that it is provided through closed services. The passive provision of content characteristic of social media depends on an open platform to which users can easily contribute. For example, social networks, such as YouTube and Facebook, need to make their platforms accessible to third parties in order to generate content and revenue. These sites fundamentally depend on users uploading content: Facebook only exists insofar as its users post status updates, and YouTube depends on individuals and organisations actively uploading videos to its site. By contrast, online TV services operate deliberately closed sites. These services may enable limited interaction and personalisation, such as rating videos or construct-ing playlists, but the primary content offered is provided by the service rather than by the user. Netflix, BBC iPlayer and Now TV do not depend on the participation of users for the video content that they offer; nor do they operate open platforms that enable any user to upload content to their service. Online TV services are, therefore, constructed as closed spaces that limit the contributions of users and are designed pri-marily to facilitate viewing. Social networks, by contrast, depend on the construction of open and networked spaces that are designed to facilitate, and are dependent on, interaction and participation.

Online TV as internet-connected services

Thus far, the definition of online TV as closed services that provide access to the viewing of editorially selected content is broad enough to encompass newer forms of VOD as well as the older forms of television channels and cable/satellite bundles. This is helpful because all of these different kinds of television service continue to coexist and intertwine in the internet era. Yet what distinguishes online TV services (whether channels, cable/satellite bundles or VOD) from earlier television services is that they are delivered through internet-connected devices and infrastructure and operate within an internet ecosystem that is fundamentally different to the broadcast, cable, satellite and even digital ecosystem. The internet infrastructure is characterised by sig-nificant fluidity between and within services. It enables channels to be integrated into VOD services and for VOD services to be offered within cable bundles. Online TV services can be delivered as standalone apps, be integrated into websites that offer other forms of television-related content and operate as one part of a broader interconnected web of services, such as the way in which Amazon Prime Video is intricately tied to Amazon's broader retail business. This is an internet ecosystem that enables high levels of fluidity between different sites, services and platforms and is characterised by the frequent and rapid development of new devices, services and infrastructures. Online TV services need to be understood, therefore, as operating in interconnection with other services and platforms in fluid and agile ways.

For example, although I have so far outlined the differences between online TV services and YouTube, many online TV services offer YouTube channels where users can access a selection of their content. This speaks to the fluid relationship between online TV and online video services. Asking why online TV services upload some of their content to YouTube reveals the benefits and limitations of operating a closed online TV service within a networked internet ecosystem. A crucial difference between an online TV service and that service's YouTube channel is the control exercised over the *frames* that organise television content within a service and shape how it is experienced by users. Within their own ser-vices online TV providers control the frames, such as **metadata** and interfaces, that determine how content is described, organised, tagged and labelled. This can shape how findable that content is and the meanings that viewers attribute to it.[8] By contrast, when online TV services place their content on YouTube they lose control over the environment within which that content sits. Online TV providers may determine which content to upload to YouTube and may have some control over the metadata attributed to that content, but they do not control the terms by which that content is uploaded or the infrastructure within which that content appears (Nixon 2016). Within the YouTube channels of online TV services, it is YouTube that controls the interface, constructs the algorithms used, determines what data is collected and sets the terms by which advertising revenue is shared.

However, although YouTube controls the frames within which content uploaded to its service is encountered, as an open service it relinquishes control over the content itself. This has left YouTube open to accusations that it enables the circulation of content that is harmful, dangerous or inappropriate (Alexander 2018; Popper 2017). By contrast, online TV services not only control the frames that shape user experience, but also control all of the content within that service, enabling them to provide highly regulated user experiences. This can help build brand trust and value, which can provide competitive advantage in a crowded marketplace where multiple services are vying for attention.

Yet one of the difficulties of operating a closed online TV service within a networked internet ecosystem is that it is less open to external search services like Google. This makes it harder for users to encounter the content within an online TV service without accessing the service directly. By contrast, an open site like YouTube is far more searchable, and users can easily share the content uploaded to YouTube, epitomising the benefits that Henry Jenkins et al. (2013) attribute to 'spreadable media.' Online TV services tend, therefore, to exploit the openness of YouTube to create channels where they upload a selection of content (typically clips and promos) that can be easily shared and discovered by users. Although YouTube channels do generate revenue for the owners of online TV services, their primary function is to promote the online TV service by making a selection of its content more accessible within the networked ecosystem of the internet (Grece 2016; Bennett & Strange 2018; Doyle 2016, p.698).

Examining the relationship between online TV services and YouTube demonstrates how online TV services operate in conjunction with other services within the internet ecosystem. Video circulates on the internet across multiple different kinds of service. Yet these services have distinct affordances and characteristics that shape the kinds of cultural functions and user experiences that they offer. Online TV services offer highly regulated and controlled experiences to viewers. By contrast their YouTube channels operate as far more open sites that facilitate marketing and promotion because the content can be more easily discovered and shared. To understand the internet era, therefore, we need to be attuned to the differences, as well as the similarities, between the range of sites where video content appears online.

At the boundaries of online TV services: platforms and products

Thus far, this chapter has laid out the key characteristics of online TV as services that facilitate the viewing of editorially selected audiovisual content through internet-connected devices and infrastructure. This definition helps distinguish online TV services from other forms of online video, from social media sites like YouTube that provide an open platform for users to upload content to news and TV-related websites that include video as a support for other activities such as reading. The next section furthers unpack this definition of online TV services by exploring two cognate concepts that emerge in the internet era: platforms and **products**. In doing so, it will continue to examine the place of online TV within the networked internet ecosystem and interrogate the sometimes fluid boundaries that sit around this book's definition of online TV.

Platforms

The internet has significantly lowered barriers to entry, allowing new services and content to be provided from a range of sources (from individuals to large conglomerates). However, the networked infrastructure of the internet has come to be dominated by a small number of global US companies. Characterised by the Silicon Valley tech companies of Google, Apple, Facebook and Amazon (GAFA), these organisations control the underlying ecosystem that shapes the internet.[9] For example, Facebook dominates social media interactions online, YouTube the sharing of online video, Amazon e-commerce and Google online search. Whereas once it was television that was seen to have the power to shape national debate, by the 2010s these tech companies were positioned at the centre of a contemporary culture enacted online.[10] While television's control over culture in the 1960s and 1970s largely operated at a national level, the corporations that preside over the internet do so on an almost global scale. Although there have been online platforms developed by national economies in the East, such as South Korea, China and Taiwan, it is the US GAFA companies that are at the centre of the global digital economy online (Yong Jin 2015).

The internet, therefore, is dominated by a small number of predominantly US corporations that exert power by developing a suite of integrated online businesses that are positioned at the heart of contemporary culture. These companies all operate as platforms. The term 'platform' has emerged largely to describe 'the online services of content intermediaries' (Gillespie 2010, p.348) whose technological architecture is designed to aggregate multiple services that facilitate connection and the exchange of data by third party users (Plantin et al. 2018, p.296). As Dal Yong Jin argues, 'The hegemonic power of American-based platforms is especially crucial because Google, Facebook, iPhone and Android have functioned as major digital intermediaries thanks to their advanced role in aggregating several services' (2015, p.6). Google, for example, offers an integrated platform for a wide range of different kinds of activities, including search, maps, document editing/sharing, video sharing, music and video streaming, email, translations, a browser, smartphones and virtual reality (VR).[11] Jean-Christophe Plantin et al. argue that this feature of platforms gives them the characteristics of an infrastructure that links heterogeneous systems together (2018, pp.295–6). The infrastructures created by platform businesses create what Phil Simon describes as a 'powerful ecosystem that quickly and easily scales, morphs, and incorporates new features…, users, customers, vendors and partners' (2013, pp.22–3). This infrastructure is designed to enable easy and flexible adjustment in order to respond to rapid changes in consumer tastes and allow consumers and businesses to undertake a range of tasks under one umbrella. Platforms, therefore, can be understood as flexible infrastructures that operate an intermediary function through the aggregation of a range of services for multiple users.

However, platforms, such as Google, Apple, Facebook and Amazon, can be understood as intermediaries not only because they aggregate a range of services, but also because these services are '*designed* to be extended and elaborated from the outside, by other actors, provided those actors follow certain rules' (Plantin et al. 2018, p.298). In this sense, platforms are open sites that facilitate the activities of others, whether to communicate, interact or sell. The terminology of the platform connotes an 'open, neutral, egalitarian, and progressive support for activity' (Gillespie 2010, p.352). Platforms, such as YouTube, Facebook and Twitter, explicitly position themselves as facilitators, rather than editors or curators, whose primary function is to support the innovation and creativity of others (Plantin et al. 2018, p.297).

The language of platforms is often used to describe online TV services, such as Netflix (see, for example, Kim et al. 2016; Mikos 2016). Such rhetoric draws attention to the ways in which many online TV services use personalisation to create highly individualised services that respond to the choices made by viewers. In this sense, online TV services do depend on the activities of third parties in that their recommendation algorithms respond to user data gathered through use of the service. Yet this use of viewer behaviour to shape an online TV service is a far cry from platform businesses such as YouTube, Facebook and Twitter that depend on users for their content. Netflix and other online TV services that use personalisation do not have the intermediary function of platform businesses, operating instead as closed online TV services designed to enable access to content that has been acquired, rather than functioning as platforms that can be extended or elaborated by others. Online TV is, therefore, quite distinct from the contemporary platform business, as Table 2.2 demonstrates.

It is worth, however, qualifying the extent to which platforms can be understood as fundamentally open. As Tarleton Gillespie (2010) argues, the language of platforms obscures the ways in which businesses such as YouTube and Google, and the design of their platforms, affect the content that they host on their sites. YouTube, for example, has rules about the content that can be uploaded to its site and will remove content that fails to abide by those rules. There is, therefore, significant debate about the extent to which platform businesses like YouTube and Facebook adopt an editorial function (Helberger et al. 2015). Furthermore, José van Dijck (2013, p.164) argues that Google, Facebook and Apple operate from quite different techno-economic principles to each other, and that these shape how open their platforms are. Google wants the social layer on the web to remain open so that its engines can crawl the content in order to generate effective search results. By contrast, Facebook wants to position itself as an identity provider to other services, and so fences off access to its pages and only lets Google index its public pages. Apple's platform is also largely impenetrable to Google. Although iTunes can be accessed by Google because it is available through the web, the value for Apple lies largely in the data generated by its mobile devices that form part of a closed and walled garden.

TABLE 2.2 Online TV vs platforms

Online TV	Platforms
Provides access to audiovisual content through internet-connected devices and infrastructure.	Provide networked ecosystems that include a range of different kinds of services and products (which can include online TV services).
Editorially selected content that is produced or licensed directly by the service.	Function as intermediaries and are designed to be extended and elaborated by third parties.
Closed services that provide editorial control over content and viewing experience.	Open or semi-closed services.
Designed to facilitate viewing experiences over other forms of activity.	Highly fluid and agile businesses that frequently experiment with new products and services.

Using the examples of the iPhone and YouTube, Pelle Snickars argues that although both can be understood as open platforms, Apple tends to exercise more control over its platform than other Web 2.0 companies. Google, for example, does not supervise the uploading process on YouTube (although it does have terms and conditions that shape what content can be uploaded). By contrast, Apple vets all apps before they can be offered through its App Store (Snickars 2012, p.158). For this reason, Snickars describes Apple as a semi-closed platform. Apple's App Store creates the tools and resources for developers to produce and upload content. In this way it is similar to YouTube's 100 channels initiative, where Google provided investment and a platform for creators to produce and upload content. However, unlike YouTube, Apple's App Store checks each app before it is made available, providing users with the reassurance that the apps will work on iOS devices. For this reason, Snickars characterises Apple's App Store as a 'structured alternative to the open Web … a controlled digital space without viruses, malware, unsecure sites, or unstable programs: a gated community of code' (2012, p.166). Although this semi-closed platform might pull against the rhetoric of the productive, open, networked platform, Snickars argues that the App Store has succeeded not despite the tight control exercised by Apple, but because of it: Apple's App Store is a 'walled garden, albeit one in which everything *always* works' (ibid.). The structured market space created by Apple provides users with guarantees about the quality and functionality of the apps that they might purchase that are not available on a completely open platform.

Snickars' analysis of Apple's App Store raises some useful insights for examining online TV. First, it draws attention to the fact that although many platform businesses are open, in the sense that they enable third parties to upload content, that does not mean that they are uncontrolled spaces, whether that is the more limited control exercised by YouTube's terms and conditions or the more editorial control of Apple App Store's vetting process. Van Dijck argues that all of the major platforms restrict the formats of content that can be uploaded to their sites and measure content in terms of its potential to draw massive numbers of users. Similarly, YouTube's and Facebook's investment in channels and more professional content can be understood as the emergence of an 'editorial filter' that pulls against any characterisation of their platforms as completely open. As such, a key question in any examination of the online video ecosystem is the extent to which services exert editorial control over the content that they provide access to. In online TV services, exerting editorial control is central to their offer to users, and this plays a key role in shaping their business models and the market within which they operate, as will be examined in Chapter 4.

Second, Snickars' analysis enables us to consider the potential positive values that might lie in closed services like online TV. For Snickars, Apple's App Store is successful because it provides an edited space that offers the guarantee of quality and ease of use. Snickars even likens the App Store to a newspaper, claiming that 'as much as we like to be free to read what we want, we also want the news to be delivered to us' (2012, p.166). This points, therefore, to a core value in online TV services. Online TV services can be understood to succeed in the online video ecosystem not despite their closed nature, but because they offer a structured alternative to the open web. This enables online TV providers to control the customer experience of viewing content by creating a managed environment within which that content is experienced.

Despite the differences outlined here between platform businesses and online TV services, it is important to recognise that a number of platform businesses provide online TV services as part of their range of products. For example, Amazon operates as a platform business providing an online retail service, cloud computing services and devices, as well as an online TV service, Amazon Prime Video. Rather than understanding platform businesses and online TV services as opposed, it is more accurate to understand online TV as a particular kind of online video service provided by a range of different kinds of businesses and organisations, including a number of platform businesses. In this sense, the definition of online TV developed here is not restricted to those services offered by broadcast, cable and satellite television businesses, and allows examination of the ways in which a number of different businesses from a range of industrial sectors are moving into the terrain previously occupied by the broadcast, cable and satellite industries.[12]

Indeed, *Variety*'s Todd Spangler claimed in 2017 that there was 'a flurry of action in the over-the-top TV space,' characterised in particular by the move of social networks into the terrain of online TV services. Given the benefits of online TV services for their providers, it is unsurprising that in 2017 both YouTube and Facebook launched online TV services: YouTube TV and Facebook Watch. YouTube TV provides online access to linear streams of US network and cable channels in major US cities. Similar to services such as TVPlayer that also provide access to streamed TV channels over the internet, YouTube TV offers an editorially managed and closed service focused on providing access to acquired/originated programming. Unlike the main YouTube site, which is predicated on allowing any user to upload content, YouTube

TV can, therefore, be understood as an online TV service.[13] Facebook Watch provides access to professionally produced video content funded directly by Facebook or created by selected companies approved by Facebook (albeit limited to users in the US at the time of writing in summer 2018). While an attempt to create a service more specifically oriented around viewing, Facebook Watch does enable users to add comments and connect with friends while watching (Sandwell 2018; Tsukayama 2017). Facebook Watch represents a significant shift for the social network platform towards offering an online TV service where it exerts more editorial control over its content and focuses user behaviour more explicitly on viewing.

At the time of writing, all of the four major US platforms are offering or developing online TV services (Apple's iTunes, Google's YouTube TV, Facebook Watch and Amazon Prime Video) alongside the other products and services that make up their platform businesses. These products and services often sit in fluid relationship with each other. A subscription to Amazon Prime Video, for example, provides free shipping on many items purchased through Amazon and can be accessed online as one section within Amazon's broader retail site. In the networked and hyperlinked ecosystem of the internet it is important to recognise the fluid interrelationships between online TV services and the other services and products that circulate around and interconnect with them. The industry has developed the language of 'products' to speak to the ways in which individual services sit within sometimes complex networks of interconnections online.

Products

Examining the relationship between online TV services and platforms reveals the ways in which online TV sits within a broader online ecosystem in which a specific online TV service can feature as one part of a broader platform business. Online TV services sit alongside a range of services and television-related content that are often referred to within the online TV industry as 'products.' In the UK context, James Bennett and Niki Strange note the adoption of the language of 'products' within the BBC around 2010 as part of a broader rationalisation of the corporation's online strategy (2014, pp.65–7). In the words of former director of BBC Future Media and Technology, Erik Huggers (2010), a product is defined as 'a self-contained entity within BBC Online, which unites technology and editorial to meet a clearly defined audience need.' At the BBC these products are defined by genre – such as Sport, Weather, News, Children's[14] – but also by service or medium, such as TV, iPlayer (the BBC's VOD service) and Radio (Grainge & Johnson 2018, p.26). The language of 'products' is also used in the tech business to refer to the different components of platform businesses. For example, Google (2018) refers to its suite of different services and technologies as 'products.' As with this book's definition of online TV, the BBC's and Google's use of the language of products attends to a new media landscape in which content is experienced across multiple technologies and media, and services and content often overlap. For example, Google's products include services (such as Google Maps and YouTube) that frequently interconnect with other services (Google Maps is embedded in Google

Search, for example), as well as the technologies that provide access to these (and other non-Google) services (such as Google smartphones or Google Chromecast). Meanwhile, CBBC, the BBC's product for children aged 6 to 12, consists of content and services that extend across multiple media, with its own website, on-demand player, television and YouTube channel, and social media presence. At the same time, however, CBBC features as a component of another BBC product, its VOD service iPlayer, where users can access CBBC content on demand and live.

A product, therefore, could be understood as one or a set of content, services and/ or technologies that meet a defined user need and are united by a clear brand. It might refer to a service, such as Google Maps, that is integrated into a number of other apps and services and accessible across a range of devices. Or it might, for example, refer to a television channel, an app, a thematic grouping of content, a website, a YouTube channel and social media accounts, all united by a master brand (such as CBBC or BBC News). In relation to online TV, the language of products is particularly helpful for articulating the ways in which television content can be extended, accessed and engaged with across multiple services, platforms and devices. At the same time, it also draws attention to the multimedia and transmedia nature of the contemporary television industry, which is not solely focused on the creation of viewing experiences or audiovisual content (Evans 2011). In doing so, it reveals the ways in which online TV services, such as BBC iPlayer, sit alongside and in relationship with other TV-related internet services (or 'products') that structure the experience of television.

An examination of broadcaster websites usefully illustrates how online TV services can be situated in relation to a number of interconnected television-related products that offer a range of media activities (beyond watching) and content (beyond video). In the mid/late-2010s these websites tended to include one or more of the following kinds of media content:

- Clips and/or full programmes of content, oriented towards watching.
- Webpages for individual programmes, particularly for high profile and popular shows. These often contain transmedia content, such as games, webisodes and behind-the-scenes footage, and offer spaces for interaction through social media feeds and competitions. They combine reading, browsing and using with watching, communicating and gaming.
- An online store where you can buy merchandise, DVDs and Blu-rays, oriented towards shopping.
- News, sport and weather pages where video supports written text, oriented towards reading.

The websites for national broadcasters and networks, such as the BBC, NBC, CBC and ABC, tend to include the full range of media content outlined above with news, sport and weather pages primarily oriented around written text with a focus on reading over viewing, programme pages with various levels of transmedia content, as well as pages that provide access to full-length content. For example, in the spring of 2018 the BBC's website (bbc.co.uk) was structured as follows (see Figure 2.3):

FIGURE 2.3 The homepage of bbc.co.uk on 18 May 2018

- Separate tabs for news, sport and weather, in which video appears as a support to written text and graphics.
- A tab for its VOD player, BBC iPlayer.
- A tab for TV, which displays the linear schedule for its channels with programme listings that link to the iPlayer and/or to individual programme pages.
- A tab for radio, which takes you to its on-demand radio player.
- A 'more' tab, which takes you to links for children's content (CBBC and CBeebies), certain genres or programme types – music, food, arts, earth, and Tomorrow's World (focused on technology) – plus services (such as Taster, a site for experimental content, Bitesize, for education content for schools, and Make It Digital, focused on supporting digital creativity) and local content.[15]

In this instance, the website as a whole offers a range of different kinds of television-related products and experiences. The BBC iPlayer page of the website facilitates the watching of acquired/commissioned audiovisual content and, therefore, functions as an online TV service. By contrast, the news, weather and sports pages follow the formal conventions of an online newspaper, oriented around text and reading with images and video as supporting content. Meanwhile, sites like Taster and Bitesize encourage user interaction. Television broadcaster and network websites, therefore, can function as online TV services, but are often used to support a wider range of activities than just watching, such as providing text-based news and interactive transmedia content. For other online TV providers, particularly those offering OTT and cable/satellite television, their websites function as marketing and retail spaces and provide access points for subscribers to log in to their VOD services and/or purchase merchandise.[16] The online TV service, therefore, might be just one component of a website that offers a number of different television-related products to the user.

At the same time, however, there has been a move by some broadcasters to seek to position their online TV services as the central access point to the rest of the products that they offer. Speaking in 2013, BBC Director General Tony Hall outlined his future vision for the corporation in which iPlayer was positioned as 'the front door to many people to the whole BBC' (Hall 2013). In the following year a new iPlayer was launched that was optimised for a multiscreen world in order to give viewers a consistent experience of the service across all devices (Grainge & Johnson 2018, p.22). Yet, despite Hall's vision of iPlayer as a front door to the BBC, on the web iPlayer remains one product within the BBC's webpage, rather than a central access point for the rest of the BBC's content and service offerings. Hall's vision, however, does seem to have been taken up by the corporation's competitors. Over 2015 and 2016 all of the other UK terrestrial broadcasters (ITV, Channel 4 and Channel 5) replaced their websites with their VOD players (Johnson 2017, p.122). This move effectively positioned their online TV services as *the* service that they offered to viewers and as *the* gateway to the TV experiences that they had to offer. As internet-connected television becomes more commonplace we may see more television providers move towards positioning their online TV services as the front door to a wider suite of products that offer a range of television-related experiences.

It is important that scholars continue to examine the different kinds of television services provided on- and offline beyond the online TV services that form the focus of this book. There is also significant benefit in considering the overall service offered by any one website or provider, such as bbc.co.uk or the BBC. However, at the same time, it is important to distinguish between the different kinds of services offered by any individual organisation or website in order to enable comparison with other similar services. For example, the news pages of the BBC website would benefit from analysis alongside other online news sites that also combine text, still and moving images to convey timely and topical news stories (such as *The Guardian, Vice* and *The Huffington Post*). Although it remains important to consider the different industrial contexts of print-originated, television-originated and online-only news sites, these websites share formal similarities that shape how they tell news stories to capture and engage audience attention that warrants comparison. Similarly, the online TV services examined in this book come from different industrial contexts (as we shall see in the next chapter) but are united by the shared objective of offering online viewing services to their users that provide access to acquired and commissioned content. Drawing attention to the form of different kinds of television service invites comparison between services with shared objectives and reveals the largely overlooked ways in which our encounters with television culture are framed.

Conclusion

The internet era challenges normative understandings of television in two ways. First, it is characterised by the fragmentation of television as a technology and cultural form, which undermines previously established definitions of television as a medium. Second, it introduces a range of other services, from social media platforms to online news websites, that also function as sites for accessing audiovisual content. In this media landscape a wide variety of different kinds of online video and television-related services coexist, often in interconnected networks.

Current academic studies that attempt to define television in the internet era have tended to focus on those newer services with the greatest difference from older forms of broadcast, cable and satellite television. However, in doing so, these studies are at risk of overlooking the ways in which older and newer forms of television intertwine and coexist. By contrast, this chapter has put forward a definition of online TV that considers the continuities as well as the changes to television as a medium as it enters the internet era, while at the same time distinguishing online TV services from other audiovisual and television-related services available online. In doing so, it has defined online TV as *services that facilitate the viewing of editorially selected audiovisual content through internet-connected devices and infrastructure*.

Identifying the specific characteristics of online TV services reveals the key stakes for this subset of the internet ecosystem. Specifically, online TV services offer their users access to audiovisual content within closed ecosystems that are designed to provide controlled and structured viewing experiences. Central to the provision of an online TV service is:

- The acquisition of content that audiences want to watch, through licensing or commissioning.
- The creation of a closed infrastructure that enables editorial control over the user's viewing experience through the use of frames, such as data, algorithms and interfaces.

At the heart of online TV services, therefore, is the ability and necessity of exerting control over content and the user experience. The ways in which online TV services attempt to exert such control will be examined in more detail in Chapters 4 (content), 5 (interfaces) and 6 (data).

Although online TV services can be identified as distinct from other forms of online video, they sit within an internet ecosystem characterised by fluid interconnections between different sites and services. Where online TV services focus on facilitating the viewing of audiovisual content, they sit alongside other TV-related sites and services that provide spaces for a range of activities, from talk and gossip about TV programmes to the purchasing of merchandise and the viewing and sharing of promotional and short-form content. All of these sites and services exist within an internet ecosystem dominated by a small number of US platforms. Online TV services are quite different from the platforms of Google, Apple, Facebook and Amazon, yet all of these companies offer online TV services. The next chapter, therefore, asks how we conceptualise the online TV industry. Through identifying the different types of company that create and manage online TV services, it draws out the key sites of competition and cooperation for this sector of the media industries. In doing so, it aims to lay out an agenda for industrial approaches to television in the internet era.

Notes

1 Chapter 5 examines in more detail some of the difficulties of distinguishing between linear and nonlinear services.
2 Chapter 3 examines the ways in which the industrial configurations of online TV enable (or inhibit) such control.
3 Although Strangelove's approach is broader than that taken by Lotz and Abreu et al., like Lotz he chooses to focus on OTT television services rather than those offered through dedicated IPTV networks by cable and telecommunications companies (2015, p.9).
4 Similarly, research focusing on how marginal communities engage with contemporary television might place user-generated YouTube channels that mirror forms of community television as central to a definition of online TV. I am grateful to Laurie Lopez for this observation.
5 The Conclusion will address the difference in meaning between this book's use of the term 'service' and the concept of public service television.
6 As discussed in Chapter 1, the transformation of television into a medium for activities beyond viewing began in the 1970s and 1980s with experiments in interactive television (such as Teletext) and the introduction of games consoles. However, at this time television services were primarily oriented around offering viewing experiences.
7 With the launch of Facebook Watch, Facebook has attempted to make watching video a more central component of its platform. Facebook Watch will be examined in more detail below.
8 For example, online TV services can determine the extent to which their interfaces indicate the identities of the organisations that originated the content that they provide access to. Perhaps the most prominent example of this has been Netflix's use of the label 'Netflix Originals' to describe programmes where it has acquired the exclusive first run rights for a series in a particular territory, as well as to describe programmes that it has originated itself. Consequently, a BBC production such as *Peaky Blinders* (2013–), first broadcast on BBC Two in the UK, is labelled as a Netflix Original in North America. Kelly Summers argues that even when brand origination (such as the originating channel, broadcaster or production company) is signalled for licensed content on online TV services, 'the brand identity gets muddled from being listed alongside the competition with little or no differentiation. Or the platform itself wants to push its brand over the content owners' (cited in Curtin et al. 2014, p.70). This is one reason why content owners might look to create their own online TV services, rather than licensing their content to other providers (Evens 2013, p.489).
9 The use of the acronym GAFA to refer to Google, Apple, Facebook and Amazon has its origins in the French press in 2012 as part of a broader discourse within Europe about the encroaching power of these new US tech corporations (Chibber 2014). US finance expert and broadcaster Jim Cramer coined a competing term in 2013, FANG, highlighting Facebook, Amazon, Netflix and Google (Cramer has since expanded the term to include Apple) as tech companies that dominate the market and represent sound stock investments (Duggan 2017).
10 At the time of writing in the summer of 2018 there is significant public and political attention on the power of Facebook, in particular, in the wake of accusations that the company Cambridge Analytica used personal data from the site without authorisation to create personalised political advertisements (Cadwalladr & Graham-Harrison 2018).
11 Google's website lists 69 different products offered by the corporation (Google 2018).
12 The constitution of the online TV industry will be explored in Chapter 3.
13 YouTube TV is also distinct from subscription service YouTube Red, which effectively functions as an ad-free version of YouTube's main open video service.
14 Children's is made up of two different products at the BBC: CBBC caters for children aged 6–12 and CBeebies for children under 6 years old.
15 It is possible to customise the homepage of bbc.co.uk to alter what content appears, such as providing your postcode to receive more relevant local content or selecting the areas of entertainment, sport and news that are of particular interest. In addition, as you increase or decrease the size of your browser window the number of tabs that appear across the top of the screen also increases or decreases.
16 Now TV is the subscription OTT VOD service offered by Sky in the UK.

Bibliography

Abreu, J. Nogueira, J., Becker, V. & Cardoso, B., 2017. Survey of Catch-up TV and Other Time-Shift Services: A Comprehensive Analysis and Taxonomy of Linear and Nonlinear Television. *Telecommunication Systems*, 64, pp.57–74.

Alexander, J., 2018. YouTube Needs More Experts to Help Tackle Dangerous Content, Says CEO. *Polygon*, 29 Jan. Available at: https://www.polygon.com/2018/1/29/16944816/youtube-ceo-experts-demonetization-content-logan-paul [Accessed August 6, 2018].

Bennett, J. & Strange, N., 2014. Linear Legacies: Managing the Multiplatform Production Process. In D. Johnson, D. Kompare & A. Santo, eds. *Making Media Work: Cultures of Management in the Entertainment Industries*. New York: New York University Press, pp. 63–89.

Bennett, J. & Strange, N., 2018. *Adapting to Social Media: Commerce, Creativity and Competition in UK Television Production*, London. Available at: https://figshare.com/articles/Adapting_to_Social_Media_Commerce_Creativity_and_Competition_in_UK_Television_Production/5951977.

Cadwalladr, C. & Graham-Harrison, E., 2018. Revealed: 50 Million Facebook Profiles Harvested for Cambridge Analytica in Major Data Breach. *The Guardian*, 17 Mar. Available at: https://www.theguardian.com/news/2018/mar/17/cambridge-analytica-facebook-influence-us-election [Accessed August 6, 2018].

Chibber, K., 2014. American Cultural Imperialism Has a New Name: GAFA. *Quartz*, 1 Dec. Available at: https://qz.com/303947/us-cultural-imperialism-has-a-new-name-gafa/ [Accessed May 11, 2018].

Cisco, 2017. *Cisco Visual Networking Index: Forecast and Methodology, 2016–2021*, Available at: http://www.cisco.com/c/en/us/solutions/collateral/service-provider/visual-networking-index-vni/complete-white-paper-c11-481360.pdf.

Cunningham, S. & Silver, J., 2013. *Screen Distribution and the New King Kongs of the Online World*, Basingstoke: Palgrave Macmillan.

Curtin, M., Holt, J. & Sanson, K. eds., 2014. *Distribution Revolution: Conversations about the Digital Future of Film and Television*, Berkeley: University of California Press.

Doyle, G., 2016. Resistance of Channels: Television Distribution in the Multiplatform Era. *Telematics and Informatics*, 33(2), pp.693–702.

Duggan, W., 2017. Jim Cramer and Bob Lang's 2013 FANG Call Was a Home Run. *Benzinga*, 25 Mar. Available at: https://www.benzinga.com/media/cnbc/17/03/9198427/jim-cramer-and-bob-langs-2013-fang-call-was-a-home-run [Accessed May 11, 2018].

Evans, E., 2011. *Transmedia Television*, Abingdon and New York: Routledge.

Evens, T., 2013. Platform Leadership in Online Broadcasting Markets. In M. Friedrichsen & W. Mühl-Benninghaus, eds. *Handbook of Social Media Management: Value Chain and Business Models in Changing Media Markets*. Berlin: Springer, pp.477–491.

Gillespie, T., 2010. The Politics of 'Platforms.' *New Media & Society*, 12(3), pp.347–364.

Google, 2018. Google: Our Products. *Google Website*. Available at: https://www.google.co.uk/about/products/ [Accessed August 7, 2018].

Grainge, P. & Johnson, C., 2018. From Catch-Up TV to Online TV: Digital Broadcasting and the Case of BBC iPlayer. *Screen*, 59(1), pp.21–40.

Grece, C., 2016. *The Presence of Broadcasters on Video Sharing Platforms: Typology and Qualitative Analysis*, Strasbourg: European Audiovisual Observatory. Available at: https://rm.coe.int/16807835ba.

Hall, T., 2013. Director-General Tony Hall Unveils His Vision for the BBC. *BBC Media Centre*. Available at: https://www.bbc.co.uk/mediacentre/speeches/2013/tony-hall-vision.html [Accessed August 7, 2018].

Helberger, N., Kleinen-von Königslöw, K. & van der Noll, R., 2015. Regulating the New Information Intermediaries as Gatekeepers of Information Diversity. *Info*, 17(6), pp.50–71.

Huggers, E., 2010. BBC Online: Putting Quality First. *BBC Website*. Available at: http://www.bbc.co.uk/blogs/aboutthebbc/2010/08/bbc-online—putting-quality-f.shtml [Accessed May 18, 2018].

Jenkins, H., Ford, S. & Green, J., 2013. *Spreadable Media: Creating Value and Meaning in a Networked Culture*, New York: New York University Press.

Jenner, M., 2016. Is this TVIV? On Netflix, TVIII and Binge-Watching. *New Media & Society*, 18(2), pp.257–273.

Johnson, C., 2017. Beyond Catch-Up: VoD Interfaces, ITV Hub and the Repositioning of Television Online. *Critical Studies in Television: The International Journal of Television Studies*, 12(2), pp.121–138.

Kim, J., Kim, S. & Nam, C., 2016. Competitive Dynamics in the Korean Video Platform Market: Traditional Pay TV Platforms vs. OTT Platforms. *Telematics and Informatics*, 33(2), pp.711–721.

Lotz, A.D., 2016. *Portals: A Treatise on Internet-Distributed Television*, Ann Arbor, MI: Maize Books.

McDonald, K. & Smith-Rowsey, D. eds., 2016. *The Netflix Effect: Technology and Entertainment in the 21st Century*, New York: Bloomsbury.

Mikos, L., 2016. Digital Media Platforms and the Use of TV Content: Binge Watching and Video-on-Demand in Germany. *Media and Communication*, 4(3), pp.154–161.

Nixon, B., 2016. The Old Media Business in the New: 'The Googlization of Everything' as the Capitalization of Digital Consumption. *Media, Culture & Society*, 38(2), pp.212–231.

Ofcom, 2017. *International Communications Market Report 2017*, London: Ofcom. Available at: http://stakeholders.ofcom.org.uk/binaries/research/cmr/cmr15/icmr15/icmr_2015.pdf.

Plantin, J.C., Lagoze, C., Edwards, P.N. & Sandvig, C., 2018. Infrastructure Studies Meet Platform Studies in the Age of Google and Facebook. *New Media and Society*, 20(1), pp.293–310.

Popper, B., 2017. YouTube Says It Will Crack Down on Bizarre Videos Targeting Children. *The Verge*, 9 Nov. Available at: https://www.theverge.com/2017/11/9/16629788/youtube-kids-distrubing-inappropriate-flag-age-restrict [Accessed August 6, 2018].

Sandwell, I., 2018. Facebook Watch Explained: Shows, App, UK Launch and Everything You Need to Know. *Digital Spy*, 14 May. Available at: http://www.digitalspy.com/tv/feature/a857044/facebook-watch-shows-app-uk-launch-platform/ [Accessed May 17, 2018].

Simon, P., 2013. *The Age of the Platform: How Amazon, Apple, Facebook, and Google Have Redefined Business* Revised Ed., Las Vegas: Motion Publishing.

Snickars, P., 2012. A Walled Garden Turned into a Rain Forest. In P. Snickars & P. Vonderau, eds. *Moving Data: The iPhone and the Future of Media*. New York: Columbia University Press, pp. 155–168.

Spangler, T., 2017. YouTube TV Launches in Five Cities, Inks Deal with AMC Networks for Internet Skinny Bundle. *Variety*, 5 Apr. Available at: https://variety.com/2017/digital/news/youtube-tv-launch-5-cities-amc-networks-1202023343/ [Accessed August 6, 2018].

Strangelove, M., 2015. *Post-TV: Piracy, Cord-Cutting, and the Future of Television*, Toronto: University of Toronto Press.

Tsukayama, H., 2017. How to Make Sense of Facebook's New Video Platform, Watch. *Washington Post*, 10 Aug. Available at: https://www.washingtonpost.com/news/the-switch/wp/2017/08/10/how-to-make-sense-of-facebooks-new-video-site-watch/?noredirect=on&utm_term=.75cf644e0dcd [Accessed August 6, 2018].

Uricchio, W., 2014. Film, Cinema, Television … Media? *New Review of Film and Television Studies*, 12(3), pp.266–279.

van Dijck, J., 2013. *The Culture of Connectivity: A Critical History of Social Media*, Oxford and New York: Oxford University Press.

Wood, H., 2009. *Talking with Television*, Urbana: University of Illinois Press.

Yong Jin, D., 2015. *Digital Platforms, Imperialism and Political Culture*, London: Routledge.

3

ONLINE TV INDUSTRY AND TECHNOLOGIES

RECAP

- Since the late 2000s, the penetration of fast broadband speeds, tablets, smartphones and internet-connected televisions has heralded a new 'internet era' for television. In this era, television and the internet are increasingly interconnected, challenging normative assumptions about television as a medium.
- Chapter 1 outlined a conceptual framework for analysing changes to television as a medium over time. It argued that television is made up of five components:

  1. *Technological infrastructures* that deliver television services to people (e.g. cable or broadband).
  2. *Technological devices* through which people directly experience television. These can be divided into *viewing devices* for watching television programming (e.g. TV set or tablet) and *add-on devices* that attach to the viewing device (e.g. personal video recorder or digital media player).
  3. *Services* that are the entry point for viewers to television content (e.g. TV channels, subscription TV services offered by cable and satellite operators or on-demand services like Netflix).
  4. *Content* such as the programmes, adverts and interstitials delivered through television services.
  5. *Frames* that organise television content and shape how it is experienced (e.g. the linear schedule, electronic programme guide or interface).

- Chapter 2 set out this book's definition of online TV as *services that facilitate the viewing of editorially selected audiovisual content through internet-connected devices and infrastructure.*
- Central to the provision of online TV services is:
  a   The acquisition of content, through licensing or commissioning.
  b   Editorial control over the user's viewing experience, through infrastructure, data and algorithms.

Introduction

In typical hyperbolic style, Hollywood producer and writer Neil Landau described the rapid expansion of the US television industry in the mid-2010s as an explosion of revolutionary proportions:

> Over the past year – from 2014 to 2015 – here's what's happened: *the digital television revolution.* It's not just an exponentially expanded chart, it's a Big Bang EXPLOSION.
>
> (Landau 2016, p.117)

To illustrate this 'Big Bang' he drew on Andrew Wallenstein's map of the US TV industry in 2015 created for the trade paper *Variety* (Landau 2016, pp.117–25; Wallenstein 2015). Wallenstein divides the US television landscape into three sectors: 'Pay-TV Powerhouses,' 'The Big Three' and 'The Big Kahuna.'

The first sector, the Pay-TV Powerhouses, maps broadly on to the US cable television business, consisting of the multichannel video programming distributors (MVPDs) that offer internet, television and phone services (such as Comcast, Verizon and AT&T), as well as the providers of cable and satellite channels (such as Scripps, Fox and Disney). Both groups of business offer subscribers access to television content online, typically as part of their cable subscription packages. The second sector, 'The Big Three,' refers to Amazon Prime, Netflix and Hulu, the main US providers of 'over-the-top' (OTT) television services direct to consumers without the need for a cable subscription. This sector also includes niche players offering OTT services around a specific genre (such as Sesame Street Go) and sports and talent-based services (such as NFL Mobile). The final sector, termed the 'Big Kahuna,' refers to YouTube, described by Landau as 'the 800-pound gorilla of the Internet space, with a global footprint so massive that few brands dare to go OTT without maintaining some YouTube presence' (2016, p.125). However, in this sector Wallenstein also includes other social media services, **multichannel networks** (MCNs) and video platforms serving specific niche audiences (often based on brands from other sectors), such as Conde Nast (publishing), Vevo (music) and Twitch (gaming).

Focused just on the US, Wallenstein's map usefully illustrates the sheer complexity and size of the contemporary industry offering audiovisual services. When I wrote my book *Branding Television* in 2010–11 about the emergence of digital television from the 1980s to the 2000s, I felt no need to explain what I meant by the 'television industry.' Just five years later, the industrial landscape of television had transformed in ways that not only challenge definitions of television (see Chapters 1 and 2) but also undermine normative assumptions about what constitutes the 'television industry.'

Wallenstein's map of the contemporary television industry includes a wide range of different kinds of service that offer access to audiovisual content. Some of these, such as the services offered by the Pay-TV Powerhouses and The Big Three, would fit into this book's definition of online TV as *services that facilitate the viewing of editorially selected audiovisual content through internet-connected devices and infrastructure*. Others, such as many of the services listed under the category of the Big Kahuna, would fall outside this book's definition of online TV because they operate as open services that depend on users uploading content or they provide video as a supplement to other activities such as reading or participating. Rather than mapping out the entire industry involved in the provision of all types of audiovisual content online, this chapter focuses specifically on how we conceptualise the industry that provides online TV services. It asks: what kinds of organisations and businesses create and manage online TV services, and what are the key sites of competition and cooperation for this sector of the contemporary media industries?

The chapter begins by recognising that the online TV industry is inherently 'messy,'[1] occupied by organisations stemming from a range of sectors and operating under varied business models. To help navigate this 'mess' the chapter presents two different, yet related, approaches to mapping the online TV industry. It begins by dividing the organisations that provide online TV services into three categories according to their business origins: **TV natives**, **online natives** and **content natives**. While this is useful in drawing attention to the dependencies and competencies that shape major segments of the online TV industry, it overlooks important intersections between the categories of organisation providing online TV services. The chapter goes on, therefore, to offer an alternative approach to mapping the online TV industry, by focusing on the core business of each organisation. Through this approach it is possible to divide the online TV industry into **content businesses** and **technology businesses**. Combining these two approaches reveals the controlling points through which different segments of the industry attempt to exert competitive advantage. The chapter ends by putting this approach into practice by focusing on industrial control over technological infrastructures and devices. In particular, it asks how the industrial battles over technology might affect the accessibility of online TV services for viewers.

Although this chapter draws primarily on examples from the UK, as with the other chapters in this book, the conceptualisation of the online TV industry developed here is designed to be adaptable to other national and transnational contexts. Irrespective of whether the categories developed in this chapter translate directly into other contexts, it should be possible to map out any online TV industry according to business origins and core business focus in order to explore the competencies, dependencies and controlling points at work. Taking such an approach also facilitates the development of comparative studies, enabling analysis of the contextual factors that might shape the ways in which different players around the globe are enacting power within this particular segment of the contemporary media industries.

Mapping the online TV industry

As with the definition of television in the internet era explored in Chapter 2, there is no consistent academic language to describe the different kinds of company that provide online TV services. In contrast to Wallenstein's map, which tends to classify according to the kind of video service offered, Stuart Cunningham, David Craig and Jon Silver differentiate between the SoCal industries of Southern California and the NoCal industries based in Northern California (Cunningham et al. 2016). The SoCal businesses of the Hollywood conglomerates can be understood as cultural industries that 'deal primarily with the industrial production and circulation of texts' (Hesmondhalgh 2013, p.16) and understand the 'fundamentals of entertainment, and content and talent development' (Cunningham et al. 2016, p.379). The NoCal companies, such as Google, Facebook, Apple and Amazon, are information technology (IT) experts that have built the underlying platforms that shape the affordances of the web. As we saw in Chapter 2, both of these sectors of the cultural industries are providing online TV services. Indeed, Cunningham et al. argue that the ecology of NoCal and SoCal can be best understood as 'an interdependent clash of cultures' (2016, p.379) in which each sector is seeking to come to terms with the fundamentals of the other's business in response to the converged online video ecosystem. Beyond the specificities of the US, Tom Evens (2013, pp.479–80) describes a contemporary television industry in which incumbents (broadcasters and cable/satellite operators) are being challenged by entrepreneurial new entrants from the tech world.[2] Although Evens uses different language, there are clear resonances with Cunningham et al.'s description of the US context. In both instances, established television providers are attempting to manage the impact of the internet on their existing business models while facing competition from new tech and online-based companies moving into television for the first time.

As with much of the literature on contemporary television, these studies point to the importance of business origins in conceptualising the contemporary online TV industry (see, for example, Wolk 2015; Lotz 2014; Lotz 2016). Taking this approach, this chapter begins by dividing the online TV industry into three categories of online TV provider: *TV natives*, *online natives* and *content natives* (see Table 3.1). *TV natives* map broadly onto Evens' incumbents (and Cunningham et al.'s SoCal businesses) in that their business origins lie in the provision of broadcast, cable, satellite and/or digital television services. Specifically, these are organisations that have extended an existing television service into the internet ecosystem. *Online natives* align with Evens' new entrants (and Cunningham et al.'s NoCal businesses) in that these are businesses

TABLE 3.1 TV natives, online natives and content natives

	TV natives *E.g. BBC, Disney,* *Sky, BT*	*Online natives* *E.g. Netflix, Amazon* *Prime Video*	*Content natives* *E.g. Globe Player,* *Arsenal Player*
Business origins	TV incumbents Broadcast, cable, satellite and/or digital TV services	Online incumbents Online services	Content businesses from a range of sectors
Business objectives	Extend an existing TV service into the internet ecosystem	Originate online TV service for the internet ecosystem	Online TV service builds on existing content business
Dependencies	Existing TV businesses	Existing online businesses (where relevant)	Existing content businesses
Competencies	Delivering viewing experiences	Creating services specifically for an online environment	Ownership of valuable intellectual property rights and brands

that have originated services for the internet. Some online natives, such as Netflix, focus solely on the provision of an online TV service. Others offer an online TV service in addition to other online services, such as Amazon, which provides Amazon Prime Video alongside its broader e-commerce business. However, all online natives have originated an online TV service specifically for the internet ecosystem. Often overlooked in studies of online TV, *content natives* have extended content businesses in sectors as varied as sport, theatre and charity into an online TV service. Their businesses are focused on brands with access to valuable content and loyal audiences.

I have chosen the language of TV, online and content natives, rather than incumbents and new entrants, as it speaks to the converged landscape of the contemporary internet ecosystem. Doing so enables us to acknowledge that while TV natives are incumbents in the TV industry, at the same time they are new entrants in the online landscape. By the same token, online natives may be new entrants in television, but they are incumbents on the internet. As we shall go on to see, these are not hard and fast categorisations, but they are helpful in revealing the ways in which existing business demands can shape the strategies of online TV providers. In developing online TV services, TV natives are having to develop the competencies of online natives, particularly in understanding the technological demands of the internet ecosystem. At the same time, online natives have to develop the competencies of TV natives, specifically in content production, acquisition and delivery. Seen from this perspective, content natives, in particular, are at a disadvantage because they do not bring with them competencies in either television or online businesses. This would help explain why content natives tend to provide niche services with relatively limited reach. The emergent online TV industry is best understood, therefore, as being situated at the intersection of online and TV corporate cultures, business practices, skillsets and ways of working.

Some studies of online TV have focused specifically on those services funded by subscription (see for example Lotz 2016). However, across the categories of TV, online and content natives a range of business models are in operation often utilising a combination of different sources of funding. Before unpacking these categories in more detail, it is helpful to outline briefly the four funding mechanisms used by online TV services:

- State/licence-fee funding, in which the service is paid for through public funds (e.g. the BBC).
- Advertiser-funding, in which the service is free to access in exchange for the viewing of advertising before and/or during the programmes selected (e.g. ITV). Advertising within advertising video-on-demand (AVOD) services is typically sold separately from the same broadcast content, with many advertisers exploiting the possibility of interactive adverts (where viewers can click on the advert or select a particular version of the advertising to watch). In addition, viewers can be prevented from fast-forwarding through or skipping the adverts embedded within the programming on AVOD services.
- Subscription-funded, in which the viewer pays a subscription, usually monthly, in order to gain access to a service. There are two broad subscription models for online TV. The first is subscription video-on-demand (SVOD), characterised by Netflix, where the viewer pays a direct subscription for an online TV service. The second is typically adopted by cable, satellite and telecoms providers, such as Sky or Comcast, where viewers pay for a cable/satellite subscription that provides them with access to a bundle of TV channels and VOD services, including many from third parties. Some cable, satellite and telecoms providers also make all of these channels and services available through a central SVOD service as part of their broader subscription package. David Waterman et al. (2013, p.727) refer to this as an 'authentication dependent' VOD service.
- Transaction-funded, in which the viewer pays to own or rent individual content (such as a television episode/series or a movie). iTunes dominates the transactional video-on-demand (TVOD) market, but this is also a common feature of cable, satellite and telecoms subscription services.

A brief overview of the different categories of organisation operating online TV services within the UK reveals the wide variety of funding models in operation within each category and the extent to which it is commonplace to combine multiple funding models within one service (see Table 3.2).[3]

TV natives

TV natives are characterised by having extended an existing TV service online. As a consequence, they need to consider the impact of their online TV service on their existing television business and to protect extant business models and revenue streams. At the same time, however, TV natives have to adapt business practices

TABLE 3.2 Examples of TV, online and content natives in the UK

	Sector	Company	Online TV service	Funding model
TV native	Free-to-air broadcasters	BBC	iPlayer	Licence fee
		ITV	ITV Hub ITV Hub+	AVOD SVOD
		Channel 4	All4	AVOD
		Channel 5	My5/ Demand5	AVOD
	Cable/satellite/ digital channel providers	BBC World-wide, Discovery	UKTV Play	AVOD
		Disney	Disney Life	SVOD
		AMC	Shudder	SVOD
	Cable/satellite service providers	Sky	Sky Go Now TV Sky Store	SVOD SVOD TVOD
		Virgin	Virgin TV Go Virgin Media Store	SVOD TVOD
	Telecoms providers	BT	BT TV BT TV Store	SVOD TVOD
		TalkTalk	TalkTalk TV	SVOD/ TVOD
Online native	Global IT firms	Netflix	Netflix	SVOD
		Amazon	Amazon Prime Video	SVOD/ TVOD
		Apple	iTunes Apple Music	TVOD SVOD
	Digital start-ups	Simplestream Ltd	TVPlayer	SVOD
		Tinizine Ltd	Azoomee	SVOD
Content native	Theatre	Shakespeare's Globe Trust	Globe Player	Freemium/ TVOD
	Sport	Arsenal FC	Arsenal Player	Free (registration)
	Charity	British Sign Language Broadcasting Trust	BSL Zone Player	Free

developed in television to the provision of services online. This involves under-standing the technological demands of the internet ecosystem and adopting ways of working more suited to an online environment characterised by faster turnaround times and more iterative ways of working (Bennett et al. 2012). Within the UK, there are four types of TV native: free-to-air broadcasters, cable/satellite/digital channel providers, cable/satellite service providers, and telecoms providers.

Free-to-air broadcasters

The four free-to-air broadcasters in the UK are the BBC, ITV, Channel 4 and Channel 5, all of which offer television channels through cable, satellite and digital, as well as VOD services funded either by licence fee (in the case of the BBC) or by advertising (in the case of ITV, Channel 4 and Channel 5).[4] These broadcasters have long histories in the production and delivery of television content and led the market in the development of VOD in the UK, with Channel 4 launching 4OD (since re-branded as All 4) in 2006, with the BBC following with BBC iPlayer in 2007 and ITV with ITV Player (since re-branded as ITV Hub) in 2008. These online TV services are sometimes referred to as catch-up services because they offer users the ability to catch up with broadcast programmes for a set period of time after transmission (typically 30 days). However, they increasingly offer features that extend beyond this description, in particular original content produced specifically for the VOD service (Grainge & Johnson 2018), live streams of broadcast channels (Johnson 2017) and access to archives and box sets of content. Channel 4, for example, makes a feature of offering box sets of content on All 4, including archive content and imported series curated under the moniker 'Walter Presents,' which aims to showcase the best of international television with series that are largely not broadcast on Channel 4's terrestrial and digital channels. BBC iPlayer, ITV Hub, All 4 and My 5 (Channel 5's VOD player) are available through the web and as apps on most major add-on and viewing devices, as well as through the on-demand services of cable and satellite providers and through Freeview and YouView (see below).

Cable/satellite/digital channel providers

Since the rise of cable and satellite television in the UK in the 1980s, a number of channels have launched that can only be accessed with a cable or satellite subscription. Digitalisation in the late 1990s further expanded the number of channels, and the launch of Freeview – a non-profit joint venture between the BBC, Channel 4, ITV, Sky and Arqiva (a leading communications infrastructure company in the UK) – made a number of digital channels available subscription-free through Freeview-enabled television sets and set-top boxes. The VOD strategies of the major cable, satellite and digital channels in the UK are highly inconsistent. UKTV, a joint commercial venture between BBC Worldwide (the commercial arm of the BBC) and Discovery (a US company providing a number of cable networks around the world), is one of the major UK cable, satellite and digital channel providers, with a suite of ten channels largely offering re-runs of programmes originated for the main free-to-air channels, combined with a small amount of original content. In 2014, UKTV announced the launch of UKTV Play, an AVOD service offering access to recently broadcast content and box sets of programming from across the UKTV channels, available through a dedicated app and through subscription to the major cable, satellite and telecoms providers.[5] Many of the other cable/satellite/digital channels in the UK are provided by overseas, often US, companies whose on-demand strategies vary. For example, Disney has launched a SVOD service in the UK, Disney Life, that provides access to Disney movies, television series, books and songs on a monthly contract. Viewers can stream and download content through an app that is available on Apple, Android and Amazon devices, TV sets, desktops, tablets and mobile. Other global cable/satellite/digital channels in the UK, such as Discovery and Universal, have been more reticent about launching VOD versions of their channels, presumably for fear of undermining their deals with the major cable and satellite services whose business models operate on the basis of providing access to these channels and their content.[6] For many cable and satellite channels, the 'carriage fees' paid to include their channels in the subscription packages of cable and satellite operators is a valuable source of income (Wolk 2015, p.5). By contrast, AMC (which is not available as a cable/satellite channel in the UK) has launched an OTT SVOD service, Shudder, in the UK, providing access to a library of horror movies.

Cable/satellite service providers

The provision of cable/satellite television services in the UK is dominated by Sky (satellite) and Virgin Media (cable). They offer access to a large number of television channels bundled into packages that are priced according to desirability, with higher subscriptions charged for premium content and channels, such as sports and movies. In addition to its satellite packages, Sky also originates content and offers a number of television channels, some of which are only available with a Sky satellite subscription.[7] Both providers offer a SVOD version of their cable/satellite service to their subscribers in the form of Sky Go and Virgin TV Go. Typically, subscriptions to Sky and Virgin's satellite/cable services include the bundling of other telecommunications services (broadband, landline and/or mobile) into 'triple and quadruple-pay packages,' and users are tied into a contract of 12 or more months.[8] However, Sky has sought to compete with the likes of Netflix and Amazon by launching Now TV, an OTT SVOD service that users can subscribe to directly without having to sign up to Sky's satellite service or be tied into a lengthy contract. The UK cable/satellite providers have also been working with OTT services to improve their offer to subscribers, with Virgin Media signing a deal to make Netflix available through its set-top boxes (although only accessible with the additional payment of a Netflix subscription). They also provide access to the VOD services of other TV natives, such as BBC iPlayer, ITV Hub and UKTV Play, through their set-top boxes. In addition, Sky and Virgin Media enable viewers to rent movies through their satellite/cable and online TV services, effectively including TVOD as part of their SVOD service. Sky and Virgin also both offer TVOD to non-subscribers through Sky Store and Virgin Media Store, where users can access movies and TV series to rent or buy online. As with the free-to-air broadcasters, the VOD services of cable/satellite providers are available through the open web and as apps.

Telecoms providers

Telecoms companies like BT and TalkTalk have extended their media infrastructure businesses into the provision of TV services. Unlike cable/satellite providers, however, telecoms companies are relative latecomers to the provision of television services. BT, for example, extended its phone and broadband service into television in the digital era with the launch of BT Vision in 2006. Other UK telecoms companies did not offer television services until the internet era, with TalkTalk launching TalkTalk TV in 2012. However, what these telecoms providers share with other TV natives is that they have extended their television services online. As with cable and satellite providers, telecoms companies offer online versions of their subscription TV packages as well as the ability to buy/rent films and TV programmes online. BT, for example, offers its SVOD service, BT TV, to its phone, broadband and TV subscribers, who can also access BT TV Store to rent and buy movies online. TalkTalk combines SVOD and TVOD into one service, TalkTalk TV, available through an app or the open web, and provides subscribers with access to a number of VOD players (such as Netflix, BBC iPlayer and All 4) integrated into its set-top box. Telecoms providers are less invested in content production and rights than the television channel providers. However, like Sky, BT has moved into the production and acquisition of content. BT and TalkTalk compete with newer **internet service providers** (ISPs), such as PlusNet, as well as with cable/satellite providers, in offering triple-pay subscription packages that bundle telephone, broadband and television services.

Online natives

If TV natives have their business origins in the world of television, online natives are businesses that focus on the delivery of internet-related services. Typically, these are organisations with origins in computing, IT and the internet, often with existing online businesses, such as e-commerce (Amazon) and home computing (Apple). With expertise and ways of working originated from the IT sector, in moving into online TV, these online natives have had to develop competencies in producing, licensing and delivering audiovisual content for viewers. In the UK, as in many other countries, the category of online native is dominated by a small number of US IT firms that operate global services.[9] However, there are also digital start-ups that can be considered as online natives in that they have originated an online TV service specifically for the internet ecosystem.

Global IT firms

In the UK, as in many countries, Netflix and Amazon dominate the OTT market. Launched in 2007, Netflix's online TV service has its origins in an internet-based DVD rental business that was founded in 1997 by Silicon Valley entrepreneurs Marc Randolph and Reed Hastings, both with backgrounds in computing.

Although Netflix still offers its DVD rental business in the USA, by the mid-2010s the company's revenues were dominated by its online TV service, which has expanded internationally since 2010, operating in over 190 countries by mid-2018.[10] Netflix has also sought to move into content production and, in doing so, has had to develop skills in television and film production, poaching key talent from the world of the TV natives to do so.[11]

As with Netflix, Amazon also has its origins in Silicon Valley, founded by Jeff Bezos (also an entrepreneur with a background in computer science) as an online bookstore in 1995. Expanding into the sale of a wide range of goods over the subsequent years, as well as into cloud computing with the launch of Amazon Web Services in 2002, Amazon launched its first online TV service, Amazon Unbox, in 2006. Initially a TVOD service where viewers could purchase or rent movies as digital files, Amazon replaced Unbox with its subscription streaming service, Amazon Prime Video, in 2011. Amazon bundles Amazon Prime Video into its broader 'Prime' subscription, which includes music streaming, e-books and magazines, photo storage and free delivery on many products ordered through Amazon's retail business. Like Netflix, Amazon has moved into the production of original content, also hiring Hollywood talent,[12] and in 2016 made Amazon Prime Video available in more than 200 territories around the world. In addition to its subscription service, Amazon still offers a TVOD service where users can rent or buy digital copies of TV series and movies. Meanwhile, Amazon has moved into the aggregation of other online TV services through Amazon Channels, launched in May 2017, which allows Prime subscribers to add extra bundles of on-demand content for an additional subscription fee. These 'channels' come from TV natives, such as cable channels Discovery and Eurosport, but also from other online natives, such as Mubi, a SVOD service that offers access to independent arthouse cinema. However, the available channels are impacted by rights deals, with HBO and Showtime, for example, not available on the UK version of Amazon Channels because of Sky's exclusive deals for these channels' content. Similarly, although both Netflix and Amazon are available across most major devices, at the time of writing Netflix was not available as a channel on Amazon Prime Video in the UK, although it was included as an app on Amazon's add-on device, the Fire TV Stick.

The other major online native operating in the UK is Apple, another company with its origins in Silicon Valley and a long history of developing computer hardware (such as desktops, laptops, smartphones and tablets) and software, such as iTunes. Where Netflix and Amazon largely operate on an SVOD model, Apple has until recently focused on its TVOD service, iTunes, that enables users to pay to download individual episodes or whole series of TV programmes to own. However, Apple does provide access to some streamed video content through its subscription music service, Apple Music, and is expected to launch an SVOD online TV service following its announcement in 2017 of significant investment in video content (Haslam 2018).[13]

Digital start-ups

Beyond the high-profile global IT firms that dominate the internet ecosystem are digital start-ups that have developed online TV services, such as TVPlayer, an online streaming service providing access to live streams of more than 85 free-to-air channels across multiple devices through a single app, and Azoomee, an SVOD service targeted specifically at children that provides access to videos, games and audiobooks. Simplestream developed TVPlayer in 2013 out of a business based on providing streaming and catch-up services to broadcast and media companies. In 2015, Simplestream added an SVOD extension, TVPlayer Plus, to the service to enable live and catch-up access to premium pay-TV channels. Tinizine's Azoomee was launched in 2014 by Estelle Lloyd, who had a background in entrepreneurship and tech/media investment and a desire to create an ad-free and age-appropriate SVOD service for children and parents that promotes online safety (Gough 2016).

Content natives

Often overlooked in studies of internet-connected television are content natives: organisations from sectors as varied as sport, theatre and charity that have developed online TV services to deliver content assets that they own the rights to in order to generate additional revenue and/or exposure. These organisations do not have origins and competencies in the delivery of TV or online services. Rather, their businesses tend to be concentrated around brands with access to valuable content and loyal, but niche, communities of viewers. For example, the major UK Premier League football teams Chelsea and Arsenal both offer VOD services, with Arsenal Player featuring as part of the club's website offering access to interviews and behind-the-scenes footage free once you have registered. Chelsea FC offers a television channel that is available for a monthly subscription (or through Sky's subscription satellite service), which is also available to subscribers as a live steam on its website. The business models for content natives vary. Globe Player (which features filmed stage productions from Shakespeare's Globe theatre in London) operates on a freemium model providing content to buy or rent online, with a limited amount of free content used primarily as a taster of the other content on offer. BSL Zone Player stands out as an unusual example of a free VOD service (without advertising), provided by the charity British Sign Language Broadcasting Trust as part of its mission to offer television programming for and by deaf people. Central to all content businesses is their ownership of content rights, alongside established brand identities associated with the content that they offer. In developing online TV services, they are seeking to exploit the value of that content by delivering it online to the niche communities that support their brands.

Distinguishing between TV, online and content natives is particularly helpful in drawing attention to the ways in which business origins might inform the practices and strategies of the different companies operating within the online TV industry.

However, dividing the online TV industry according to business origins overlooks important differences between the companies within the categories of online and TV native in particular. I want to suggest, therefore, another way of dissecting the online TV industry. This approach examines the core business focus of each organisation and argues that it is possible to distinguish between *content businesses* and *technology businesses*. *Content businesses* are those that focus primarily on the production, acquisition and delivery of audiovisual content to viewers. *Technology businesses* are those that are responsible for the provision of the technological infrastructures and devices needed to access online TV services. Again, these are not rigid categorisations. Indeed, all online TV providers are concerned with the delivery of audiovisual content to viewers, and many also produce content. In addition, some content businesses have sought to move into the provision of technological devices. However, as we shall see from a brief overview of the content and technology businesses operating online TV services in the UK, this approach is particularly helpful in drawing attention to the sites through which different segments of the online TV industry attempt to exert control over their competitors (see Table 3.3).

Content businesses

Content businesses are those focused primarily on the production and delivery of audiovisual content to viewers. All *content natives* can be understood as content businesses because they have their basis in the production of content, whether theatrical performances, sporting events or signed programming. *TV natives* operating content businesses would include the free-to-air broadcasters and cable, satellite and digital channel providers, such as the BBC, Channel 4, Disney and UKTV. Netflix and Azoomee are examples of *online natives* that operate as content businesses because they are focused on the provision of an online TV service. Central to all content businesses is the production, acquisition and delivery of content, alongside the development of a strong brand identity associated with the content and/or services that they offer. BBC, Channel 4 and UKTV, for example, have all utilised their established brand reputations in the delivery of television services when developing their online TV services. Meanwhile, Globe Player can be understood as a brand extension that rests on the brand equity of the Globe Theatre as a leading producer of Shakespearean theatre. Content businesses attempt to extend their brand reputations in content provision to become the default online TV service in their particular area, whether attempting to become the default provider of safe online spaces for children to engage with audiovisual material (Azoomee) or the default provider of long-form audiovisual content online (Netflix). A key benefit for content businesses in running their own online TV service is that they control the frames within which their content is provided to (and experienced by) viewers.

TABLE 3.3 Content businesses and technology businesses: the controlling points of the online TV industry

Business focus	Business origins	Sector	Company	Technological infrastructure	Technological device	Content
Content business	TV native	Free-to-air broadcasters	All			Content production and owning rights
		Cable/satellite/ digital channel providers	All			Content production and owning rights
	Online native	Global IT firms	Netflix			Content production and owning rights
		Digital start-ups	Azoomee			Content production and owning rights
	Content native	Theatre/sport/ charity etc.	All			Content production and owning rights
Technology business	TV native	Cable/ satellite service providers	Sky	Internet/ broadband	Set-top boxes	Content production and owning rights
		Telecoms providers/ ISPs	BT PlusNet	Internet/ broadband	Set-top boxes	Content production and owning rights
	Online native	Global IT firms	Amazon	Cloud computing	Digital media player	Content production and owning rights
			Apple		Desktops, laptops, tablets, smartphones, digital media players	Content production and owning rights
	Digital start-ups	TVPlayer	Streaming services			

Technology businesses

Where content/service businesses are focused exclusively on the provision of content and services, for technology businesses the provision of TV services supports a wider portfolio of business operations focused on controlling the technological infrastructures and devices necessary to access online TV. *TV natives* operating technology businesses would include the cable, satellite and telecoms providers, such as Virgin Media, Sky and BT. As well as providing online TV services, these companies control the technological infrastructures that provide consumers with access to broadband, whether through satellite or fibre optic cable. As will be examined in more detail below, this offers them a commercial advantage over their competitors by owning and controlling the core infrastructures that other online TV services need to access in order to operate. Telecoms providers and ISPs, such as TalkTalk and PlusNet, are perhaps better understood as technology businesses than TV natives. Although they have extended a TV service online, they lack the long history of offering television services more characteristic of other TV natives. However, they do share with technology businesses a focus on the provision of the technologies that all online TV services rely on.

Online natives operating technology businesses in the UK would include the major platform businesses Amazon and Apple. As with the UK's cable, satellite and telecoms providers, these companies exert control over the technologies required to access online TV services. Although it might seem anomalous to refer to online retailer Amazon as a technology business, the single most profitable part of Amazon's business in 2017 was its cloud computing platform, Amazon Web Services (AWS) (Hern 2017). AWS provides many of the internet infrastructure services necessary to run an online TV service – such as hosting applications and websites, storage backup, content delivery and database software – to a range of high-profile clients including Channel 4, Discovery, 21st Century Fox and Netflix. This points to a key distinction between Amazon and Netflix as businesses. As a content business, Netflix is purely focused on its online TV service, while Amazon Prime Video operates as a subset of Amazon's broader platform business. As industry analyst Guy Bisson claimed, 'Netflix is a pure content businesses, while Amazon clearly is not. If it boosts Amazon Prime, Amazon Prime Video doesn't necessarily have to make lots of money or any money' (cited in Barraclough 2016).

Where Amazon exerts control over online infrastructure, Apple is a particularly dominant player in the production of devices such as smartphones, tablets, laptops and desktops, which are increasingly central to the delivery and experience of online TV. At the same time, both Apple and Amazon have developed digital media players (Apple TV and Amazon Fire TV Stick) that can be attached to a television set to provide access to a wide range of audiovisual content and services. Control over devices enables these online natives to shape users' access to services by, for example, determining which services come pre-loaded or are even available on a particular device. Cable, satellite, telecoms and internet service providers also exert some control over devices by providing set-top boxes as part of their TV packages that can shape which content and services are most easily available and accessible to viewers. Furthermore, control over these add-on and viewing devices gives technology businesses the ability to generate significant data about the viewing experiences of users that could provide them with a competitive advantage in the development of content and services.

There are also digital start-ups that could be considered technology businesses, although the control that they exercise over online TV's technological infrastructures and devices tends to be less pronounced. For example, Simplestream developed its online TV service, TVPlayer, out of a technology business based on offering streaming services to media companies. As a technology service provider for the online TV industry, Simplestream does not exert control over core internet infrastructure or devices in the same way as cable/satellite providers, global IT firms or telecoms companies. However, the example of Simplestream does point to the way in which relevant technological know-how might provide a competitive advantage in developing an online TV service.

A further feature of technology businesses is that they tend to aggregate the content and online TV services of other providers. All of the companies examined above aggregate TV services from third parties. This gives them control over the frames within which viewers experience their competitors' services. Virgin TV Go, for example, controls the interface and algorithms that shape which programmes and/or channels are prioritised and how content is categorised within its service. Technology businesses can, therefore, use their control over devices to shape which content and services are most easily available and accessible to viewers.

Segmenting the online TV industry according to business focus draws attention to the ways in which content and technology can operate as controlling points in the online TV industry. Tom Evens (2013, p.489) defines controlling points as the aspects of an industry that new entrants would rely on in order to enter the business. Control over the rights to content can provide a strategic advantage both in launching a new service and in determining what content is (and is not) made available to competitor services. In addition, companies that already offer content services can utilise an existing brand reputation with core communities of users to launch a new service. Control over technological infrastructures can be used to shape users' access to online TV services, such as through the speed of broadband services, while the companies that produce technological devices like digital media players and set-top boxes can exert control over the user experience and gain access to valuable consumer data.

From Table 3.3 it is clear that control over content and technology is not enacted evenly across the online TV industry; there is significantly more competition at the level of content than technology. As will be examined in more detail in Chapter 4, many technology businesses have made aggressive moves into content, whether in the form of producing and licensing sports content (BT and Amazon) or investing in the origination of drama, documentary, comedy and entertainment programming (Sky, Amazon and Apple). In the companies listed in Table 3.2 only Simplestream, Virgin, TalkTalk and PlusNet have not moved into content production. Content origination and ownership of content rights have, therefore, become a particularly competitive battleground for online TV providers. By contrast, content businesses have not moved into the provision of the technological infrastructures and devices needed to access online TV services. As a consequence, technology businesses have the potential to exert significant control over the online TV industry. As we shall go on to see, this creates an environment in which they can enact unfair practices over their competitors.

There has been some pushback from content businesses. At the level of devices, the major UK-based free-to-air broadcasters (BBC, ITV and Channel 4) have sought to exert some control by working together with technology businesses to develop Freeview and YouView. Freeview is a non-profit UK digital TV service launched in 2002 by DTV Services Ltd, a company owned and run by the BBC, Channel 4, ITV, Sky and Arqiva. It began as a subscription-free alternative to cable/satellite television providing access to digital terrestrial channels through Freeview-enabled television sets and set-top boxes. In 2015, DTV added Freeview Play, which enables on-demand access to Freeview's channels. YouView is a commercial joint venture between the BBC, ITV, Channel 4, Channel 5, BT, TalkTalk and Arqiva, providing subscription-free access to linear channels and a range of VOD services through purchase of a set-top box or YouView-enabled Sony television set.[14] YouView set-top boxes are included in the TV bundles of BT TV, TalkTalk and Plusnet. However, it is noticeable that such moves by TV natives into devices involve collaboration with technology businesses and the involvement a number of different companies. By contrast, the move into content origination does not necessitate such partnerships. This points to the significant barriers to entry that exist around the controlling points of online TV technologies and the power exerted by technology businesses in this area.

However, although technology businesses tend to exert significant control in the online TV industry through their provision of technological infrastructures and devices, there are co-dependencies at work here. All online TV services are shaped by the content that they offer to users, the frames that construct user experiences of that content, and the technological infrastructures and devices through which the service is accessed. Although technological infrastructures and devices can be used to exert control over access to online TV services, they are also dependent on services and content. For example, the ability to access a popular online TV services can drive increased use of technological infrastructure and devices, such that accessing online TV services could be a factor in users choosing to subscribe to the more expensive superfast broadband services.[15] Meanwhile, as we shall see below, the presence of popular online TV services can have an impact on the success of devices. At the level of content, although a significant number of online TV services have moved into content origination, many (particularly the services of online natives that do not have access to back catalogues of content) depend on licensing content from third parties.[16] At the same time, the sale of intellectual property rights is a crucial revenue source for many TV natives, particularly those that operate as content businesses. Finally, all online TV services use control over the frames of online TV services to shape how content is made available to users. If content businesses can use these frames to control how users experience their content, those technology businesses that aggregate online TV services from third parties can use frames to structure how users experience their competitors' services by, for example, determining the prominence of content and services within their interfaces.

Technological devices, infrastructures, services, frames and content, therefore, exist in interdependent relationships with each other. Recognising these co-dependencies is important in understanding the dynamics of the online TV industry, which is characterised by significant volatility. This volatility emerges not only in the wide range of organisations providing online TV services with competing business models, but also in the complex ways in which these different businesses exist in interrelation with each other. This chapter has so far considered the online TV industry as being characterised by different types of company exerting competitive advantage through the controlling points of technology and content. However, it might be more productive to understand the online TV industry as a series of battlegrounds through which power is enacted and negotiated between different parties with varying competencies, dependencies and areas of control.

The rest of this book will focus on four key battlegrounds that shape online TV services: technology, content/rights, interfaces and data/algorithms. Content/rights has emerged over this chapter as a site of significant competition in the online TV industry. The battleground of content/rights, and its impact on the services provided by online TV, will be explored in more detail in the next chapter. Interfaces and data/algorithms are both powerful frames that can be used by services and devices to shape access to content. All online TV providers use frames to shape how users experience their services. This can have specific ramifications for the kinds of cultural experiences that online TV services provide, as will be examined in more detail in Chapters 5 and 6. Finally, this chapter has argued that technological infrastructures and devices emerge as sites through which technology businesses in particular can enact control. The final section of this chapter will end by examining the technological battleground of online TV in more detail in order to ask what impact the struggles for control enacted through technology has on the provision of online TV services to users. Online TV services are offered within an internet ecosystem characterised by the promise of ubiquity and accessibility. Yet, at the same time, this is a media landscape in which the assurances of being able to move seamlessly from watching television on a TV set to a smartphone, tablet or laptop is frequently hampered by proprietary standards. We end this chapter, therefore, by looking at the ways in which the interoperability of technology emerges as a key battleground in the provision of online TV services.

Online TV technologies: ubiquity, interoperability and incompatibility

Unlike broadcast television, online TV services are not tied to the technological infrastructure of broadcasting and the device of the TV set, but operate within a connected media ecosystem in which television can be delivered via broadcast, cable, satellite, broadband, wifi, 4G and cloud-based infrastructures to a range of viewing devices, such as a smartphone, tablet, desktop or TV set. For example, I can access Netflix directly on my smartphone when out of the home using 4G infrastructure or I can access it through the set-top box attached to my television set at home using cable and broadband infrastructures. In between the technological infrastructures and viewing devices used to access online TV services are a growing number of add-on devices, particularly digital media players like Apple TV, Slingbox and Google Chromecast, that facilitate the use of online TV services across a range of viewing devices. These technologies have different affordances and interdependencies, but typically depend on connection to a television set and use of broadband infrastructure. For example, the add-on device of my Virgin TV cable set-top box is dependent upon the television set as a viewing device, as well as the cable infrastructure that delivers television and broadband to my home. Meanwhile, the experience of accessing my cable TV service on a television set differs from accessing it through the VOD app Virgin TV Go on a tablet, because of the affordances of each viewing device. Online TV services cannot exist without the infrastructures and devices to deliver them, much as infrastructures and devices have no value if they are not delivering content and services of some kind. Recognising these interdependencies is important given that convergence is one of the core characteristics of the online TV ecosystem, but also because not all services are available across all devices, not all content is available across all services and not all devices are compatible with all infrastructures. As such, central to understanding what is at stake in the industrial ecosystem of online TV is recognising the battles that take place across the lines of technological infrastructures and devices.

As José van Dijck (2013, p.156) argues, connective media do not operate within a neutral technological ecosystem. At the level of infrastructure, the merging of cable/satellite and internet distribution to the home has made control over internet traffic a key battleground, particularly within markets like the US where there are significant monopolies over internet provision. Online TV services depend on the technological infrastructures of copper and fibre optic cables, wireless radio connections and satellite links. In many countries there is significant consolidation in the ownership of these infrastructures. For example, in many US cities there is only one ISP, creating problematic monopolies in the internet infrastructure upon which online TV depends. As we have seen in the UK context, TV natives that operate as technology businesses, such as BT, Virgin and Sky, combine domestic broadband with television, mobile and telephone services to consumers in triple-pay and quadruple-pay packages. New OTT services, such as Netflix, frequently depend on the broadband internet infrastructures that are controlled by the technology businesses with which they are competing in the provision of online TV services. These OTT streaming services have been particularly disruptive to ISPs because video streaming uses a lot of bandwidth. In the US, the rapid expansion of Netflix streaming in late 2010 led the US ISPs to claim that they needed to place caps on video services that made extensive use of broadband capacity, resulting in a flurry of debates about the need for 'net neutrality' regulation to ensure that ISPs did not exploit their monopoly over internet infrastructure and ensure that they treated all internet traffic equally (Lotz 2014, p.159; Stiegler 2016, p.241).[17]

However, the control of streaming and downloading speeds lies not only with ISPs but also with the companies that own the routers and servers that act as intermediaries in the delivery of content over the internet (Wolk 2015, p.52). For example, Netflix does not upload files directly to ISPs, but rather to content distribution networks (CDNs) that deliver them to transit providers like Cogent, that then provide them to the ISPs (like Comcast) that bring the files from the internet to the consumer's home. The creation of fast and slow lanes that might privilege certain forms of data over others on the internet could take place at the level of the transit providers and CDNs that operate out of public view (ibid.). Amazon, for example, runs CloudFront, a global content delivery network integrated into its cloud computing platform, Amazon Web Services, which provides internet infrastructure services to a number of online TV services, including Netflix. However, although AWS is a significant player in the area of cloud computing, many online TV providers adopt a multicontent delivery network approach, often including developing their own proprietary CDN (Rayburn 2017). The BBC, for example, uses multiple CDNs, including its own 'BBC Internet Distribution Infrastructure' (BIDI) (Benedetto 2016). Meanwhile, although Netflix uses AWS to track its users and organise its content catalogue, it uses its own CDN, Open Connect, to stream its content to users. This enables Netflix to store its video content in data centres around the world to be as close to its end users as possible (Butler 2016). As high data services such as video streaming become a central part of the internet, control over cloud computing and CDNs will become as important to the operation of online TV services as control over internet service provision.

The control that TV native technology businesses (cable, satellite and telecoms companies) have over both television and broadband infrastructure, however, provides them with a significant market advantage through their ability to offset potential losses from users switching from cable/satellite/digital television to OTT services by charging more for broadband usage. These charges can be made direct to consumers by, for example, charging per data usage or for faster download speeds, or they can be made directly to the OTT service providers. For example, Netflix and other OTT providers pay US cable, satellite and telecoms companies to connect directly to their services in order to prevent network congestion and poor viewer experience (Lotz 2014, pp.159–60). Meanwhile, in Europe Netflix has been making alliances with telecommunications companies Telekom (that operates across Germany and Central Europe) and Vodaphone (that operates across 26 countries around the world) in exchange for free access to Netflix for their subscribers (Stiegler 2016, p.242). This demonstrates the ways in which content businesses can leverage the power of a strong brand in negotiations with technology businesses.

Although control over broadband tends to lie with TV native technology businesses, in 2011 online native Google attempted to move into the provision of broadband infrastructure through its Google Fiber initiative, which installed fibre optic cables to homes in a number of cities across the US with the promise of vastly increased internet speeds and a package of television channels to replicate those offered by the cable, satellite and telecoms providers (Lotz 2014, p.156; Wolk 2015, p.54). By 2017, Google announced that it was pausing development of Google Fiber in a number of cities (Forrest 2016). Conner Forrest cites low subscriber numbers, high costs and lack of expertise and partnerships in infrastructure delivery as reasons for the failure of this initiative. However, others have argued that the roll-out of Google Fiber acted as a catalyst for other US ISPs to develop faster speeds (Whittaker 2015), leading one industry analyst to speculate that Google's goal was to stimulate the development of the high-speed networks needed for the delivery of its products and services (Lotz 2014, p.156). Whatever the truth, the failure of Google Fiber reveals the high barriers to entry in the provision of physical infrastructure, and demonstrates the competitive advantage that ownership of broadband infrastructure provides technology businesses in enabling them to shape the experience of online TV by controlling the speeds at which video is streamed or downloaded and combining the provision of internet and other services within one package.

Beyond the level of infrastructure, producers of add-on and viewing devices can attempt to lock in online TV service providers and/or users through built-in incompatibility. Phil Simon (2013, p.146) argues that the platform businesses of the global IT companies like Google, Amazon, Apple and Facebook (see Chapter 2) are built upon internal synthesis. The fundamental principle of a platform business, according to Simon, is to produce a range of integrated products that combine to fulfil multiple different needs for users. Apple, for example, produces a range of devices that are designed to operate seamlessly together and that come pre-loaded with Apple services, such as iTunes. The aim in platform businesses is to make it easy for users to move within and across the platform's suite of integrated products, but difficult to move between the products of different platforms. Apple's platform business, for example, is designed to keep users within its different services and devices by deliberately building in incompatibility with other devices. For example, Apple's video calling service, FaceTime, only works on Apple devices and the 'screen mirroring' feature on Apple TV (that enables users to mirror the screen on their mobile or tablet on a television set) only works with iPhones, iPads and Macs.

Gregory Steirer refers to the principle of 'switching costs' to explain the ways in which built-in incompatibility functions in the online video ecosystem. Switching costs refer to 'the additional expenses incurred by a consumer when he or she changes from one product to a competing or substitute product' (2015, p.187). These costs can be financial, such as the costs involved in having to buy new content or devices, or implicit, such as the time involved in learning how to use a new operating system or device. There are two ways in which switching costs operate. The first is through 'lock-in,' where the costs of switching outweigh the value to be gained by switching. The second is 'path dependency,' where a product dominates not by offering a better consumer experience but by locking consumers in at an early stage in the market's development, although Steirer notes that there is some disagreement as to whether path dependency actually exists. Within the electronic sell through (EST) and TVOD markets in particular (where viewers buy digital copies of audiovisual content), **digital rights management** (DRM) is used to bind consumers, so that users often have to use the same service through which they purchased a video in order to view it.[18] Where a company such as Apple has high market penetration and consumer popularity, high switching costs can become a significant barrier for new entrants into the market. As Steirer writes:

> Whether or not path dependency is at work, Apple's large market share and locked-in customers give it tremendous negotiating power with the studios, allowing it not only to influence general EST policies, such as DRM systems and storage rights, but also to effectively set both wholesale and retail pricing for the entire EST industry.
>
> (Steirer 2015, p.188)

Issues of interoperability extend beyond the specificities of the EST and TVOD market. There are many manufacturers producing smart, internet-connected television sets; yet there are no consistent industry standards, which means that sets from different manufacturers cannot speak to each other and app developers have to produce new versions for each manufacturer/set (Wolk 2015, pp.24–5). Indeed, while Steirer draws attention to the costs inherent in built-in incompatibility for consumers, there are also costs for service providers that have to create different versions of their online TV services to run across the range of available add-on and viewing devices. A key strategy for many online TV providers has been to enable their services across as many devices as possible. A number of commentators have argued that Netflix owes much of its success to the ubiquitous availability of its service across multiple devices (Cunningham & Silver 2013, pp.90–1; Lindsey 2016, p.176; Ulin 2014; Ward 2015, p.229). However, offering a service across a number of devices can be a costly endeavour because of the need to produce and update multiple versions enabled for different technologies and operating systems (Medina et al. 2015, p.156). Channel 4's AVOD service, All 4, for example, offers a very similar service and interface across its app, website and on the Amazon Fire TV Stick. However, Virgin Media's set-top box offers a limited 'catch-up' version of the service without the branding and interface design characteristic of All 4 on other devices. In 2014 the BBC addressed this problem in the re-launch of iPlayer, which aimed to offer a consistent experience across all devices, having previously developed and operated 14 different versions of the service for specific devices (from YouView to PlayStation to the iPad) (Grainge & Johnson 2018, p.22). The lack of standardisation across devices can, therefore, present barriers not only to viewers, but also to the ability of online TV providers to offer their users consistent experiences regardless of where their service is accessed.

However, the relationship between online TV service and add-on device can be reciprocal where the service has developed particular brand equity. Jeff Ulin argues, for example, that it was the ability to view Netflix on television sets that initially drove adoption of the digital media player Roku, which provided access to online TV services through a dongle that attached to the USB port in a television set.

According to Ulin, Roku's offer to consumers depended specifically on the services it was able to provide access to, claiming that in this instance Roku needed Netflix more than Netflix needed Roku (2014, p.396). For device manufacturers, the availability of particular services can offer a competitive advantage. At the same time, for the major technology businesses that offer services and devices, a lack of compatibility and ubiquity can be used to attempt to create consumer lock-in. The technological ecosystem of online TV is, therefore, one in which issues of interoperability and ubiquity between competing platforms, devices and services function as a crucial staging ground in the battle for control over the online TV ecosystem.

Although television studies has long raised concerns about the increased consolidation of broadcasters/networks, studios and distributors within the industry (Evens & Donders 2016), the interdependencies between online TV services, devices and infrastructures indicate that attention also needs to be paid to mergers and acquisitions across and between different facets of the IT/technology and media/entertainment sectors that play an increasingly significant role in the delivery of television. As Tom Evens and Karen Donders (2016, p.676) argue, however, mergers and acquisitions, particularly across sectors, do not guarantee success. The majority of mergers fail to produce benefits for shareholders, and over half even destroy value, with the overwhelming cause of failure due to differences of culture and corporate values (ibid.). The interdependencies between infrastructures, devices and services in the online TV ecosystem are as likely, therefore, to play out in the negotiations and deals enacted between different players within the market as through the activity of mergers and acquisitions. Therefore, to understand the stakes in this market we need to be particularly attuned to the ways in which online TV providers leverage their controlling points.

Although the market for online TV services is certainly crowded and far more complex than that of broadcast (or even satellite/cable) television, this does not mean that controlling points do not exist or that certain companies cannot leverage those to create an unfair competitive advantage that is not always in the interests of consumers. Indeed, the current lack of industry standards in online TV technology has created an online TV ecosystem in which consumers' access to content and services can be constrained by the ISP and device that they use. Although the increased variety of technologies for accessing television brings with it the promise of being able to watch whatever, whenever and wherever we want, in reality the interdependencies between infrastructure, device and service providers can work to limit access and choice. In this ecosystem interoperability emerges as a battle line that compromises the extent to which online TV fulfils the utopian promise of ubiquitous access to content.

Conclusion

The aim of this chapter has been to examine the industry that provides online TV services. The online TV industry sits at the intersection of television and IT, but involves players from a broad range of sectors. This is a highly volatile industry made up of organisations operating multiple different business models which exist in dynamic and often dependent interrelationships with each other. To make sense of this varied and distinctly 'messy' industry, this chapter has offered two approaches to categorising the industry. First it argued that it is possible to distinguish three kinds of online TV providers according to business origins, competencies and dependencies: TV natives, online natives and content natives. *TV natives* are incumbents in the world of television, bringing the benefits and dependencies of existing TV businesses and competencies. *Online natives* are incumbents on the internet, focused on the delivery of internet-related services and often dominating core components of the internet ecosystem, such as search and e-commerce. Both have to learn each other's business and ways of working. *Content natives* operate more niche services extended from an existing content business and focused on specific communities of viewer. Each category of online TV organisation brings with it a set of competencies and dependencies that shape how their business operates.

However, this chapter has argued that the categories of TV, online and content native overlook significant intersections between these segments of the online TV industry. Categorising the online TV industry according to core business focus rather than business origins drew attention to the ways in which different segments of the industry attempt to exert competitive advantage over their competitors. Using this approach, the chapter distinguished between *content businesses* and *technology businesses*. *Content businesses* are focused on the production, acquisition and delivery of content. *Technology businesses* control the technological infrastructures and/or devices required to access online TV services. This approach revealed that there is significantly more competition at the level of content than technology. While a large number of technology businesses have moved into content production, the barriers to entry around online TV technologies have tended to exclude content businesses from moving into the provision of infrastructures or devices. At the same time, however, it is important to recognise that there are dependencies between the different segments of the online TV industry. Control over technology can shape access to services, but control over services can impact the success of devices, and control over content can affect the success of services. We can understand these dependencies as the dynamics of the online TV industry.

These dynamics play out on a series of battlegrounds through which power is enacted and negotiated. Through examining the controlling points of the online TV industry, this chapter has argued that there are four key battlegrounds for online TV: technology, content/rights, interfaces and data/algorithms. As we have seen in relation to technology, these battlegrounds can affect the user's experience of online TV services. This chapter has argued that the control that technology businesses exert over broadband infrastructure and the lack of industry standards in viewing and add-on devices can be used to constrain access to online TV services, undermining the promised ubiquity that often accompanies the industry and media rhetoric around online TV (see Chapter 1). Where Chapters 5 and 6 will examine the battlegrounds of interfaces and data respectively, the next chapter will turn its attention to content and rights. It will examine the ways in which content functions as a site of competition and co-dependence for TV and online natives in particular, and will ask how this might work to restrict or enhance users' access to online TV content in the internet era.

Notes

1 I have borrowed the concept of the 'messiness' of the online TV industry from John Caldwell's analysis of the 'mess' of the contemporary screen industries, characterised by increasingly blurred boundaries between film, television and marketing (2013, p.163).

2 The language of incumbents and new entrants is used by other scholars examining the contemporary television industry (see, for example, Ganuza & Viecens 2014; Zhao 2017).

3 In Table 3.2 the online TV services selected are all VOD players of some kind. However, an online TV service can be any service that facilitates the viewing of editorially selected audiovisual content through internet-connected infrastructure and devices. For TV natives, therefore, this could include linear channels made available through internet-connected infrastructure and devices.

4 ITV has experimented with offering an ad-free version of its online TV service (ITV Hub +) for a small subscription fee, which is available as an app, on some smart TVs or as a channel through Amazon Prime Video. Meanwhile, UK public service broadcaster BBC experimented with a TVOD service, BBC Store, that ran alongside iPlayer (its free VOD service funded through the licence fee). However, the corporation announced the closure of BBC Store in November 2017 following weaker than expected demand for the service.

5 Some of UKTV's channels are also available without subscription through Freeview. In July 2018 all of UKTV's channels were pulled from the cable provider Virgin Media's TV subscription package after a dispute concerning carriage fees and the VOD rights to UKTV content. Specifically, the BBC does not automatically provide UKTV Play with the VOD rights to its content, preferring to retain those rights for the iPlayer or sell them to other online TV services, such as Netflix. Virgin Media sought to cut the fees that it pays to UKTV for its channels, pointing to the lack of VOD rights to BBC content as a sticking point in negotiations in a media landscape in which Virgin customers expect to be able to access the content provided within their channel bundles through Virgin's on-demand services (Munn 2018). The dispute was resolved by August 2018 after UKTV saw significant losses in ad revenue and Virgin faced the move of subscribers to other services (Anon. 2018a).

6 Discovery has, however, launched a 'channel' on Amazon Prime Video and a SVOD service, DPlay, within a number of other European territories.

7 Virgin Media used to operate its own television channels, but sold them to Sky in 2010.

8 Triple-pay refers to the bundling of television, internet and landline telephone services into one subscription package. Increasingly, cable and satellite operators are moving into 'quadruple-pay' packages that also include mobile phones.

9 China has sought to keep out the major US platforms and support the development of its own internet companies, dominated by Baidu, Alibaba and Tencent (BAT). As with the major US corporations, these companies operate as platforms (see Chapter 2), developing a range of different, but linked, online services, including online TV services (Zhao 2018).

10 Netflix's DVD rental business lost 4.8 million subscribers between 2013 and 2018 (D'Onfro 2018) and contributed revenues of just over $450,000 in 2017, compared to revenues of just over $11 million from Netflix's domestic and international streaming services (Anon. 2018b). Netflix introduced efficiency measures to minimise the costs of continuing to run its DVD rental business, cutting the number of distribution centres across the US from 50 to 17 (as of 2018) and reducing its expenditure on DVDs (D'Onfro 2018).

11 For example, in 2017 Netflix poached Bela Bajaria from Universal TV to oversee unscripted TV production (Sakoui 2018).

12 For example, Roy Price (Head of Prime Video Global Content and Amazon Studios) is a former vice president of series development and programming at Disney.

13 As with Netflix and Amazon, Apple has also poached staff with backgrounds in television content production. For example, in 2017 Apple hired two former Sony Television executives, Jamie Erlicht and Zack Van Amburg, to be the co-heads of video programming worldwide (Anon. 2017).

14 Sony is an interesting company that sits at the intersection of content and technology businesses, given that it combines content production and the provision of media technologies (from games consoles to television sets). However, it is probably best understood as a technology business because its online TV service, PlayStation Video, largely supports its development of the PlayStation games console as a media entertainment system.

15 However, as will be discussed below, OTT services such as Netflix can take up significant bandwidth and negatively affect the quality of the service provided by an ISP.

16 As we shall examine in more detail in Chapter 4, there are significant differences between the ways in which online and TV natives approach the ownership and sale of content rights.

17 In 2015, President Barack Obama's Democratic government in the USA introduced legislation that barred internet service providers from blocking or slowing access to content online or charging consumers more for certain content. The intention was to ensure that internet providers did not favour their own material or services over that of their competitors. However, in December 2017 the Federal Communications Commission (FCC) repealed these rules. In May 2018, the US Senate voted to overturn the FCC's decision, but this measure would need to be approved by the House of Representatives or the White House in order to take effect (Shepardson 2018).

18 See also Richard Berger (cited in Curtin et al. 2014, p.56), who argues that the digital EST market needs to learn from DVD, which was so successful because there was a standard format around which manufacturers could build technology to enable all DVDs to play.

Bibliography

Anon., 2018a. UKTV: Dave and Gold Channels Return to Virgin Media. *BBC News Website.* Available at: https://www.bbc.co.uk/news/uk-45154707 [Accessed August 11, 2018].

Anon., 2018b. 2018 Quarterly Earnings. *Netflix.com.* Available at: https://ir.netflix.com/quarterly-earnings [Accessed June 4, 2018].

Anon., 2017. Jamie Erlicht and Zack Van Amburg Joining Apple to Lead Video Programming. *Apple.com.* Available at: https://www.apple.com/newsroom/2017/06/jamie-erlicht-and-zack-van-amburg-joining-apple-to-lead-video-programming/ [Accessed June 4, 2018].

Barraclough, L., 2016. Amazon Prime Video Goes Global: Available in More Than 200 Territories. *Variety,* 14 Dec. Available at: https://variety.com/2016/digital/global/amazon-prime-video-now-available-in-more-than-200-countries-1201941818/ [Accessed August 13, 2018].

Benedetto, F., 2016. BIDI: The BBC Internet Distribution Infrastructure Explained. *BBC Blogs,* 22 Sept. Available at: http://www.bbc.co.uk/blogs/internet/entries/8c6c2414-df7a-4ad7-bd2e-dbe481da3633 [Accessed August 11, 2018].

Bennett, J. et al., 2012. *Multiplatforming Public Service Broadcasting: The Economic and Cultural Role of UK Digital and TV Independents,* London: Royal Holloway, University of London, University of Sussex, London Metropolitan University.

Butler, B., 2016. Netflix is (Not Really) All in on Amazon's Cloud. *Network World,* 24 Feb. Available at: https://www.networkworld.com/article/3037428/cloud-computing/netflix-is-not-really-all-in-on-amazon-s-cloud.html [Accessed August 11, 2018].

Caldwell, J.T., 2013. Para-Industry: Researching Hollywood's Blackwaters. *Cinema Journal,* 52(3), pp.157–165.

Cunningham, S. & Silver, J., 2013. *Screen Distribution and the New King Kongs of the Online World,* Basingstoke: Palgrave Macmillan.

Cunningham, S., Craig, D. & Silver, J., 2016. YouTube, Multichannel Networks and the Accelerated Evolution of the New Screen Ecology. *Convergence: The International Journal of Research into New Media Technologies,* 22(4), pp.376–391.

Curtin, M., Holt, J. & Sanson, K. eds., 2014. *Distribution Revolution: Conversations about the Digital Future of Film and Television*, Berkeley: University of California Press.

D'Onfro, J., 2018. What It's Like to Work at Netflix's Dying DVD Business. *CNBC.com*, 18 May. Available at: https://www.cnbc.com/2018/01/23/netflix-dvd-business-still-a live-what-is-it-like-to-work-there.html [Accessed August 11, 2018].

Evens, T., 2013. Platform Leadership in Online Broadcasting Markets. In M. Friedrichsen & W. Mühl-Benninghaus, eds. *Handbook of Social Media Management: Value Chain and Business Models in Changing Media Markets*. Berlin: Springer, pp. 477–491.

Evens, T. & Donders, K., 2016. Mergers and Acquisitions in TV Broadcasting and Distribution: Challenges for Competition, Industrial and Media Policy. *Telematics and Informatics*, 33(2), pp.674–682.

Forrest, C., 2016. Why Google Fiber Failed: 5 Reasons. *Tech Republic*, 20 Dec. Available at: https://www.techrepublic.com/article/why-google-fiber-failed-5-reasons/ [Accessed August 11, 2018].

Ganuza, J.J. & Viecens, M.F., 2014. Over-the-Top (OTT) Content: Implications and Best Response Strategies of Traditional Telecom Operators. Evidence from Latin America. *Info*, 16(5), pp.59–69.

Gough, O., 2016. Interview with Innovation of the Year Winner Azoomee. *smallbusiness.co.uk*. Available at: http://smallbusiness.co.uk/innovation-year-azoomee-interview-2534830/ [Accessed August 11, 2018].

Grainge, P. & Johnson, C., 2018. From Catch-Up TV to Online TV: Digital Broadcasting and the Case of BBC iPlayer. *Screen*, 59(1), pp.21–40.

Haslam, K., 2018. Apple Subscription TV On-Demand Service Rumours. *Macworld*, 11 Jun. Available at: https://www.macworld.co.uk/news/apple/apple-streaming-movie-tv-con tent-3610603/ [Accessed June 11, 2018].

Hern, A., 2017. Amazon Web Services: The Secret to the Online Retailer's Future Success. *The Guardian*. Available at: https://www.theguardian.com/technology/2017/feb/02/ama zon-web-services-the-secret-to-the-online-retailers-future-success [Accessed June 11, 2018].

Hesmondhalgh, D., 2013. *The Cultural Industries* 3rd ed., London: Sage.

Johnson, C., 2017. Beyond Catch-Up: VoD Interfaces, ITV Hub and the Repositioning of Television Online. *Critical Studies in Television: The International Journal of Television Studies*, 12(2), pp.121–138.

Landau, N., 2016. *TV Outside the Box : Trailblazing in the Digital Television Revolution*, New York: Focal Press.

Lindsey, C., 2016. Questioning Netflix's Revolutionary Impact: Changes in the Business and Consumption of Television. In K. McDonald & D. Smith-Rowsey, eds. *The Netflix Effect: Technology and Entertainment in the 21st Century*. New York: Bloomsbury, pp.173–184.

Lotz, A.D., 2014. *The Television Will Be Revolutionized* 2nd ed., New York: New York University Press.

Lotz, A.D., 2016. *Portals: A Treatise on Internet-Distributed Television*, Ann Arbor, MI: Maize Books.

Medina, M., Herrero, M. & Guerrero, E., 2015. Audience Behaviour and Multiplatform Strategies: The Path towards Connected TV in Spain. *Austral Communicacion*, 4(1), pp.153–172.

Munn, P., 2018. UKTV Set to Go Dark on Virgin Media Due to Carriage Dispute. *TV Wise*, 19 Jul. Available at: https://www.tvwise.co.uk/2018/07/uktv-set-to-go-dark-on-virgin-media-due-to-carriage-dispute/ [Accessed August 11, 2018].

Rayburn, D., 2017. Clearing up the Cloud Confusion Re: Amazon, Disney, Hulu, BAM-Tech, Akamai and Netflix. *Streaming Media Blog*, 15 Aug. Available at: https://www.streamingmediablog.com/2017/08/clearing-up-the-cloud-confusion.html [Accessed June 11, 2018].

Sakoui, A., 2018. Netflix's Talent-Poaching Strategy: Pay 'Em Double. *Seattle Times*, 30 Mar. Available at: https://www.seattletimes.com/explore/careers/netflixs-talent-poaching-strategy-pay-em-double/ [Accessed August 11, 2018].

Shepardson, D., 2018. Senate Approves Bill in a Bid to Retain US Net Neutrality. *Reuters*, 16 May. Available at: https://www.reuters.com/article/us-usa-internet/u-s-net-neutrality-bill-gets-enough-senate-votes-to-advance-idUSKCN1IH2DS [Accessed June 11, 2018].

Simon, P., 2013. *The Age of the Platform: How Amazon, Apple, Facebook, and Google Have Redefined Business* Revised Ed., Las Vegas: Motion Publishing.

Steirer, G., 2015. Clouded Visions: UltraViolet and the Future of Digital Distribution. *Television & New Media*, 16(2), pp.180–195.

Stiegler, C., 2016. Invading Europe: Netflix's Expansion to the European Market and the Example of Germany. In K. McDonald & D. Smith-Rowsey, eds. *The Netflix Effect: Technology and Entertainment in the 21st Century*. New York: Bloomsbury, pp.235–246.

Ulin, J., 2014. *The Business of Media Distribution* 2nd ed., Abingdon: Focal Press.

van Dijck, J., 2013. *The Culture of Connectivity: A Critical History of Social Media*, Oxford and New York: Oxford University Press.

Wallenstein, A., 2015. The OTT View-niverse: A Map of the New Video Ecosystem. *Variety*, 29 Apr. Available at: https://variety.com/2015/digital/news/ott-map-video-ecosystem-1201480930/ [Accessed June 11, 2018].

Ward, S.J., 2015. *Branding Bridges: Imported Drama and Discourses of Value in the British Digital Television Industry*. PhD Thesis. University of Nottingham.

Waterman, D., Sherman, R. & Wook Ji, S., 2013. The Economics of Online Television: Industry Development, Aggregation, and 'TV Everywhere.' *Telecommunications Policy*, 37 (9), pp.725–736.

Whittaker, Z., 2015. Google Fiber is Forcing its Rivals into Offering Cheaper, Faster Service. *ZD Net*, 13 Apr. Available at: https://www.zdnet.com/article/i-wish-google-fiber-was-in-my-neighborhood/ [Accessed August 11, 2018].

Wolk, A., 2015. *Over the Top: How the Internet Is (Slowly But Surely) Changing the Television Industry*, CreateSpace Independent Publishing Platform.

Zhao, E.J., 2017. The Bumpy Road towards Network Convergence in China: The Case of Over-the-Top Streaming Services. *Global Media and China*, 2(1), pp.28–42.

Zhao, E.J., 2018. Negotiating State and Copyright Territorialities in Overseas Expansion: The Case of China's Online Video Streaming Platforms. *Media Industries*, 5(1). Available at: https://quod.lib.umich.edu/m/mij/15031809.0005.107?view=text;rgn=main.

4

ONLINE TV CONTENT PRODUCTION AND DISTRIBUTION

RECAP

- Since the late 2000s, the penetration of fast broadband speeds, tablets, smartphones and internet-connected televisions has heralded a new 'internet era' in which television and the internet are increasingly interconnected.
- The internet era has created the conditions for the emergence of online TV, defined in Chapter 2 as *services that facilitate the viewing of editorially selected audiovisual content through internet-connected devices and infrastructure.*
- Central to the provision of online TV services is:

    a   The acquisition of content, through origination or licensing.
    b   Editorial control over the user's viewing experience, through infra-structure, data and algorithms.

- Chapter 3 examined the industry responsible for providing online TV services. It argued that the industry can be divided into three categories of company according to business origins:

    1   *TV natives*, that have extended an existing TV service into the internet ecosystem (e.g. BBC, Disney, Sky).
    2   *Online natives*, that have originated online services for the internet ecosystem (e.g. Netflix, Amazon, Apple).
    3   *Content natives*, that have extended a content-based business in another field into an online TV service (e.g. Globe Player, Arsenal Player).

- The online TV industry can also be categorised according to business focus into:

a   *Content businesses*, that focus primarily on the production, acquisition and delivery of video content to viewers (e.g. BBC, Disney, Netflix).

b   *Technology businesses*, that are responsible for the provision of the technological infrastructures and devices needed to access online TV services (e.g. Sky, Amazon, Apple).

• Both content and technology businesses have moved into the production of content, making content a particularly competitive battleground in the online TV industry.

Introduction

There has been a long-standing debate within film and television studies about whether control of distribution or of content provides greater competitive advantage. This is a debate that has been rekindled in the internet era. Stuart Cunningham and Jon Silver argue that a small number of largely US tech companies, such as Google, Facebook and Apple, have come to dominate the online ecosystem by controlling the platforms that deliver content to audiences. Confirming the power and profitability of distribution over content in the contemporary screen industries, they claim that 'if content is *king*, then distribution is *King Kong*. The power and profitability in screen industries have always resided in distribution' (Cunningham & Silver 2013, p.4). In the online TV industry, however, content is a valuable asset. All online TV services depend on audiovisual content in order to attract viewers, and this differentiates online TV from online video services like YouTube that create an infrastructure through which users can upload their own content (see Chapter 2). As services that *facilitate the viewing of editorially selected audiovisual content through internet-connected devices and infrastructure*, the acquisition of content is at the heart of online TV. Online TV services hope that by producing or licensing the most desirable content – from *Game of Thrones* to high-profile sports – they can distinguish themselves in the market and attract viewers within a competitive attention economy. Content rights are also valuable financial assets that can be licensed to third parties. As more online TV services seek to build up large catalogues of content to attract viewers, the sale of content rights to third parties can generate significant revenue for content owners. This would seem to support Neil Landau's insistence on the value of content to the contemporary TV industry when he writes: 'Perhaps the biggest lesson learned from all media companies is that ownership of content has far greater value than distribution' (2016, p.133).

However, there are two problems with characterising the internet era as a battle between owners of content and of distribution. The first is that it overlooks the extent of consolidation within the industry. As we saw in Chapter 3, ownership of content and distribution frequently falls within the same hands, as most online TV service providers have moved into content production (Lotz 2016; Evens & Donders 2016).[1] The second is that there is often a lack of clarity about what 'distribution' refers to and how it intertwines with content production in practice. Amanda Lotz

(2014, p.113) argues that in industry and academic discourse the term 'distribution' is often used interchangeably to refer to two separate industry practices: the delivery of content to viewers and the sale of content rights to third parties. Where Cunningham and Silver argue that distribution is 'King Kong' they are referring primarily to ownership of the means by which content is delivered to viewers. By contrast, where Landau argues that the primary value lies in content he is referring to ownership of content rights. In the online TV industry the owners of most online TV services produce content, own content rights and control the means to deliver content to viewers. The role of content within the online TV industry is far more nuanced, therefore, than a simple battle between content and distribution.

This chapter asks how audiovisual content functions as a site of competition and co-dependence in the online TV industry, and what impact online TV has on the production and distribution of video content. The chapter examines the ways in which established industry practices for producing and distributing audiovisual content have been destabilised with the growth of online TV. In doing so, it focuses in particular on the interrelationships between content production, content delivery and the sale of rights as sites of competition and cooperation in the online TV industry. Chapters 5 and 6 will then turn in more detail to examine the delivery of content to users of online TV services, looking at the role that interfaces and data play respectively in this process.

In examining the battlefield of content production and distribution this chapter unpacks the strategies used by different segments of the industry, drawing on the analysis developed in Chapter 3, which outlined two approaches to mapping the industry that provides online TV services. The first approach focused on business origins and identified three kinds of online TV provider: TV natives, online natives and content natives. *TV natives* are organisations that have extended an existing television service onto the internet (e.g. BBC, Disney, Sky). *Online natives* are businesses that have originated online services for the internet ecosystem (e.g. Amazon, Apple, Netflix). *Content natives* have extended a content-based business in another field into an online TV service (e.g. Globe Player, Arsenal Player). The second approach categorised the online TV industry according to core focus business and distinguished between *content businesses* (such as BBC, Disney, Netflix, Globe Player and Arsenal Player) that focus primarily on the production, acquisition and delivery of content to viewers, and *technology businesses* (such as Sky, Apple and Amazon) that are responsible for the provision of the technological infrastructures and devices needed to access online TV services.

Chapter 3 demonstrated how technology businesses can use their control over technological devices and infrastructures to exert competitive advantage in the online TV marketplace. In relation to control over content production and distribution, however, the picture is more complex. Although content businesses focus on the production, acquisition and delivery of content to viewers, many technology businesses have moved into the origination of content for their online TV services. This makes content production an especially competitive sector of the online TV industry. The move of online natives into content production has been particularly disruptive for those TV natives that operate as content businesses centred on the production, acquisition and delivery of content and services. By contrast, TV natives that operate as technology businesses (such as the cable, satellite and telecoms providers) are not as dependent on revenues generated from the production and/or sale of content.

This chapter will focus on the impact that online natives are having on the long-standing industry practices developed by TV natives for the production and circulation of audiovisual content.[2] However, the chapter also stresses the dependencies between TV and online natives, arguing that online natives rely in particular on TV natives that operate as content businesses for a significant proportion of their content. In the midst of this conflict lies the viewer, and the chapter ends by asking what this battle over content production and distribution might mean for online TV users. Traditionally, content distribution practices have been utilised to create artificial scarcity that works to limit the free circulation of content. To what extent do the content production and distribution strategies of online TV providers continue to create artificial scarcity and restrict the ubiquity of access to audiovisual content promised in the internet age?

Online TV and content production

There are two broad models for the production of audiovisual content by the television industry: in-house and independent. In-house production refers to the creation of content through production facilities that are owned by the TV service. This mode of production is most common amongst the free-to-air terrestrial channels with origins in broadcasting, which often own studio facilities. Over time, however, there has been a gradual shift away from in-house production in many countries. As a consequence, many free-to-air broadcasters have sold off much of their studio space, choosing instead to rent facilities on a per-production basis or to commission audiovisual content directly from external production companies. It is, therefore, increasingly common for online TV service providers to finance content that is produced by independent studios. In the UK, the shift from in-house to independent production has been actively encouraged through media policy since the 1980s, which led to a significant increase in the independent production sector (Doyle 2016b). In other markets, such as the US, media conglomerates often run TV networks and production studios as separate but linked businesses. These studios will produce programming not only for their partner networks but also for competing networks.[3] As such, it is worth treating the term 'independent' here with caution. Many 'independent' production companies are part of large conglomerates, with Mark Sweney (2014) noting in 2014 that the leading production companies in the UK are owned by 'foreign giants, mostly from the US, including NBC Universal, Warner Bros, Sony and Rupert Murdoch's 21st Century Fox.'

There are two main models through which online TV service providers fund content production: **deficit financing** and **cost plus.** Deficit financing is the practice of paying production companies less than the costs required to make a programme. In exchange the production company retains some or all of the secondary rights to the final content. This enables the production company to recoup the costs of production by selling the rights to the programme after its initial broadcast. For example, an independent production company might make a programme for BBC One. After it has been aired on BBC One the production company could sell the rights to a UK digital channel, a streaming service and to numerous services overseas. Deficit financing enables TV service providers and independent production companies to share the financial risks of TV production (Doyle 2016b, p.83). The benefit for production companies is that by retaining the rights to the content they have the potential to generate significant profits by licensing that content in national and international markets.

By contrast, cost plus is the practice of paying producers 'the full production costs plus a small production fee or "profit" up-front' (Doyle 2016b, p.83). In the cost-plus model the TV service provider retains all rights, not only for initial transmission but also in secondary markets. Here the TV service provider takes on the risk of production but will also reap the financial rewards of a successful programme. For smaller production companies, cost plus can remove the need to secure additional capital investment to make up for the financial shortfall of deficit financing (ibid.). Due to media policies designed to stimulate the development of a competitive independent production market, deficit financing has been the dominant practice in the UK since the early 2000s. In much of the rest of Europe and the USA cost plus is more prevalent (ibid.). However, it is not always possible for online TV service providers to be able to afford all of the costs of creating original content, whether it is produced through deficit or cost-plus financing. It has become increasingly common, therefore, for TV service providers to engage in co-production deals. Co-productions are a valuable way of sharing the costs of content origination, and generally involve sharing the profits and/or the rights to the content produced.

The internet era presents particular challenges to established practices for content production in the TV industry. There are three key facets that are crucial to understanding the internet's impact on television production. The first is that the internet is *geographically expansive*, facilitating the movement of content across national boundaries. The second is that the internet has significantly *increased capacity* when compared to linear television, enabling the storage of vast amounts of content not limited by the temporal constraints of a channel schedule (Lotz 2016, p.24). The third is that the internet is *networked and participative*, offering audiences more control over the viewing and circulation of content. These three facets of the internet disrupt many of the dominant practices that have shaped the production of television since the broadcast era.

One of the most overt changes to content production in the internet era has been the massive investment from new online natives, primarily Netflix and Amazon, in producing original drama series, movies, documentaries and comedies. In 2017 Netflix reportedly spent $6 billion on content and Amazon $4.5 billion (McAlone 2017). Josef Adalian (2018) claimed in 2018 that Netflix makes more television than any US network in history. The move of online natives such as

Netflix and Amazon into content origination is particularly associated with investment in big statement drama and documentary productions (Doyle 2016b, p.87). Gillian Doyle describes this as a marketing-oriented model of production which focuses on creating high-impact programmes that elicit buzz in order to generate and maintain subscribers (2016a, p.638). In this move they have adopted many of the strategies developed by US premium cable services since the 1990s and associated with the rise of 'quality TV' (McCabe & Akass 2007). For example, Ted Sarandos (Chief Content Officer, Netflix) has claimed that, when commissioning original content, Netflix aims to produce series that are not 'already on television or would be difficult to put on television. ... I'm not looking for something that could easily be made somewhere else' (cited in Landau 2016, p.15).[4] Along with the emphasis that Netflix places on providing showrunners with creative freedom, Sarandos' rhetoric here chimes with that adopted by HBO (and other US premium cable channels) in the 1990s with its mantra of producing programming that is 'not TV' (Johnson 2007; Leverette et al. 2007). As with US premium cable channels, subscription video-on-demand (SVOD) services like Netflix are unburdened by commercial interruptions and the limitations of standards and practices departments that can shape the kinds of content produced by advertiser-funded services, enabling them to create more risky content that might otherwise upset advertisers or audiences. Many of the strategies adopted by the major online natives as they enter into content origination, therefore, stem from practices developed in premium cable, and can be better understood as a feature of subscription and ad-free business models rather than online TV services per se. This extends to their focus on niche subject matter, as subscription-based services focus content origination on attracting and retaining subscribers. Amanda Lotz (2016, p.26) refers to this as a 'conglomerated niche' strategy in which content is valued according to its appeal to specific niche groups of consumers rather than its ability to generate overall ratings.

However, there are some specific characteristics of online TV that can affect the kinds of programmes produced for these services. The increased storage capacity of online TV services removes the temporal limitations on programming that shaped the broadcast and, to a lesser extent, cable/satellite and digital eras of television. Standardised lengths for television programmes tended to emerge from the mid-1950s as television became more competitive and as an international distribution market for television programmes emerged (Jacobs 2000, p.115). Producing programmes to fit 30-minute or 1-hour timeslots in a linear schedule enabled broadcasters to attempt to poach viewers from one channel to another at key points in the day (Ellis 2000). Programmes that could be easily placed within existing schedules were also more attractive on the burgeoning international distribution market.[5] By contrast, online TV services are not constrained by the temporal limitations of the linear schedule, often producing programmes of varying lengths (Sandberg 2017). For example, Netflix's original comedy series *Master of None* (2015–) included one episode that lasted for 21 minutes, and another that ran at nearly an hour.[6] This freedom from the standardised 30-minute and 1-hour time slots of the linear schedule broadens the ways in which stories (both fictional and factual) can be told within individual programmes/episodes and across whole series.

The lack of capacity constraints in online TV services has also led to new delivery and consumption patterns that can have an impact on storytelling. Mareike Jenner argues that Netflix's strategy of releasing all the episodes of many of its series in one go (rather than adopting the more typical weekly release schedule of linear television) has led to more highly serialised and complex narrative structures that encourage **binge viewing** (2017, p.305). Traced back to the emergence of DVD box sets of television programmes in the 1990s, binge viewing refers to the practice of watching several episodes of a television series in one sitting (Jenner 2017, p.306). Where linear services adopt scheduling strategies to encourage viewers to remain tuned to a flow of different programmes on their channels, VOD services have been associated with encouraging binge-viewing practices, including through the production of shows that particularly reward sequential viewing.

However, these changes to the kinds of content produced by the television industry are not evident across all online TV services. Many online TV services still produce much of their content in standard lengths and release it weekly. This speaks to the continued relevance of linear television strategies to online TV, particularly for TV natives that are often seeking to create content that they can release on both linear and nonlinear services. For example, most of the BBC's content production budget is spent on programmes that are shown on its linear channels *and* made available through its VOD service, iPlayer. Furthermore, programmes of standard lengths are easier to sell to the large number of linear channels looking for content on the international market.

Beyond the need to produce content for linear environments, some online TV services have argued for the continued value of standardised lengths and weekly releases within on-demand environments. For example, SEESO, the now defunct US, comedy-focused SVOD service, offered mainly 30-minute programmes (the traditional length for comedy on linear television), with live streaming and weekly launches being a characteristic feature of the service. Evan Shapiro (Executive VP of Digital Enterprises, SEESO) argued that binge-viewing models based on simultaneous release of all episodes were not always desirable as they could pressurise viewers to watch immediately to avoid spoilers, rather than allowing a series to build and sustain buzz over time (cited in Landau 2016, pp.48–9). In this instance, weekly release strategies have a marketing dimension in which audiences for series can be generated gradually over time. Aficionados can watch weekly, eagerly awaiting new episodes. As the buzz filters down to other viewers, they can engage in binge viewing by accessing the back catalogue of episodes within the online TV services. Here, linear and nonlinear strategies support each other, rather than operating in opposition. Online TV services have the capacity to make episodes released weekly available for a number of weeks or months so that new audiences can discover them over the run of a series.

Other online TV services have sought to create programming that can be easily shared online. For example, Beatrice Springborn (Head of Original Programming,

Hulu) notes the value of commissioning weekly variety series because such content is 'clippable' and can be distributed to third party platforms (such as social media sites) in order to enhance discovery of new programmes and drive viewers to their service (cited in Landau 2016, p.28). Meanwhile, Victoria Jaye (Head of TV Content, BBC iPlayer), described the content origination strategy for iPlayer as focusing not just on 'long-form TV shows and series, but shorter form content, feature-length films and events, all originated for the platform and aimed at on-demand audiences' (cited in Grainge & Johnson 2018, p.35). This has included producing short-form drama and comedy specifically designed to be shared and to stand out online (ibid.). The production of this kind of 'spreadable' (Jenkins et al. 2013) content speaks to the ways in which some online TV providers are seeking to create programming that extends beyond the closed infrastructure of their online TV services and moves out into the broader internet ecosystem. This is perhaps most apparent in experiments with social media storytelling found in entertainment, news, sports and fictional genres (Bennett & Strange 2018, p.33). One of the more high-profile examples of social media storytelling is Norwegian broadcaster NRK's drama series *Skam* (2015–17). In this series the story was told through short clips released through the series' website as they were happening to the character. Between videos, NRK uploaded text conversations and social media updates from the characters. The videos were then gathered into a weekly episode that aired on NRK's linear channels. In this example, NRK experimented with the formal construction of the drama by telling the story across short-form video and social media posts while simultaneously presenting the narrative in more conventional weekly episodes on linear television.

It is notable that SEESO, Hulu, NRK and the BBC are all TV natives.[7] This may account for their commitment to traditional television practices such as standardised lengths, weekly release of content and commissioning a range of genres. Even in the case of *Skam*, NRK produced the programme to be experienced on linear television as well as through the web and social media. For each TV provider, this enables their online TV services and linear channels to support each other, for example, through the movement or repurposing of content from one service to another.

Despite these links between the production practices of online TV services and broadcast/cable/satellite television, there have been attempts to distinguish linear and nonlinear television services according to the kinds of content that they commission and acquire. For example, Jorge Abreu et al. (2017, p.69) argue that you can distinguish between three broad groups of TV programme: those that require an instant audience and lose relevance over time (news, live sports); those that can be watched at any time and don't date so quickly (drama series, some documentary series); and programmes that blend the two and that benefit, but don't depend on, being watched live (reality TV, talent shows, series finales). They argue that time-shifted services (such as VOD) might be best suited to content without any temporal significance, and that linear TV will focus on programmes with immediacy appeal (see also Bruns 2008, p.91).

However, although temporally significant content, such as news and live sports, might seem most suited to linear television, such arguments over-simplify the dynamics of the online TV ecosystem. In practice, linear broadcasters are increasingly operating online TV services that combine the streaming of broadcast schedules with access to on-demand content (Johnson 2017), and VOD services are acquiring rights to some temporally significant content, particularly live sports. For example, in 2017 Amazon Prime Video purchased the rights to the NFL (American football) and the ATP World Tour (men's tennis), aping the strategy of pay-TV cable/satellite services in using sports content to entice new subscribers to their service (McMullan 2017; Ruddick 2017). Sports rights are particularly attractive to subscription-based services because they engage loyal viewers who are prepared to pay a premium for access to live games. As such, it is not possible to argue that online TV services only (or even primarily) produce and/or acquire content that lacks temporal significance.

However, although all three groups of TV content identified by Abreu et al. are available across the range of different online TV services, it is notable that the online natives that have moved into content origination have tended to focus on drama, documentary and sport, and have not sought to produce news, soaps and live entertainment. The reasons for this are complex. Soaps and live entertainment are tied to the particular practices of linear television, encouraging regularised viewing at specific times of the day/week. Soaps also require investment in standing sets and ongoing casts that run counter to the production models adopted thus far by online natives for TV drama and lack the prestige and marketing buzz of the high-end dramas favoured by online natives. Meanwhile, news is typically produced in-house (although with some footage sourced from third parties), is often nationally specific in its tone of address and tends to have little value in secondary markets, making it less suitable to the business models of online natives. As such, the reasons for the different kinds of television produced by TV and online natives may have as much to do with established production practices and business models as it does with the characteristics of on-demand and nonlinear modes of delivery.

In moving into the production of high-end dramas and documentaries, online natives such as Amazon and Netflix have not just extended and innovated with new forms of storytelling but have also challenged the ways in which content is commissioned, particularly in the US. Historically, the US television industry has operated a highly regulated commissioning process in which studios would produce pilots in January, with the successful series being picked up and put into production for transmission in September. Netflix has been critical of this practice and introduced a new commissioning process that is closer to that operated in Europe, where series are put into production from a story idea, treatment and/or spec script (Curtin et al. 2014, p.185). Beyond Netflix, online TV services have introduced more variety into the commissioning process. Amazon, for example, has reinvented the pilot process for the internet era by allowing viewers to vote on pilots that they would like to see produced as series. At the same time, however, Amazon does still commission direct to series for shows that come from established and high-profile creatives (Landau 2016, pp.18–21). Similarly, Hulu combines straight to series commissions, particularly for established talent, with a more traditional pilot process (ibid., p.27). In the internet era, therefore, commissioning practices can be variable.

Despite this variety of practice, however, it is notable that the track record of the creative talent plays a significant role in the commissioning process, with established writers more likely to have their ideas commissioned straight to series, particularly for high-end content. Although this is in part a strategy designed to minimise risk by going with tried and tested talent that is known by the audience, it also reflects the dynamics of the US market in which there is a perceived scarcity of experienced showrunners. Beatrice Springborn claims of the US context: 'there is huge competition for high-end showrunners and creators. So with those, we'll typically go straight to series' (cited in Landau 2016, p.27). In 2015 John Landgraf, president of US cable channel FX, argued that there was 'too much television' being produced in the US, claiming that the number of scripted series on air had increased from around 280 in 2012 to over 400 in 2015 (Littleton & Ryan 2017). Coining the term 'peak TV' to describe what he saw as an over-supply of content in the television industry, Landgraf argued that it was harder for TV services to find the talent able to tell compelling and original stories that will stand out from the competition (Rose & Guthrie 2015). Cynthia Littleton and Maureen Ryan go further in arguing that Peak TV has transformed the job market for television writers in the US, creating a 'gulf between the haves and have-nots among WGA [Writers Guild of America] members'.[8] In the US context, where writing teams have been the norm for scripted series, Littleton claims that pressures on production costs have led some companies to eliminate mid- and lower-level writing jobs altogether. Where lower-level writers are still employed, longer production times for shorter seasons has led to employment on a per-episode basis, leading to writers working longer hours for less pay. As well as raising questions about the ways in which writers should be compensated for their work, these changing production practices also raise concerns about how emerging writers will learn the trade of being a writer-producer without the experience of working with more senior writer-producers in a writing-room environment.[9]

Beyond the US, where the system of commissioning from pilots is less dominant and highly formalised, online TV has been used as a site to experiment with new forms of talent development. For example, the BBC has used workshops with new talent to generate script ideas to be developed into short-form content for iPlayer (Grainge & Johnson 2018, p.37). Here, the lack of capacity constraints within online TV services is seen to provide the space for experimental content. In production contexts like the UK, without the tradition of the writers' room, writers and producers have often cut their teeth on soap operas and other continuing series. It is too early to say whether changing content origination practices will have an impact on the production of continuing series, which can be important in providing regular and significant ratings to terrestrial television channels. However, the move towards commissioning online series of a range of lengths suggests that online TV might open up opportunities for new forms of, and spaces for, talent development.

Beyond the television industry, online video services like YouTube represent a new source of content and talent for online TV services (Morreale 2014; Van Esler

2016). There are companies that specialise in trawling online video services for content that is sold on to TV networks (Lobato 2016, p.352). Many multichannel networks (MCNs) on YouTube (a number of which are owned by major media conglomerates) perform the intermediary functions of media buyers and agents in helping talent repackage their content for distribution on online TV services (Cunningham et al. 2016, p.386). However, Stuart Cunningham, David Craig and Jon Silver (ibid.) argue against understanding online video as simply a stepping-stone for talented writers and directors to break into television. They claim that for many online video writers and producers, working for traditional media companies would involve relinquishing the creative control that they experience in the more open context of online video services.[10]

Beyond changes to commissioning and talent development, the internet era has also been characterised by a rise in international co-productions, particularly for high-end drama. Doyle argues that the emergence of high-end drama as a key site of competition, especially for subscription services, has 'greatly increased producers' reliance on international sources of [co-production] finance' to off-set rising production costs (2016a, p.639). A further reason for the reliance on international co-production finance is the expansion of online TV services into overseas markets. Here Netflix is the most overt example, operating its online TV service in more than 190 countries as of 2018.[11] As Netflix has entered new markets, it has sought to produce more localised content, co-producing a number of non-English language dramas outside of the USA, such as *3%* (2016–, Brazil), *Dark* (2017–, Germany) and *Ingobernable* (2017–, Mexico).[12] In the Asian context, the move of major Chinese online TV service iQiyi into Taiwan has also been accompanied by investment into co-productions with local companies, in many ways mirroring Netflix's localisation strategy (Zhao 2018).

Such international co-productions can have an impact on national production ecologies. For example, iQiyi has invested heavily in South Korean drama productions that are particularly popular with the younger audiences that watch online TV in China. Typically, South Korean dramas are created via a 'live-shoot' model whereby forthcoming episodes are written and filmed while a series is being transmitted (Zhao 2018, p.114). However, since 2014, online TV services in China have been required to register foreign films and TV shows with the State Administration of Press, Publication, Radio, Film and Television (SAPPRFT) for advance approval (ibid., p.115). To avoid a delay in release between the South Korean and Chinese markets (which could lead to increased piracy), co-productions with iQiyi have been produced in advance of their transmission in both South Korea and China (ibid.). Here co-productions designed to satisfy the interests of young Chinese audiences in South Korean drama have led to changes in established local ‚ industry production practices.

International co-productions have also been understood to impact the kinds of programmes produced. For Ib Bondebjerg the increase in European co-productions has had positive consequences, leading to a new form of transnational European television drama that counters both the national and American dominance of television and contributes to a 'better feeling for and understanding of the "us" and "them" in European culture' (2016, p.12). At the same time, however, increased dependence on co-financing may make it harder, particularly for countries with small local markets, to get investment in the production of high-quality content that tells stories of importance to national and local audiences that might not have international appeal. Jock Given et al.'s interviews with television executives in Australia revealed significant concerns that new online TV services like Netflix would not be interested in producing nationally specific programmes, particularly given the relatively small size of Australia's national television market (Given et al. 2015, p.9). For example, Courtney Gibson (Programming Production Executive, Nine Network, a major free-to-air commercial network in Australia) claimed, 'Netflix has a great brand and a great business but they're not here to tell idiosyncratic Australian stories: they're rolling out a global footprint and they're here largely to extract money, rather than invest it' (cited in Given et al. 2015, p.45).

Even where Netflix is investing money in local productions, its business model depends on originating programmes that can be exploited transnationally across the large number of countries within which it operates. Netflix has even argued that algorithmic analysis of its viewers' habits reveals that nationality has little impact on viewing preferences (Roettgers 2017). Instead, Netflix claims that it can segment its consumers into around 2,000 taste communities according to their viewing habits (Laporte 2017). One consequence of this is that Netflix is seeking to create content with transnational appeal even when engaged in localised productions. For example, Netflix's production of *The Crown* (2016–) could be seen as localised investment in a nationally specific story of British post-war society told through the lens of its monarchy. The series certainly draws on British writing, acting and directing talent. Yet its subject matter has significant global appeal given the widespread interest in the British royal family around the world (see, for example, Otnes & Maclaran 2015). Even iQiyi's investment in South Korean drama is focused on the production of programming that will appeal primarily to audiences in China and Taiwan.

As Ramon Lobato (2019) argues, the internet era creates a media ecosystem in which the global and the national sit in tension. Although the internet is characterised by increased geographic expansiveness, it operates within a media ecosystem that is frequently national in its production practices and regulations. The move of online natives like Netflix and iQiyi into new markets is often accompanied by concerns that they will undermine national media systems and cultures. For example, in the Australian context, international services like Netflix entered the market without being subject to the local content policy requirements of TV natives, such as quotas on nationally specific programmes (Turner 2016, p.23). Meanwhile, iQiyi's move into the Taiwanese market was accompanied by concerns that the service would act as external propaganda for China (Zhao 2018, p.112).

Similarly, the increase in international co-productions has led to concerns that television programming that serves the needs and interests of national and local audiences will be undermined. As Jeanette Steemers argues of the UK context,

> The national orientation of policy-making and public service broadcasting with its obligations to a national public sit uneasily next to the international strategies of some producer-distributors, who are increasingly less aligned to the United Kingdom as they distribute more non-U.K. product, produce overseas, and succumb to overseas or U.S. ownership.
>
> (Steemers 2016, p.747)

Jinna Tay and Graeme Turner see this as part of a broader disruption of the Reithian ideal that television has a valuable role to play in constructing national audiences (2008, p.74). Within this rhetoric, online TV services like Netflix fracture the imagined national community of broadcast television into commercialised taste cultures and introduce programming originating from other countries that tend to address global audiences, rather than national or local ones (ibid.). This represents a broader decline in the value placed on television's social role as audiences become increasingly fragmented and media policy, particularly in the West, has shifted focus towards regulating competition over national culture (Turner 2016, p.18).[13] At the same time, however, as Lobato (2019) argues, evaluations of the international expansion of online TV services like Netflix and the increase in international co-productions are context specific. It could be argued, for example, that these developments in transnational television increase access to a broader range of multicultural content and produce programming that, as Bondebjerg argues, has the capacity to strengthen understanding between and across nations.

In sum, online TV has upset a number of established industry practices for the production of content. The increased capacity of online TV has facilitated experimentation in the form of television programming. At the level of high-end drama, this has involved the production of programmes with complex, highly serialised narratives of non-standard lengths, often released in one go in order to encourage binge viewing. Beyond high-end drama, TV natives, such as the BBC and NRK, are using online TV services as spaces to experiment with new content forms and to develop talent. The increasingly globalised nature of television production has also led to the origination of content by online and TV natives designed with transnational appeal.

However, despite these changes, there are also significant continuities in content production practices. Many online TV services still produce much of their content in standard lengths and release it weekly. This speaks to the continued relevance of linear television strategies to online TV, particularly for TV natives that are often seeking to create content that they can release on both linear and nonlinear services. Furthermore, programmes of standard lengths are easier to sell to the large number of linear channels looking for content on the international market. Many TV natives also function under regulatory remits that require them to produce content that serves the needs of domestic, national audiences. As Evens and Donders argue (2013, p.420), despite increased globalisation, television markets remain bound by regulatory, political, geographic, cultural, economic and historical factors that are highly national.

To a significant extent, the battlefield of online TV content production can be understood as a fight between online natives, which are investing heavily in content origination for nonlinear environments, and TV natives that are still bound to the demands of linear broadcasting. However, it is important to recognise that many TV natives are embracing the possibilities that online TV represents to experiment with content production, as we have seen with NRK and the BBC. At the same time, many online natives have adopted the strategies of TV natives, particularly when they seek to sell the rights to their content to linear channels on the international market. To understand fully the impact of online TV on content production, therefore, we need to examine how online TV is challenging distribution, particularly the licensing of content to third parties.

Online TV and content distribution

In film, television and media studies 'distribution' is used to refer to what happens to content after it is produced in order for it to be accessed by viewers. There are broadly two ways in which online TV content travels to viewers after being produced:

1. The TV service provider that originated the content delivers it to viewers through their own service.
2. The company that originated the content sells the rights to a third party who delivers that content to viewers through their own service.[14]

Distribution, therefore, involves two related processes: the delivery of content to viewers and the licensing of content to third parties through the sale of rights (Lotz 2014, p.133). As we have seen, increasingly the online TV services that are responsible for the delivery of content to viewers are also involved in the production of original content. However, it is also common practice for TV service providers to buy in additional programming to fill the airwaves of linear channels and the catalogues of on-demand services. Between the producers of audiovisual content and the TV service providers that deliver that content to viewers, therefore, are distributors that sell the rights to content into different markets. Some distributors are part of the same conglomerates or organisations as studios and TV service providers, while others are independent. As with television production, TV service providers don't always use an in-house distributor, particularly when selling their content into foreign markets.

Central to the distribution practices related to the sale of rights and the delivery of content to viewers is the construction of 'artificial scarcity.' The television industry, as with most creative industries (Hesmondhalgh 2013, p.31), depends on creating artificial scarcity around its content. This is because the products of the creative industries are public goods with high production costs and low reproduction costs that are not used up at the point of reception. If I watch a television programme, that television programme is still available for you to watch, whereas if I were to eat a burger, that burger would no longer be available for you to eat. As a consequence, the television industry has to manufacture scarcity of access to its content in order to make a profit. The conventional industry logic within the television industry has been that without some form of restriction on distribution it is difficult for producers to recoup the costs of production and there would be few incentives for the creation of programming (Doyle 2016b, pp.77–8).

The television industry restricts the distribution of content primarily through the sale of intellectual property (IP) rights and the industry practice of 'windowing.' When the IP to content is sold (referred to as licensing) industry players are given the rights to deliver that content to viewers within a specified market and time period, typically referred to as a 'window.' These windows are constructed across geographic territories, technologies and services, and depend on mobilising four factors that shape how content value is optimised: time, repeat consumption, exclusivity and differential pricing (Ulin 2014, p.5). Time refers to the practice of constructing windows that stagger the release of content temporally across markets, such as transmitting a TV programme in the US before releasing it to the international market, then selling it on to cable and subsequently DVD months, or even years, later. Such temporal release patterns support repeat consumption by leaving a gap between release to different markets in the hope that viewers will pay a second time to watch the content again. Maximising value depends on each window being exclusive, so that one window does not cannibalise the audience of another window. Finally, differential pricing attaches value to each window, such that viewers may pay more to watch a movie in the cinema on first release than they would pay to watch the same movie on television one year after release. For example, a programme might first air exclusively on a free-to-air national channel. A number of months later, it might then be shown on a cable/satellite channel within the same country, as well as being transmitted on terrestrial, cable or satellite channels in other countries. Perhaps a year after first broadcast, it might be released on DVD or be available to download and own. These distribution practices enable the industry to control how content circulates, restrict the availability of content and construct artificial scarcity.

This section will identify five challenges that the geographic expansiveness, increased storage capacity and networked and participative nature of the internet ecosystem present to established distribution practices associated with the licensing of content for television. As with content production, these challenges play out in part as a battle between online natives that are introducing new disruptive practices and TV natives that are seeking to maintain existing ways of working. Yet there are also significant dependencies between online and TV natives that must be recognised if we are to understand fully the battlefield of content production and distribution in the online TV industry.

Expansion of windows

Since the late 1950s there has been a vibrant market for the sale of rights to content to be shown on television channels around the world. As more countries launched television services and extended the number of broadcast hours, licensing content from other countries became a cost-effective way of filling the schedules. The growth of cable and satellite (and later digital) television from the 1980s further expanded the number of television channels, increasing international demand for licensed content. The development of new online TV services has further increased demand for licensed content. However, a key difference is that online TV services do not share the temporal limitations of linear channels, and often depend on offering their users deep and expansive catalogues of content. Although many of the new online TV services have sought to originate their own content, they still rely significantly on the back catalogues of TV natives to fill their services. This has created what Richard Finlayson (Director of Television, Australian Broadcasting Company) referred to as a 'goldrush' for back catalogues of television programmes and movies (cited in Given et al. 2015, p.31; see also Medina et al. 2015, p.154; Curtin et al. 2014, p.46).

The purchase of content rights is particularly important for subscription services targeted at broad audiences, such as Netflix and Amazon Prime Video, that depend on aggregating a significant amount and variety of content with appeal to a number of different taste cultures. For TV natives, this has opened up new markets for content that previously had little value through traditional distribution routes. In particular, the emphasis within SVOD services, such as Netflix, on conceiving of the audience as taste cultures rather than demographics has expanded the market for non-US content, niche programming and series of varying lengths (Steemers 2016, p.745).[15]

Increase in availability of content

The increased storage capacity of online TV services not only creates greater demand for content but also alters the value of the windows for content distribution by making content available for longer. Doyle (2016a, p.635) argues that while, in the pre-internet era, it was possible to partition the audience into discrete segments and control the release of content across available windows, with the development of online TV services windows have become more porous and overlapping. The internet ecosystem enables vast amounts of content to be made available to viewers over long periods of time within one window/service and facilitates the ease with which viewers can copy and share content. In this sense, windowing could be understood as a strategy born of the capacity limitations of linear channels as a mode of content delivery. Online TV services can provide viewers with access to vast catalogues of content made available over extended periods of time and across geographic boundaries, potentially flattening out and removing the need for windows organised according to time, repeat consumption, exclusivity and differential pricing.

The impact of the increased availability of and access to content made possible by online TV challenges industry perceptions of the value of content. Content that is first made available through a SVOD service is often understood by the industry to have less value in secondary markets. As Doyle claims, 'It is widely acknowledged that sale of first window rights to a SVOD service is apt to reduce the opportunities available to content suppliers to exploit any residual value in their intellectual property assets in subsequent release windows' (2016b, p.90). This reduction in value can also be attributed to the different ways in which viewing is valued and measured. For SVOD services, traditional ratings have less value than the ability for a programme to attract new subscribers and maintain existing ones. Therefore, SVOD services tend to use different measures of success. However, ratings have been the traditional mechanism for determining the value of a programme on the distribution market. The lack of traditional ratings for a show licensed to a SVOD can, therefore, make it harder to value that programme when it comes to be licensed to other windows (ibid.).

Exclusive, cross-platform and global rights

One consequence of the perceived difference in value between VOD and linear television as windows for content has been a move towards exclusive, cross-platform and global rights. Rather than seeking to maximise revenues by selling content across different windows, this strategy works on the basis that content has more value within one service that acts as the sole window for repeat consumption of that content over time. Adopted in particular by online natives that operate SVOD services, the assumption here is that by making content available exclusively within one service it can be used to attract subscribers who will not be able to access that content elsewhere. Netflix has, for example, used cost-plus financing to retain exclusive and cross-platform rights to some of its original programmes in order to ensure that they are available only within its service. This pulls against the long-standing industry practice of generating revenue from content by licensing it to multiple windows.

The conflict between the Cannes Film Festival and Netflix in the summer of 2017 gives an insight into the ways in which exclusive rights challenge traditional windowing practices. The conflict arose around Netflix's attempt to enter two original movies into the competition for the prestigious Palme d'Or: Noah Baumbach's *The Meyerowitz Stories* (2017) and Bong Joon-ho's *Okja* (2017). Although both films received a limited theatrical release in the USA, neither was shown in cinemas in France. The National Cinema Centre in France, which coordinates the public financing of films and underwrites more than half of the budget for the Cannes Film Festival, criticised the inclusion of these films within Cannes because they had not had a theatrical release in France. At the heart of the conflict was the French 'cultural exception' law, which requires that a percentage of all box office, DVD, VOD, television, streaming and downloading revenues be pooled to help finance home-grown films. The law also includes a 'media chronology' that legally enshrines windowing by setting 'a strict time frame in which a film moves from theatres to video-on-demand after four months, to cable television after 10 months, to free television after 22 months and finally to a streaming service [after 36 months]' (Donadio 2017).[16] By maintaining a strict windowing strategy, the law aims to keep the French cinema industry buoyant by maximising the funds that come to the state to finance domestic production. It also supports the business models of key players within the French film industry, such as cable television operators like Canal Plus, which help finance movies for theatrical release and want to ensure that those films come to their television channels before moving to other distribution sites, such as SVOD services (ibid.). Such a media chronology, however, conflicts with Netflix's business model, which is based on funding original content, such as *The Meyerowitz Stories* and *Okja*, in order to drive subscriptions to its services around the world. It is, therefore, not in Netflix's interest to distribute its movies widely in other windows, particularly as a theatrical release in France would mean withholding these movies from its own streaming service in that territory for 36 months. The Cannes–Netflix clash perfectly encapsulates the ways in which exclusive and cross-platform rights threaten the established practices of windowing.

This battle over windowing reveals an underlying conflict of business models. Netflix's business model relies on restricting circulation of the content it produces to its own delivery service. By contrast, the business models of many TV natives are tied to generating revenue through the licensing of content across multiple windows. As Jon Penn of BBC Worldwide (the BBC's commercial arm and one of the largest distributors of content outside of the US) describes, 'We've built our business around very careful windowing of content across pay television, free-to-air, online, DTO [download to own], SVOD' (cited in Given et al. 2015, p.68). This conflict particularly comes to the fore in Netflix's attempts to secure global rights to the content that it licenses from third parties. Markets such as those in Europe and Australia have been formed on the bedrock of the territorial licensing of content, creating revenues for rights owners, producers and national broadcasters that cross-subsidise the production of content that has little value in the international market, such as news and certain domestic productions (Steemers 2016, p.737). However, as Netflix has expanded into new territories it has increasingly sought global rights so that it can offer the same content across all of its services.

These changes to established windowing strategies also disrupt the organisational structures for the sale of rights to content. Television markets tend to be organised territorially, making the practice of securing global rights a challenge. For example, while the US market is dominated by a small number of distribution companies, there are no equivalent European majors, which means that online TV services have to negotiate with each European content provider separately, making content acquisition a time-consuming process. As Anders Sjöman, Vice President of Communication for Scandinavian online TV service Voddler argues, 'There's simply a lack of infrastructure to facilitate face-to-face interactions with folks outside of America to make those content deals' (cited in Curtin et al. 2014, p.200). Content for international distribution also needs dubbing or subtitling (which carries additional costs), and in many territories the most valuable content has already been licensed to existing services (Given et al. 2015, p.31; Stiegler 2016, p.242). With most major distributors also having different divisions running each window, such as a separate television and retail division, exclusive, cross-platform and global licensing pulls against the traditional ways in which media businesses are organised. Any move towards licensing of exclusive, cross-platform and global rights as a standard industry practice, therefore, may be hampered by existing industry practices and organisational structures.[17]

Reconstructing windowing within one service

An alternative response to the challenge that online TV presents to traditional windowing strategies has been to reconstruct release windows within one service. For example, Voddler combines three different 'windows' within one service. The newest material, such as movies, is available to purchase or rent a few months after cinema release. That material then moves into Voddler's SVOD service after 6 to 12 months, with the oldest titles subsequently being made available without a subscription, but with the addition of advertising. Effectively, Voddler collapses a number of windows into one service, but still segments the market temporally in order to extract as much value as possible from the content it has acquired (Curtin et al. 2014, pp.194–5). Another way in which windowing might be reimagined within online TV services could be through the adoption of 'freemium' models (Ball 2016). More common in the games industry, freemium works on the basis of extracting value from content 'according to an individual viewer's attachment to or desires for a given piece of content' (ibid.). For example, games such as *Candy Crush* are made available for free (sometimes ad-supported) but revenue is generated from the small (but significant) number of users who are prepared to pay for additional features. In the context of online TV services, viewers might pay extra for premium content, no adverts or ease of access (such as being able to download content). These strategies combine traditional windowing practices with newer models of exclusivity, where the rights to content are restricted to one service but access is segmented according to time and/or differential pricing.

Restricting user behaviour

The geographically expansive, networked and participative nature of the internet ecosystem increases the ability for users themselves to circulate content. Content distributed over the internet is easier to share and to pirate (Doyle 2016b, p.84). The industry has responded by introducing simultaneous global release of some content (Doyle 2016a, p.634), placing additional pressures on the traditional practice of segmenting windows temporally and geographically. Beyond windowing, the industry has also sought to restrict user control over the circulation of content through digital rights management (DRM). Digital rights management refers to the technologies used to control access to and use of content (Landau 2016, p.82). DRM can be used to prevent users from sharing or modifying content, and can also restrict use of that content to a particular technology (see Chapter 3). One form of DRM that is widely used by online TV services to limit access to content is geoblocking. For example, the BBC uses geoblocking to prevent users outside the UK from accessing its online TV service iPlayer. Geoblocking relies on Internet Protocol addresses that indicate the geolocation of any device used to send and receive data online (Lobato 2019), and can be used to restrict access to online TV services by country. For the online TV industry, geoblocking is particularly important because, despite Netflix's attempts to acquire global rights, most audiovisual content rights are still sold according to geographically determined windows. Therefore, geoblocking functions as a way of maintaining geographic boundaries between markets and separate territorial windows. DRM, and geoblocking specifically, can be understood as an industry strategy that aims to retain artificial scarcity within the geographically expansive, networked and participative internet ecosystem by restricting user behaviour online.

What becomes apparent from examining these five ways in which distribution practices are changing in the online TV industry is that there is no single industry response to the challenges presented by the geographic expansiveness, increased storage capacity and networked and participative nature of the internet ecosystem. As with content production, the industry response can be understood as a battle between TV natives that are protecting their existing television businesses and online natives that are adopting new strategies more attuned to the internet ecosystem. TV natives, particularly content businesses such as the main terrestrial, cable and satellite television channels, have sought to protect traditional windowing strategies developed in the broadcast era in order to retain the revenues generated through the sale of content. Online natives, particularly the major global IT firms like Netflix and Amazon, have challenged these established industry practices and sought to adopt distribution strategies more adapted to the characteristics of the internet ecosystem. Rather than developing business models that depend on the sale of rights across multiple windows, the major online natives have sought to acquire exclusive rights in order to build up vast catalogues of content in an attempt to drive subscriptions. For SVOD services in particular, 'Exclusivity becomes very important; to earn monthly payment, subscriber-funded portals need to provide content viewers want to watch – rather than just something to watch' (Lotz 2016, pp.25–6). Meanwhile, the strategy of developing services that offer vast catalogues of content exploits the increased storage capacity enabled in the internet age. At the same time, Netflix's push towards global and cross-platform rights responds to the increased ease with which content can travel across national and technological boundaries online.

However, although it might appear that the business models of online and TV natives are fundamentally at odds, there are co-dependencies at work here. Crucially, online natives that offer access to large catalogues of content do not have the resources to produce all of that content themselves. As such, the business models of online natives, such as Netflix, are fundamentally dependent on TV natives to provide content for their catalogues. As long as this dependency continues, it is in the interests of online natives to ensure that their strategies do not completely undermine the business models of TV natives. Furthermore, although the move towards global rights threatens the revenues gained from traditional windowing strategies, for many online TV services the sale of rights to content that they own within international markets where they do not operate remains a valuable source of income. In the future it is likely that we will see more companies attempt to launch international services to compete with Netflix and Amazon. For example, in 2018, Disney announced plans to launch a streaming service to rival Netflix in 2019, initially in the US before expanding overseas. If more major industry players move towards business models based on international SVOD services, then the sale and purchase of global rights may become more common.

Even within national markets we may see a flattening of windows as online TV services seek to purchase rights for longer periods of time in order to shore up the value of their catalogues of content for viewers. For example, in 2018 it was revealed that the BBC was seeking to make increasing numbers of its programmes available for extended periods of time on its VOD service, iPlayer (Lawson 2018). This was an expansion of the 30-day time period that the BBC traditionally made content available on iPlayer after it had aired on one of its channels. Seen by Mark Lawson as an attempt to fulfil viewer demand created by Netflix for longer access to content, this move also has the potential to derail relationships between the BBC, independent production companies and Netflix itself. At present, the BBC tends to deficit finance content in exchange for handing over the secondary rights to independent production companies. If the BBC were to extend the amount of time that its programmes were available on iPlayer this could undermine the revenues that independent producers could generate from selling that content within secondary markets. One of those secondary markets has been Netflix itself, which currently holds a significant number of BBC programmes. This perfectly encapsulates the ways in which online natives like Netflix are both disrupting and dependent upon traditional distribution practices based on windowing.

Conclusion

Over this chapter we have seen how, in the internet era, long-established industry practices for the production, sale and delivery of content have been disrupted, but not in a consistent or uniform manner. In relation to production, the geographic expansiveness and increased storage capacity of the internet have created the conditions to engender new forms of storytelling. Building on developments that can be traced back to the expansion of the cable, satellite and digital eras, programmes are less bound by the standardised lengths associated with linear television production, and the increased availability of content has led to experiments with more serialised and complex narratives that reward binge viewing. Meanwhile, Netflix's global expansion, combined with an increase in international co-productions to offset rising budgets, has led to a growth in transnational storytelling designed to appeal across national boundaries. These changes to the form of television programming are mirrored by changes to the industrial practices for programme production, including greater variety in commissioning models and new routes for talent development. Where some providers are using their online TV services to offer opportunities to experiment with new talent, new commissioning models where series of shorter lengths are bought from established writer-producers threaten to reduce opportunities for new writers to learn their trade within the writers' rooms that have characterised US television production.

In relation to the licensing and delivery of content, new industry strategies challenge the use of windowing as the primary mechanism to create artificial scarcity. The increased storage capacity of the internet enables online TV services to make content available for longer, which threatens to undermine its value in secondary markets. Netflix's move to secure more exclusive, cross-platform and global rights undermines the logic of windowing by seeking to become the only window where its original content can be accessed. Other online TV services have sought to reconstruct windows within one service, such that the availability of content to users is determined by the willingness to pay for immediate and/or ad-free access. Digital rights management, such as geoblocking, also works to enforce the logic of windowing within an internet ecosystem by using technological means by which to restrict users' ability to circulate and access content.

These changes to the industrial practices for television production and distribution can be understood in part as a battle between TV and online natives. TV natives have sought to maintain production and distribution strategies that protect their existing business models. As such, TV natives are more likely to retain standardised lengths of programmes and weekly release strategies that both support their linear channels and facilitate the sale of the content they produce into secondary markets. By contrast, online natives have been at the forefront of the new and disruptive production and distribution strategies that are designed to exploit the global expansiveness, increased storage capacity and networked and participative nature of the internet ecosystem.

However, to characterise the production and distribution of online TV content as a simple battle between online and TV natives would be to overlook the significant dependencies at work between these two segments of the online TV industry. Online natives that offer large catalogues of content, such as Netflix and Amazon, base their business models on the ability to license content from TV natives. It is not in the interests of online natives, therefore, to undermine completely a secondary market for television content.[18] Furthermore, although Netflix and Amazon have extended their online TV services internationally, many online TV services are limited to one or a small number of countries. As a consequence, the international market for the sale of rights to content remains a primary way in which content travels across national boundaries.

The continued resilience of windowing as a strategy is threatened, however, by the logic of online TV services which locates greater value in exclusive rights. Although Lotz (2016) sees exclusivity as a particular feature of SVOD services, it could be argued that online TV services, regardless of their funding model, benefit from creating long-term access to content. A key feature of online TV services is that they are not constrained by the limited capacity of a linear TV schedule. Online TV services can, therefore, add new content without having to remove old content, and promise to make content available to viewers when, where and how they want to watch it. This promise of ubiquitous availability pulls against the temporal limitations imposed by traditional windowing strategies. Part of the value of online TV services to users is the availability of content over extended periods of time. By the same token, a key way for online TV services to attract new users is by being the only site where valued content can be accessed. It is unsurprising, therefore, that we have seen online and TV natives seek to acquire extended exclusive rights to content. As the online TV market matures, we may move towards a distribution model in which within each national territory, content is licensed exclusively to one service. This would undermine the existing windowing strategies within national markets (e.g. selling the rights to a programme trans-mitted on terrestrial TV to a cable or satellite channel within the same country) while retaining an international market for the sale of rights to content.

Yet what of the viewer within this picture? To what extent does the viewer seek to gain or lose in the ongoing battle around online TV content production and distribution? The global expansiveness, increased storage capacity and networked and participative nature of the internet would seem to offer opportunities for viewers to have greater access to and control over content. However, the online TV industry has responded to these changes by seeking new ways to restrict access to content and maintain artificial scarcity. By making content permanently available, exclusive, cross-platform and global licensing might at first glance appear to be a challenge to the industry practice of constructing artificial scarcity. Yet this strategy is predicated on exclusivity that aims, fundamentally, to restrict access within one particular service. As such, exclusive rights can be understood as replacing windowing as a mechanism for achieving scarcity in the market. What is at stake in the battle for control over content, therefore, is the conflict between different mechanisms for the construction of artificial scarcity, rather than the removal of artificial scarcity altogether. Far from providing ubiquitous programming on demand, the online TV industry still seeks to contain and constrain our access to content.

Notes

1 It is worth noting that the media industries have a tendency towards vertical and hor-izontal integration, and that this consolidation cannot be seen as a specific feature of online TV but rather a broader tendency within the creative and cultural industries (Hesmondhalgh 2013, pp.30–1).
2 This chapter focuses on online and TV natives as these are the main players in the pro-duction and distribution of online TV content. Content natives are less centrally involved in the production and/or sale of audiovisual content to the television industry.
3 This model is increasingly being adopted in the UK, where the terrestrial broadcasters operate studios (such as BBC Studios and ITV Studios) that compete to produce work for a wide range of channels.
4 In a similar vein, Beatrice Springborn (Head of Original Programming, Hulu) claims to be seeking to produce comedy series with 'very singular points of view' (cited in Landau 2016, p.28).

5 There is national variation to this, depending on context. However, many countries adopted 30-minute and 1-hour time lengths to facilitate sale of content on the international market or in response to competition so that programmes across different broadcasters finished at the same time. It is also worth noting that in the US and other advertising-funded contexts programme lengths would run at closer to 22 and 42 minutes in order to accommodate advertising within 30-minute and 1-hour slots (Sandberg 2017).

6 Non-standard episode lengths can also be traced back to premium US cable channels – such as the extended finale of HBO's *The Sopranos* (1999–2007) (Sandberg 2017) – but appear to be more commonplace in online TV services.

7 NBC Universal helped set up SEESO, and Hulu was launched as a joint venture between Fox, Disney and NBC Universal.

8 The Writers Guild of America is the labour union representing film, television, radio and new media writers in the US.

9 In 2017 these concerns about writers' pay led to a renegotiated contract between the WGA and the Association of Motion Picture and Television Producers (AMPTP).

10 See Chapter 2 for a discussion of the differences between more open online video services (such as YouTube), where users can upload content, and the more closed online TV services that actively acquire their content through commissioning and licensing.

11 Amazon has also expanded internationally, operating in more than 200 countries and territories since 2016 (Barraclough 2016).

12 It is important to note that the majority of Netflix's content is not local, as will be discussed in more detail in Chapter 5 (see also Lobato 2019).

13 Such arguments are less applicable to the Chinese context, where media policy remains significantly concerned with protecting national culture and socialist ideologies. However, online TV services like iQiyi have increased access and exposure to foreign films and TV programmes, and led to a rise in co-productions with companies outside of China (Zhao 2018).

14 It is important to note that it is not just TV providers that finance the production of content for television services. For example, TV services often show movies that have been produced by studios without direct financing from the TV service itself.

15 The standard practice in the US syndication market was that a series needed 100 episodes before it could be licensed to secondary markets in order to provide enough episodes to fill the schedules of linear channels. However, SVOD services such as Netflix are no longer bound by the temporal constraints of linear channels, increasing the value of shorter-length series across international distribution markets. Landau argues that as few as eight episodes will now qualify for syndication because that is what Netflix and Hulu will buy (2016, p.78). However, it is also worth noting that although SVODs like Netflix do include non-US content, they are dominated by US content, and so these new markets are not equally available to all content producers.

16 Video on demand and streaming are often used interchangeably, and there are no accepted industry definitions of the two terms. In this context, video on demand refers to transaction video on demand, where viewers pay to rent or download movies, and streaming refers to subscription video on demand, where viewers gain access to a movie as part of a larger service (see Lauvaux n.d.).

17 For example, according to Kelly Summers (former Vice President of Global Business Development and New Media Strategy, Walt Disney Company), Disney was the first US studio to structure its organisation in order to manage distribution holistically. However, Summers recognises that this remains a challenge as exhibition, retail and television tend to operate as separate industries despite the flattening out of windows (cited in Curtin et al. 2014, pp.71–2).

18 The co-dependency between the business models of TV and online natives is even greater for those online natives whose business is based on streaming the linear channels of TV natives (such as YouTube TV and TVPlayer).

Bibliography

Abreu, J. et al., 2017. Survey of Catch-up TV and Other Time-Shift Services: A Comprehensive Analysis and Taxonomy of Linear and Nonlinear Television. *Telecommunication Systems*, 64, pp.57–74.

Adalian, J., 2018. Inside the Binge Factory. *Vulture*, 10 Jun. Available at: http://www.vulture.com/2018/06/how-netflix-swallowed-tv-industry.html [Accessed August 13, 2018].

Ball, M., 2016. Letting It Go: The End of Windowing (and What Comes Next)? *ReDef*, 26 Aug. Available at: https://redef.com/original/letting-it-go-the-end-of-windows-and-what-comes-next [Accessed August 13, 2018].

Barraclough, L., 2016. Amazon Prime Video Goes Global: Available in More Than 200 Territories. *Variety*, 14 Dec. Available at: https://variety.com/2016/digital/global/amazon-prime-video-now-available-in-more-than-200-countries-1201941818/ [Accessed August 13, 2018].

Bennett, J. & Strange, N., 2018. *Adapting to Social Media: Commerce, Creativity and Competition in UK Television Production*, London. Available at: https://figshare.com/articles/Adapting_to_Social_Media_Commerce_Creativity_and_Competition_in_UK_Television_Production/5951977.

Bondebjerg, I., 2016. Transnational Europe: TV-Drama, Co-Production Networks and Mediated Cultural Encounters. *Palgrave Communications*, 2(May), pp.1–13.

Bruns, A., 2008. Reconfiguring Television for a Networked, Produsage Context. *Media International Australia*, 126(1), pp.82–94.

Cunningham, S. & Silver, J., 2013. *Screen Distribution and the New King Kongs of the Online World*, Basingstoke: Palgrave Macmillan.

Cunningham, S., Craig, D. & Silver, J., 2016. YouTube, Multichannel Networks and the Accelerated Evolution of the New Screen Ecology. *Convergence: The International Journal of Research into New Media Technologies*, 22(4), pp.376–391.

Curtin, M., Holt, J. & Sanson, K. eds., 2014. *Distribution Revolution: Conversations about the Digital Future of Film and Television*, Berkeley: University of California Press.

Donadio, R., 2017. Why the Netflix-Cannes Clash Couldn't Be Avoided. *New York Times*, 16 May. Available at: https://www.nytimes.com/2017/05/16/movies/why-the-netflix-cannes-clash-couldnt-be-avoided.html [Accessed August 13, 2018].

Doyle, G., 2016a. Digitization and Changing Windowing Strategies in the Television Industry: Negotiating New Windows on the World. *Television & New Media*, 17(7), pp.629–645.

Doyle, G., 2016b. Television Production, Funding Models and Exploitation of Content. *Icono 14*, 14(2), pp.75–96.

Ellis, J., 2000. *Seeing Things: Television in the Age of Uncertainty*, London and New York: I.B. Tauris.

Evens, T. & Donders, K., 2013. Broadcast Market Structures and Retransmission Payments: A European Perspective. *Media, Culture & Society*, 35(4), pp.417–434.

Evens, T. & Donders, K., 2016. Mergers and Acquisitions in TV Broadcasting and Distribution: Challenges for Competition, Industrial and Media Policy. *Telematics and Informatics*, 33(2), pp.674–682.

Given, J., Brealey, M. & Gray, C., 2015. *Television 2025: Rethinking Small-Screen Media in Australia*, Melbourne: Swinburne Institute for Social Research.

Grainge, P. & Johnson, C., 2018. From Catch-Up TV to Online TV: Digital Broadcasting and the Case of BBC iPlayer. *Screen*, 59(1), pp.21–40.

Hesmondhalgh, D., 2013. *The Cultural Industries* 3rd ed., London: Sage.

Jacobs, J., 2000. *The Intimate Screen: Early British Television Drama*, Oxford: Oxford University Press.

Jenkins, H., Ford, S. & Green, J., 2013. *Spreadable Media: Creating Value and Meaning in a Networked Culture*, New York: New York University Press.

Jenner, M., 2017. Binge-Watching: Video-On-Demand, Quality TV and Mainstreaming Fandom. *International Journal of Cultural Studies: The International Journal of Television Studies*, 20(3), pp.304–320.

Johnson, C., 2007. Tele-Branding in TVIII: The Network as Brand and the Programme as Brand. *New Review of Film and Television Studies*, 5(1), pp.5–24.

Johnson, C., 2017. Beyond Catch-Up: VoD Interfaces, ITV Hub and the Repositioning of Television Online. *Critical Studies in Television*, 12(2), pp.121–138.

Landau, N., 2016. *TV Outside the Box: Trailblazing in the Digital Television Revolution*, New York: Focal Press.

Laporte, N., 2017. Netflix Offers a Rare Look Inside Its Strategy for Global Domination. *Fast Company*, 23 Oct. Available at: https://www.fastcompany.com/40484686/net flix-offers-a-rare-look-inside-its-strategy-for-global-domination [Accessed June 11, 2018].

Lauvaux, E., n.d. Media Chronology in France. *Independent Film and Television Alliance*. Available at: http://www.ifta-online.org/media-chronology-france-2017 [Accessed August 13, 2018].

Lawson, M., 2018. Box, Set and Match: How On-Demand Became TV's New Battleground. *The Guardian*, 25 May. Available at: https://www.theguardian.com/tv-and-ra dio/2018/may/25/box-set-and-match-how-on-demand-became-tvs-new-battleground [Accessed August 13, 2018].

Leverette, M., Ott, B.L. & Buckley, C.L. eds., 2007. *It's Not TV: Watching HBO in the Post-Television Era*, New York and London: Routledge.

Littleton, C. & Ryan, M., 2017. WGA Deal: Extended Talks Highlight Major Shift in Peak TV Era. *Variety*, 2 May. Available at: https://variety.com/2017/tv/features/wga-strike-p eak-tv-labor-strife-1202405696/.

Lobato, R., 2016. The Cultural Logic of Digital Intermediaries: YouTube Multichannel Networks. *Convergence: The International Journal of Research into New Media Technologies*, 22(4), pp.348–360.

Lobato, R., 2019. *Netflix Nations: The Geography of Digital Distribution*, New York: New York University Press.

Lotz, A.D., 2014. *The Television Will Be Revolutionized* 2nd ed., New York: New York University Press.

Lotz, A.D., 2016. *Portals: A Treatise on Internet-Distributed Television*, Ann Arbor, MI: Maize Books.

McAlone, N., 2017. Amazon Will Spend about $4.5 Billion on Its Fight against Netflix this Year, According to JPMorgan. *Business Insider UK*, 7 Apr. Available at: http://uk.businessinsider. com/amazon-video-budget-in-2017-45-billion-2017-4 [Accessed August 13, 2018].

McCabe, J. & Akass, K. eds., 2007. *Quality TV: Contemporary American Television and Beyond*, London: I.B. Tauris.

McMullan, C., 2017. Amazon's NFL Deal Paves the Way for a Sports Rights Arms Race between Streaming Companies. *Digital Sport*, 6 Apr. Available at: https://digitalsport. co/amazons-nfl-deal-paves-the-way-for-a-sports-rights-arms-race-between-stream ing-companies [Accessed August 13, 2018].

Medina, M., Herrero, M. & Guerrero, E., 2015. Audience Behaviour and Multiplatform Strategies: The Path towards Connected TV in Spain. *Austral Communicacion*, 4(1), pp.153–172.

Morreale, J., 2014. From Homemade to Store Bought: Annoying Orange and the Professionalization of YouTube. *Journal of Consumer Culture*, 14(1), pp.113–128.

Otnes, C.C. & Maclaran, P., 2015. How the British Royal Family Became a Global Brand. *The Atlantic*, 21 Oct. Available at: https://www.theatlantic.com/international/archive/ 2015/10/british-royal-monarchy-queen-elizabeth/411388/ [Accessed August 13, 2018].

Roettgers, J., 2017. How Netflix Wants to Rule the World: A Behind-the-Scenes Look at a Global TV Network. *Variety*, 18 Mar. Available at: https://variety.com/2017/digital/news/netflix-lab-day-behind-the-scenes-1202011105/ [Accessed June 11, 2018].

Rose, L. & Guthrie, M., 2015. FX Chief John Landgraf on Content Bubble: 'This is Simply Too Much Television.' *Hollywood Reporter*, 7 Aug. Available at: https://www.hollywoodreporter.com/live-feed/fx-chief-john-landgraf-content-813914 [Accessed August 13, 2018].

Ruddick, G., 2017. Amazon TV Hints at Significant Expansion into Sport Broadcasting. *The Guardian*, 25 Aug. Available at: https://www.theguardian.com/tv-and-radio/2017/aug/25/amazon-tv-hints-at-significant-expansion-into-sport-broadcasting [Accessed August 13, 2018].

Sandberg, B.E., 2017. TV's Age of Entitlement: Why Episodes Are Now So Damn Long. *Hollywood Reporter*, 8 Jun. Available at: https://www.hollywoodreporter.com/news/tvs-age-entitlement-why-episodes-are-damn-long-1010621 [Accessed August 13, 2018].

Steemers, J., 2016. International Sales of U.K. Television Content: Change and Continuity in 'the Space in between' Production and Consumption. *Television & New Media*, 17(8), pp.734–753.

Stiegler, C., 2016. Invading Europe: Netflix's Expansion to the European Market and the Example of Germany. In K. McDonald & D. Smith-Rowsey, eds. *The Netflix Effect: Technology and Entertainment in the 21st Century*. New York: Bloomsbury, pp. 235–246.

Sweney, M., 2014. British Indie TV Producers a Victim of Own Success as Foreign Owners Swoop. *The Guardian*, 10 Aug. Available at: https://www.theguardian.com/media/2014/aug/10/british-indies-tv-production-companies-americans-coming [Accessed August 13, 2018].

Tay, J. & Turner, G., 2008. What is Television? Comparing Media Systems in the Post-Broadcast Era. *Media International Australia*, 126(1), pp.71–81.

Turner, G., 2016. Surviving the Post-Broadcast Era: The International Context for Australia's ABC. *Media International Australia*, 158(1), pp.17–25.

Ulin, J., 2014. *The Business of Media Distribution* 2nd ed., Abingdon: Focal Press.

Van Esler, M., 2016. Not Yet the Post-TV Era: Network and MVPD Adaptation to Emergent Distribution Technologies. *Media and Communication*, 4(3), pp.131–141.

Zhao, E.J., 2018. Negotiating State and Copyright Territorialities in Overseas Expansion: The Case of China's Online Video Streaming Platforms. *Media Industries*, 5(1). Available at: https://quod.lib.umich.edu/m/mij/15031809.0005.107?view=text;rgn=main.

5

ONLINE TV INTERFACES

RECAP

- Chapter 1 outlined a conceptual framework for analysing television as a medium. It argued that television can be understood as being made up of five components: technological infrastructures and devices, and cultural services, content and frames.
- Since the late 2000s, the penetration of fast broadband speeds, tablets, smartphones and internet-connected televisions has heralded a new 'internet era' in which television and the internet are increasingly interconnected.
- The internet era has created the conditions for the emergence of online TV, defined in Chapter 2 as *services that facilitate the viewing of editorially selected audiovisual content through internet-connected devices and infrastructure.*
- Chapter 3 examined the industry responsible for providing online TV services. It argued that the industry can be divided into three different categories of company according to business origins:

    1   *TV natives*, that have extended an existing TV service into the internet ecosystem (e.g. BBC, Disney, Sky).
    2   *Online natives*, that have originated online services for the internet ecosystem (e.g. Netflix, Amazon, Apple).
    3   *Content natives*, that have extended a content-based business in another field into an online TV service (e.g. Globe Player, Arsenal Player).

- The online TV industry can also be categorised according to business focus into:

    a   *Content businesses*, that focus primarily on the production, acquisition and delivery of video content to viewers (e.g. BBC, Disney, Netflix).

> b   *Technology businesses*, that are responsible for the provision of the technological infrastructures and devices needed to access online TV services (e.g. Sky, Amazon, Apple).
>
> • Central to the provision of online TV services is:
>
> a   The acquisition of content, through origination or licensing.
> b   Editorial control over the user's viewing experience, through infrastructure, data and algorithms.

Introduction

In the internet era there is a dominant industry discourse that proclaims the consumer as the new controller of online TV. In its 2016 report on the growth of video on demand (VOD), the global media measurement company Nielsen (2016) was keen to assert that consumers are 'in the viewing driver's seat' in this new on-demand media ecosystem:

> For most of us around the world, gone are the days where 'watching TV' means sitting in front of the screen in your living room, waiting for a favorite program to come on at a set time. Today, the growth of video-on-demand (VOD) programming options (via download or stream) gives consumers greater control over what they watch, when they watch and how they watch.
>
> (Nielsen 2016)

Meanwhile digital strategy and consultancy firm Accenture's 2013 report on the future of TV stated in no uncertain terms that the consumer is the 'undisputed king' of this brave new world (Murdoch et al. 2013, p.3). As Murdoch et al. explained, 'Over the past decade, control of the viewing experience has shifted rapidly to the one who holds the remote. ... So who wins in a new media world? The consumer does, of course' (ibid., pp.3–6). This discourse, however, obfuscates the ways in which the online TV industry continues to exert significant control over the consumers' experience of television. Chapter 3 examined the ways in which control over technological infrastructures and devices can be used to constrain access to online TV services, while Chapter 4 explored how the sale and management of rights is used to create artificial scarcity that restricts the availability of online TV content. This chapter and the following chapter turn attention to the role that interfaces and data/algorithms respectively play in shaping our experience of online TV.

Chapter 1 of this book argued that since the late 2000s the penetration of fast broadband speeds, tablets, smartphones and internet-connected televisions has heralded a new 'internet era' of television. This internet era creates the conditions for the emergence of online TV: *services that facilitate the viewing of editorially selected content through internet-connected devices and infrastructure*. Most online TV services can be accessed through desktops, laptops, tablets, smartphones and smart TVs, as well as set-top boxes and digital media players (like Amazon Fire TV Stick) that attach to the TV set. Crucial to the experience of all television services are *frames* that organise content and shape what users can and cannot do within the service. For example, within the service of the TV channel, the frame of the linear schedule organises content according to time of day, shaping which programmes are more and less prominent within the service, with those programmes shown in the mid-evening typically attracting higher viewing figures. Frames play a crucial, yet largely overlooked, role in constructing our experiences of watching television. While the linear schedule has been the dominant television frame for many decades, within online TV services the primary frames are interfaces and algorithms. Interfaces utilise user-experience design to display the content on offer within online TV services and to facilitate certain forms of user behaviour over others. Algorithms sit behind the visible surface of the interface, responding to user interactions in order to shape which content is prioritised and how it is organised. Where Chapter 6 examines the role of data and algorithms, this chapter examines how interfaces function to create an *illusion of content abundance and user agency* that belies the highly structured nature of online TV services.

Analysing online TV interfaces is a tricky enterprise because of their inherent ephemerality (Johnson 2017, p.123). Interfaces are ephemeral in two senses: they are transient and they are peripheral (Grainge 2011, p.2). Interfaces consist of a relatively stable wire frame and **graphical user interface** (GUI) within which content (images, video, text and so on) is placed. However, that content is transient in that it is frequently updating, changing according to the day/time of access, who is accessing the service and where they are located. The GUI of an online TV service can also vary depending on the device used to access the service. Lisa Gitelman's definition of web documents as 'continuously present and yet constantly subject to change' (2008, p.145) is, therefore, particularly apposite when thinking about online TV interfaces that can vary according to when, where, through what technology and by whom they are accessed. Online TV interfaces need to be approached, therefore, as dynamic objects subject to change depending on time, date, location, technology and user (Johnson 2017, p.124).

Interfaces can also be understood as transient in that they are sites designed to be passed through. Daniel Chamberlain writes that interfaces operate as 'functional environments that offer up their own characteristics yet are not in themselves destinations' (2011, p.234). One consequence of this transient nature is that interfaces have been culturally positioned as peripheral and throwaway. Unlike the content that they provide access to, interfaces are not routinely archived, analysed or valued, despite the role that they play in organising the viewing experience of television. It is easy to look through interfaces and to take their role in our experience of culture for granted. Part of the aim of this chapter is to subject the ephemeral and increasingly quotidian surface of the online TV interface to critical analysis and to place online TV interfaces more centrally on the agenda of academics, industry, regulators and archivists.

Given their ephemerality, studying online TV interfaces is methodologically challenging. However, it is possible to undertake textual analysis of the GUI of an online TV interface in order to examine how its design shapes the experience of using the service (Johnson 2017, p.124). As José van Dijck (2013, p.33) argues in relation to social media, when discussing people's experiences of media it is important to distinguish between *implicit usage* as it is inscribed in the design of the service and the *explicit use* that people make of a service when they interact with it. Analysis of online TV interfaces (and algorithms) cannot tell us about the explicit use that people make of online TV services. However, through analysis of the design of online TV interfaces it is possible to identify the functions that are enabled and inhibited within an online TV service. For example, whether an interface allows users to search or not tells us something about the kinds of behaviours that the online TV service encourages or inhibits. Such analysis can reveal how interface design is used by organisations in an attempt to engender certain kinds of user behaviour over others.

The interfaces of online TV services can vary according to the service provider and the device used to access the service. For example, as discussed in Chapter 3, cable, satellite and telecoms providers tend to provide set-top boxes that combine access to linear TV channels with a range of online TV services from different providers. This makes their interfaces particularly complex. When using the subscription television service from cable provider Virgin Media, the interface of my set-top box can be used to select a particular linear channel, to select a specific programme from its array of on-demand content or to go into the interface of another online TV service, such as BBC iPlayer or Netflix. Rather than focusing on the detailed analysis of one specific online TV interface (as I have done elsewhere, see Johnson 2017), this chapter aims instead to unpack in more general terms the characteristics and functions of online TV interfaces. Although it focuses its analysis on the interfaces of VOD services, it also draws on the more complex interfaces of cable/satellite set-top boxes in order to reveal the ways in which usage is implicitly inscribed within online TV services.

Such analysis is based on examples of online TV interfaces gathered in two ways. First, I have drawn on my own experience of online TV interfaces in the UK and the US, where I have documented my use of as many different kinds of online TV services as possible across multiple devices. Here I have paid particular attention to the home pages of online TV services and the ways in which the GUI designs and organises user experience. For example, I have noted which functions are available and how they are arranged within the interface, alongside the organisation of content and text, focusing on those aspects of design that are consistent across the devices used to access the service. Second, I have sought images of the home pages of the interfaces of online TV services from friends, colleagues and students in order to ascertain the extent to which the design features of online TV interfaces in the UK/ US are mirrored in other territories. This has included examples from advertiser- and subscription-funded services in Malaysia, Denmark, Germany, Greece, Brazil, China, Taiwan and Australia. This method has enabled me to draw some more general conclusions from a small sample of online TV interfaces around the globe. More detailed and comparative work is needed to unpack fully how online TV interfaces construct the experience of television in the internet age. The analysis offered here aims to operate as a conceptual model for such research in the future.

The chapter begins by defining online TV interfaces. It asks how online TV interfaces differ from the frame of the linear TV schedule, which has played a dominant role in structuring the experience of television since the beginning of the broadcast era. It also draws comparison between the features and functionality of online TV interfaces and those commonly associated with desktop computer interfaces, such as the icons, menus and windows found on Macs and PCs. Asking why the features commonly found in the interface design of desktop computers have not been adopted in the design of online TV interfaces helps unveil the implicit assumptions about usage that sit behind the surface of interface design in online TV services. The chapter uses this analysis to outline the three core functions that interfaces play in online TV services, arguing that interfaces create an illusion of content abundance and user agency that belies the highly structured experiences offered by online TV. The chapter goes on to argue that despite the apparent differences between linear and online TV, an analysis of interfaces challenges any easy distinction between linear and nonlinear television. The chapter concludes that interfaces can be understood as mechanisms through which the online TV industry is attempting to exert control over the viewer experience within an increasingly networked and participative internet ecosystem.

Defining online TV interfaces

Interfaces may be easy to overlook, but they play a crucial role in shaping the experience of watching television (Chamberlain 2011, p.233). Much like the interstitials and schedules of linear television channels in the broadcast era, interfaces perform a paratextual function. Jonathan Gray, drawing on Gérard Genette, argues that media paratexts affect our experience of watching films and TV programmes. He writes,

> paratexts tell us what to expect, and in doing so, they shape the reading strategies that we will take with us 'into' the text, and they provide the all-important early frames through which we will examine, react to, and evaluate textual consumption.
>
> (Gray 2010, p.26)

Online TV interfaces also play a paratextual role in shaping our encounters with media texts. The still image and description chosen to represent a particular programme, the rating given to it and its prominence within an interface can all function to inform and frame our encounter with the content of online TV services. However, online TV interfaces not only perform a paratextual function in relation to specific texts. They also shape our expectations of online TV more broadly. The layout of an online TV interface and the menus, tabs and buttons that help users navigate within that service offer and encourage certain behavioural choices (to watch, search, browse and so on). In doing so, interfaces inform what we expect to experience when we use an online TV service.

Online TV interfaces have some specific characteristics that differentiate them from the television frames that developed in the broadcast era, such as the linear schedule. Chamberlain (2010, p.85) argues that contemporary television interfaces result 'from the intersection of networks and microprocessors' or, in other words, television and computing. Essentially, interfaces are features of software that function to convert the language of binary code, through which computers operate, into the textual language of images, words and sounds that humans can easily understand. Steven Johnson defines the interface as 'software that shapes the interaction between user and computer. The interface serves as a kind of translator, mediating between the two parties, making one sensible to the other' (1997, p.14). In the context of online TV services, therefore, interfaces can be understood as a visual (and sometimes aural) language for representing online TV as a cultural form and a technology to its users. In doing so, interfaces construct online TV as a particular kind of service and experience.

A further difference from linear television channels is that computer interfaces are far more malleable than the frames of analogue TV, being designed to facilitate and enable two-way communication between users and computers. When interfaces convert binary code into a language that humans understand, this is a language that is designed not only to be read but also to be enacted upon. Interfaces, therefore, are not just surfaces; they are *sites of action*. However, we should be wary of equating the possibility of manipulation offered by interfaces with user agency and control. Johnson (1997, p.21) argues that by adding a layer of direct manipulation, whereby users can click, drag, resize and so on, interfaces can create a sense of 'tactile immediacy' that gives the impression that users are doing tasks themselves.[1] Yet, in fact, each action by the user is simply a means of telling the computer to perform an action on behalf of the user.[2]

Interfaces matter, therefore, in part because they function to downplay the control of the computer that sits behind the interface. As Chamberlain argues, 'the visible and compelling interactive scripted space of the media interface draws attention away from the relatively unscrutinized aspects of the networks and code that make the interfaces function' (2011, p.243). Interfaces are sites that mask the work of the computers that they represent and the industries that produce them. The masking of computerisation is not necessarily a bad thing. Interfaces function to make computers usable and accessible to people without specialist knowledge. At the same time, however, interfaces are designed with specific objectives in mind. All computer-based systems make use of protocols, described by van Dijck as 'formal descriptions of digital message formats complemented by rules for regulating those messages in or between computing systems' (2013, p.31). Protocols effectively function as sets of rules that govern how users can behave when using a particular site or service. Computer-savvy users can subvert protocols by altering a service's software or designing a subversive app; but for most users protocols shape what actions can (and cannot) be taken on a particular site or service. And although computers are malleable, interfaces are often characterised by default settings designed to channel behaviour in certain ways. Such defaults are described by van Dijck as 'often the literal stakes in the battle for social meaning' (2013, p.32). Interfaces are, therefore, *the visible manifestations of protocols that aim to shape the experiences of users.* Analysing the design of interfaces can reveal how the industry constructs online TV services as sites of action and the kinds of audience behaviours that it wants to encourage and discourage. In this regard, this chapter will argue that online TV interfaces can be understood to have three related functions:

1. Online TV interfaces create an illusion of abundance and plenty.
2. Online TV interfaces minimise interactivity while creating an illusion of user agency.
3. Online TV interfaces orient user behaviour towards viewing.

One of the key differences between online TV services and television channels is the elimination of the capacity constraints that characterise linear broadcasting. Where linear television channels can only provide access to a programme at the moment of broadcast, online TV services offer viewers vast databases of content that are available over extended periods of time (Lotz 2016, p.24).[3] However, this does not mean that there are no limitations on the content available through online TV services. In addition to the constraints of licensing discussed in Chapter 4, which restrict the programmes available in specific markets, online TV services are also limited by the physical space available on the screens of the viewing devices used to access them. The limits of the screen space on smartphones, tablets, laptops/desktops and television sets act as capacity constraints on what content can be presented to users. Therefore, although online TV services have the capacity to store vast catalogues of content, their interfaces can only show us a selection of that content because of the limited space available on the screens of contemporary viewing devices.

Computer interfaces have developed mechanisms to manage what Johnson (1997, p.47) refers to as the limited 'real estate' of computer screens. Johnson argues that a recognition of this problem led to the conceptualisation of early computer interfaces as 'desks,' with each project visualised as equivalent to a piece of paper. This resulted in the contemporary desktop interface in which individual documents are filed within different folders and opened with specific applications (such as Word, Keynote or Adobe). Typically, desktops utilise file system trees to organise content, in which individual files can be named and filed within folders and subfolders managed by the user. File managers, such as Finder for Mac and My Computer for PC, enable users to store their files, much like an electronic filing cabinet. Users need only call up individual files to be opened on the desktop when they are needed, functioning as a way of managing the limited space within the real estate of the computer screen itself (see Figure 5.1).

FIGURE 5.1 The desktop computer interface

Online TV interfaces also need to manage the limited screens of viewing devices; but, rather than adopting the desk metaphor, their visual iconography is closer to that of a row of shelves or a catalogue. Typically, online TV interfaces present rows of images of the programmes and movies on offer (see Figures 5.2 and 5.3). The visual design of the online TV interface invites the viewer to browse, as if flicking through an electronic catalogue or perusing the shelves of a library. Where desktops tend to layer files on top of one another, online TV interfaces scroll, either horizontally, vertically or both. This visual design functions to create a sense of abundance, of a catalogue without limits, of which only a small part is revealed at any one time. This is enhanced by the lack of a visible filing system, making the limits (and organising hierarchies) of the catalogue hard to determine.

Online TV interfaces do offer their users other modes of discoverability, primarily through tabs that enable search or order content according to pre-designated categories, such as type (TV, movie), genre, channel, producer/studio, popularity, newness, exclusivity and so on. However, these modes of engagement tend not to be prioritised within the interface design, usually appearing as small text at the top or side of the interface that is dwarfed by the images of programmes that dominate the screen. Search functionality is also often limited, rarely offering users the ability to filter or organise search results.[4] By downplaying search functions in favour of a pre-organised catalogue of content, online TV interfaces prioritise content selected for the user.[5] The design of online TV interfaces, therefore, encourages users to scroll through rows of images of content selected by the service and to choose from the programmes and movies made visible and easily accessible by the interface, rather than emphasising and facilitating the users' ability to search for content themselves. As a consequence, online TV services have the potential to exert significant control over what users watch by determining what content is prioritised in the interface.

FIGURE 5.2 The homepage of All 4 on 22 August 2018

In emphasising the content selected for the viewer, online TV services operate as 'gatekeepers' with the ability to 'affect user choices and diversity of exposure' (Helberger et al. 2015, p.63). Natali Helberger, Katharina Kleinen-von Königslöw and Rob van der Noll argue that the rise of search engines, social networks and apps challenges the terms of the debate about media diversity. As well as focusing on diversity of supply (such as ensuring that there is diversity in the companies producing and providing media content) and output (such as ensuring that there is a wide range of media content produced and distributed), they argue that contemporary media policy needs to examine 'diversity of exposure' which 'relates to the audience dimension of media diversity, and the question of to what extent the diversity of content and supply actually results in a (more) diverse programme consumption' (ibid., p.52). In the context of online TV services, this means examining how content delivery might limit the kinds of programming that viewers choose to consume.

Writing largely in a Western context Mark Stewart (2016, p.698) examines the kinds of content most valued on the major television streaming services. He argues that there is a prioritisation of Anglophone (particularly US and, to a lesser extent, UK) content and an emphasis placed on 'types of dominant masculine culture' – such as prestige, quality scripted series – at the expense of genres more typically coded as feminine, such as talk shows, soap operas and reality television. The 'myth of televisual ubiquity,' Stewart argues, belies these limits on online TV services:

FIGURE 5.3 The homepage of Netflix on 27 July 2018

By privileging masculine, mainstream, and narratively complex television, digital streaming services negate the importance of the variety of television that appeals to much more diverse audiences. Streaming services claim to offer content for all audiences but in fact prefer the specific type of content on which television has come to pride itself in the twenty-first century. These types of 'quality' serial television, often referred to as literary or cinematic, are still used to legitimate television as an art form, but simultaneously, their privileging as 'important television' obfuscates the lived experience of much of the television audience.

(Stewart 2016, p.698)

Stewart's argument here may seem to run counter to ways in which online TV services offer an increasingly personalised viewing experience to their users. For example, in 2017 Netflix claimed that more than 80 percent of what people watched on its service came from some sort of recommendation (Plummer 2017). Yet, as will be explored in more detail in Chapter 6, these personalised recommendations are primarily based on user behaviour within the online TV service itself and that behaviour is shaped, in part, by the design of the interface. The content and behaviours that the interface privileges or downplays, therefore, have the potential to impact what content is recommended and what taste communities are formed.

A number of studies on the accessibility of local content on Netflix and other online TV services support Stewart's claims that despite the appearance of content abundance there are limits to the catalogues of the major online TV services. For example, Alexa Scarlata and Ramon Lobato note that in 2017 only 2–2.5 percent of the content on Netflix Australia was Australian in origin. Even Australia's first local subscription video-on-demand (SVOD) service, Stan, only featured 9.5 percent of Australian content in the same period (2017, p.2). A European Audiovisual Observatory report found that in the European context, Netflix's catalogue was dominated by American movies and TV programmes, with the Netflix service in smaller European markets offering little or no local content (Fontaine & Grece 2016; see also Scarlata & Lobato 2017, p.10). This speaks to the arguments laid out in Chapter 4 about the ways in which licensing continues to shape the kinds of content available on online TV services around the globe. However, beyond the actual content available within the service, the design of online TV interfaces can affect the user's ability to discover content. For example, Scarlata and Lobato note that while Netflix Australia's browse function does include the categories of 'Australian movies' and 'Australian TV shows,' equivalent categories for local content are not available on Netflix in New Zealand, Iceland, Indonesia and Thailand (2017, p.14). They also claim that Australian content is more prominent in Stan's interface than in Netflix's.

The problem of discoverability has been addressed by the EU's Audiovisual Media Services Directive, which imposes on member states the obligation to ensure that on-demand services promote European works. However, the tools used to implement this directive vary from country to country. A European Commission report on the promotion of European works in VOD services noted that three successive evaluations have argued that 'it is difficult to see a relation between the presence of films in a catalogue and their consumption' (European Commission 2014). Just because certain content is available within an online TV service does not automatically mean that people are going to watch it. Quotas on European content are not enough, therefore, if you want to encourage viewing of local content. The report goes on to argue for the importance of online TV interfaces in actively promoting the consumption of European content, recommending design features such as indicating country of origin, enabling search by country of origin and more prominent placement of European content and trailers (ibid.). The interfaces of online TV services, therefore, have the potential to play a significant role in increasing diversity of exposure to content, and this has particular implications for the distribution and consumption of non-US and local content, particularly in services outside of the US.

Reports such as those produced by Scarlata and Lobato and the European Commission draw attention to the ways in which, despite creating an appearance of abundance, online TV interfaces can work to reduce exposure to a diversity of audiovisual content. Online TV interfaces do this not just through the ways in which they select and present content to viewers, but also through the ways in which they function to limit or contain user interactivity. Despite the dominant industry rhetoric that online TV services give users 'greater control over what they watch, when they watch and how they watch' (Nielsen 2016), online TV interfaces tend to discourage user agency while, paradoxically, seeming to encourage interactivity. Pyungho Kim and Harmeet Sawhney define interactivity as two-way communication that is malleable, programmable and creative, offering users tools that they can use 'to control the production and exchange of information' (2002, p.221). Historically, Kim and Sawhney argue, broadcast television has lacked interactivity, functioning primarily as a one-to-many communication technology with relatively limited feedback routes from viewer to producer.[6] By contrast, the malleability of computer-based systems offers the promise of increased interactivity. The interfaces of desktop computers usefully illustrate this. Johnson (1997, pp.45–7) argues that although desktop computers have a fixed and consistent visual layout, significant components of a desktop's interface are designed to be malleable. The clearest example of this is the desktop window. The windows found in desktop interfaces are the spaces within which individual files and applications appear and can be manipulated. As well as often being able to alter the content within windows, users can also open and close windows, resize them, layer them on top of each other and rename them.[7] The malleability of windows, alongside the ability to specify some (if not all) of the icons that appear on the desktop itself, gives users significant control over the layout of the desktop interface. By contrast, online TV services provide few opportunities for such manipulation and control.

Where desktops enable users to manipulate the visual appearance of their interfaces and to control how and where files are stored and arranged, online TV interfaces are far more structured spaces. Most online TV interfaces do include some features that enable user interaction, such as the ability to construct a wishlist of programmes to watch, to download programmes, to share links to programmes on social media, to rate content and/or to post reviews. Yet, unlike desktops, users do not control how the content on online TV services is organised or displayed. Users generally cannot attach their own metadata, organise the content according to their own filing system, manipulate the content (for example by editing clips or adding tags), rename individual files or move them to new or alternative sub-folders. Kim and Sawhney argued that interactive television in 2002 operated as an 'instant query-response/request-delivery conduit offering mechanical interactions over the system. It is in short a hierarchical, centralised and closed network system' (2002, p.226). Sixteen years later, the online TV services of 2018 continue to function as hierarchical, centralised and closed network systems where interaction is largely relegated to the activity of choosing what to watch.

In presenting users with seemingly endless rows of programmes and movies, online TV interfaces create the appearance of an abundance of content in which users have control over what, when and how to watch. Yet that control is limited not only because the service itself plays a significant role in selecting which content is prioritised, but also because the interface functions to minimise the opportunities for users to actively interact with and personalise the database. Part of the reason for the limited interaction in online TV interfaces compared to desktop computers lies in the need for online TV interfaces to operate across a range of viewing devices. Despite the rise of desktop and laptop computers, tablets and smartphones as devices for viewing screen media, the television set remains a primary site for viewing online TV.[8] In addition, although it is possible to enable a television set to operate as a computer monitor, at the time of writing television sets continue to be positioned as viewing devices operated by remote controls that do not facilitate complex interactions.[9]

The minimising of interaction in online TV services works to support the final function of online TV interfaces, which is to encourage viewing-related activities over other forms of engagement, despite the fact that the convergence of television and the internet makes it possible to offer a wide range of activities within one service. Van Dijck argues that 'platforms discipline their users into particular roles and modes of behaviours' (2013, p.159). Online TV services are no different, and the primary role of their interfaces is to drive user behaviour towards the activity of viewing. In 2016 UK media regulator Ofcom undertook a quantitative diary study examining adult and child media consumption in the UK. The research identified five broad forms of media and communications activities engaged in by its respondents: watching, listening, communicating, gaming and reading/browsing/using (Ofcom 2016, p.18). Online TV interfaces focus user behaviour around one primary activity – the selection and viewing of content – rather than creating sites where viewers can discuss, share, edit, read and/or communicate about television. The presentation of rows of programming, the use of recommendation algorithms and the de-emphasis on the manipulation and malleability of the interface all function to address the user as a viewer, first and foremost.

Once again, comparison with the desktop computer brings this aspect of the online TV interface to the fore. The primary aim in developing the window as a core component of the desktop interface was to enable what programmers call 'mode switch' (Johnson 1997, p.81). As a spatial device, the window allows users to switch easily back and forth between modes, for example, from writing a word document to browsing a website, to composing an email (see Figure 5.1). In this sense, the interface of the desktop computer is primed to enable multitasking. By contrast, online TV interfaces lack the layering characteristic of desktop interfaces. Users are encouraged to scroll through the icons of programmes and, once selected, the interface usually plays the programme immediately in full screen, effectively replacing the activity of selection with the activity of viewing.[10] In addition, many online TV services adopt autoplay, such that as soon as one episode ends a new episode starts playing.[11] Services that use autoplay tend to provide viewers with a visible countdown to the start of the next episode. However, in a strategy not dissimilar to the scheduling strategies of linear broadcasters designed to prevent viewers from switching channels (Johnson 2012), it is not uncommon for the new episode to start playing during the credits of the previous episode. The lack of windows and the automatic full screen and autoplay functions in online TV interfaces work together to discourage mode switching and multitasking, and focus user behaviour on one mode of engagement – viewing.

Infrastructural techniques such as autoplay and automatic full screen push back against multitasking in a period in which the media industries are understood to be operating within an 'attention economy' where competition for attention is a key battleground (Webster 2014, p.6). Numerous studies have drawn attention to the ways in which the television industry is having to operate in a media ecosystem in which audiences are increasingly engaged in what Ofcom (2013, p.33) refers to as 'media multi-tasking' (see also Red Bee Media 2012a; Red Bee Media 2012b; Red Bee Media 2012c). Here audiences are characterised as distracted by multiple calls on their attention from competing screens (laptops, smartphones, tablets) and services (such as social media, email and websites). The industry has sought to develop strategies to address media multitasking, particularly in the development of second screen apps that can be accessed on tablets, smartphones and laptops before, during and/or after viewing a specific programme. These second screen apps aim to channel viewer multitasking onto the spaces and sites owned by the television provider (Grainge & Johnson 2015; Gillan 2011; Holt & Sanson 2014).

It is striking that, with some notable exceptions, the industry has not sought to integrate media multitasking into its online TV interfaces. Some online TV interfaces offer the opportunity for viewers to share links to content on social media or to follow hyperlinks to other sites (usually programme pages owned by the provider of the service rather than third party sites), but they tend not to integrate second screen content. This is surprising given that the possibility of mode switching would enable online TV interfaces to facilitate simultaneous viewing and commenting (or other forms of interaction). There are a number of possible reasons for this. Second screen activity varies according to genre (Red Bee Media 2012a, p.5). As such, there may be little incentive in integrating such activities into online TV interfaces when they might only be utilised around a small percentage of the content. Integrating social interaction into an online TV interface also increases the work involved in managing that service. For example, providing the ability for viewers to comment on content as it is screened would necessitate some level of moderation of viewer input, which would involve significant resources.[12] Finally, in limiting interaction, online TV services mirror the social practices of television that have been in place since the broadcast era in which television has been associated with watching audiovisual content on a television set while other forms of interaction take place elsewhere. In this sense, we might understand that lack of interaction on offer in online TV interfaces as an example of the continuing power of social conventions associated with television viewing.

It is useful, however, to consider outlier examples where online TV interfaces have sought to integrate various forms of interactivity. VOD service Viki, created by Japanese company Rakuten, has constructed an interface that, in addition to selecting and viewing, encourages viewers to assist in the subtitling of its content. The Viki interface includes a 'community' tab in which users are invited to join a team of volunteers that facilitate subtitling on the service. Those without language skills can volunteer as segmenters, cutting videos into timed parts into which subtitles can be written. Volunteer subtitlers translate videos into new languages, recruited by channel managers and overseen by moderators and editors. Viki operates a perks package whereby contributors get rewards (such as a free subscription to Viki) depending on the amount of work undertaken. Subtitlers can only apply to be channel managers once they have contributed a sufficient number of subtitles, and appointment is subject to approval. Although Viki offers more interactivity than many other online TV services, this interactivity is ultimately in aid of its primary aim, which is to encourage viewing of its content. By contrast, Chinese online TV services typically integrate user-generated content (UGC) into their interfaces (Gilardi et al. 2017; Curtin & Li 2018). For example, Youku's interface displays a user rating and the number of views, comments and likes for videos as well as providing a link to audience reviews on social media. iQiyi also includes a 'comment zone' and Tencent Video includes user-generated videos within its page for season seven of *Game of Thrones*.[13] Michael Curtin and Yongli Li argue that for iQiyi, creating a social component to its service that enables communication and interaction has served an important promotional function which is particularly important because 'a substantial amount of iQiyi's content comes from foreign producers that do not have the capacity for conducting promotional campaigns in China' (2018, p.345). Here we can see how cultural and industrial differences may shape the normative conventions in online TV interfaces. The screens of Chinese and Japanese television have historically been far busier than UK screens, with textual information commonly layered over audiovisual content. In addition, in China the major online TV services tend to operate other internet services, such as social media and UGC platforms (Curtin & Li 2018). It is important, therefore, to recognise that the ways in which online TV interfaces are designed are not natural, but are shaped by industrial, social and cultural factors. More comparative research would be beneficial to identify what conventions are shaping the ways in which online TV services construct television experiences for their users within specific contexts.

Online TV interfaces and the illusion of control: beyond the linear/nonlinear divide

So far, this chapter has argued that online TV interfaces tend to focus on creating seamless viewing experiences that limit the work involved in finding something to watch. They do this by creating an illusion of control that belies the ways in which the service is structured. In doing so, online TV services actually operate contra to the dominant industrial discourse that claims that these services give viewers more control over their experience of television. This industry rhetoric is echoed (albeit in a more measured way) in academic scholarship that argues that digitalisation has led to a shift from linear to nonlinear television.

Both linear and nonlinear forms of television aggregate content for viewers. However, the ways in which they aggregate content has been understood as fundamentally distinct. Definitions of linear television largely originate with Raymond Williams' theorisation of broadcast television as flow. Williams argued that when broadcasting was established it introduced a distinct new form of cultural experience. Rather than the discrete experience of reading a novel or watching a play, broadcasting unified different forms of communication into a singular continuous flow (1990, p.87). In this context, broadcast television is linear in that it organises programmes into a schedule that flows from one piece of content to the next. Schedules are organised according to established assumptions about viewer behaviour at particular times of day (Ellis 2000). For example, most countries will schedule the most popular programmes in the evening 'prime time' hours, and many countries adopt a 9pm 'watershed' after which adult programmes not suitable for children are broadcast. The flow of linear television is designed to encourage continuous viewing and, as the number of television channels has increased and channel-hopping has been facilitated by the emergence of the remote control, broadcasters have adopted new scheduling and branding strategies designed to keep viewers watching their channels (Bruun 2016; Johnson 2012; Johnson 2013). The structure of linear television means that it is characterised by capacity constraints (viewers can only watch the programme being broadcast) and by time specificity (content is only available at the moment it is broadcast) that limit what is available for the viewer to watch at any given moment. See Table 5.1 for an overview of the characteristics of linear television.

Developments in digital and, later, online television have been understood to introduce a new form of nonlinear television that challenges the fundamental characteristics of linear television. Jason Mittell, writing in 2011 and analysing the viewing habits of his children, argued that this new 'DVR [digital video recorder] generation' experiences television as files, 'digital objects to be accessed in menus and manipulated via an interface' rather than as a flow (2011, p.50). Also writing in 2011, James Bennett argued that in a digital media context, 'instead of flow … we have an interface, hyperlink, and a database structure experienced via broadband rather than broadcasting' (2011, p.1). Nonlinear forms of television are understood to

TABLE 5.1 The characteristics of linear television

Characteristic	Description
Flow	Different forms of communication flow into each other in one seamless experience
Schedule	Programmes are organised into a sequence according to assumptions about viewer behaviour
Continuous	Scheduling creates a continuous, unending flow of content
Viewing	Content is organised to maintain viewing and prevent switching off/over
Capacity constraints	Viewers are limited to watching the programme being broadcast
Temporal standardisation	Programming of standard lengths is scheduled according to the time of day
Immediacy	Programming is only available when broadcast

free viewers from the temporal logic of the broadcast flow, providing programmes within the fragmented and hyperlinked structure of the internet or personal video recorder (PVR) in which 'a vast array of audiovisual files sit side by side often pulling our attention in several different directions at once' (Kelly 2011, p.126). In doing so, nonlinear television services are understood to eliminate the time specificity and capacity constraints characteristic of linear TV. Amanda Lotz (2016) argues that as a consequence value in nonlinear SVOD services is based more on availability, with specific emphasis placed on the acquisition of large catalogues of content that viewers can access over an extended period of time, in contrast to the immediacy that characterises the temporal relationship between linear television channel and viewer. See Table 5.2 for an overview of the characteristics of nonlinear television.

However, these arguments that digital and online television introduces new forms of nonlinear television tend to overlook the ways in which linear logics continue to structure online TV services. Most fundamentally, such arguments do not account for the number of online TV services that include the streaming of linear television channels as a core part of their offer.[14] A number of online TV services, such as YouTube TV in the US and TVPlayer in the UK, have launched that focus specifically on providing access to streams of linear television channels (see Figure 5.4). Here viewers can select from a number of different channels, effectively integrating the linear flow into a nonlinear database.

Beyond this, the ability to watch live streams of TV channels is a common feature of the VOD services offered by TV natives that have extended existing linear TV services online. UK free-to-air broadcaster ITV found that over 30 percent of the usage of its VOD service, ITV Player, was to live stream one of its linear channels. As a consequence, when ITV re-launched ITV Player as ITV Hub in 2015, it introduced a 'swipe to live' option for mobile users and privileged the option to 'watch live' at the top of the app and website versions of its interface (Johnson 2017, p.126). Indeed, UK broadcasters increasingly recognise the value of

TABLE 5.2 The characteristics of nonlinear television

Characteristic	Description
File	Programmes are removed from the flow and offered as discrete and individual files
Database	Programmes are organised into a database for selection by viewers
Fragmented	Hyperlinked databases create a fragmented experience in which viewers can flit from one piece of content to another
Interacting	Viewers can choose from a range of content options and control when, what, where and how they watch
Abundance	Viewers can access large catalogues of content
Lack of temporal constraints	Content is not limited by temporal constraints
Extended access	Content can be accessed over an extended period of time

FIGURE 5.4 The homepage of TVPlayer on 23 July 2018

live television as a key part of their multiplatform strategy (Sørensen 2016, p.382) and the continued 'supremacy of channels as a vehicle for the distribution of television content … to make choices easier for viewers in an environment of ever greater abundance and choice' (Doyle 2016, p.701). Here linear and nonlinear modes of distribution are not opposed but function together as different ways of engaging viewers in a media environment characterised by 'choice fatigue' (Vonderau 2014, p.726).

Beyond the integration of streams of linear television, the online TV services of TV natives often adopt the structure of the television channel and schedule as a central organising device. For example, the online TV services of the UK's three main terrestrial broadcasters (BBC, ITV and Channel 4) have interfaces that are structured in part by the temporal logic of the schedule, often prioritising those programmes most recently broadcast (Johnson 2017, p.134). Furthermore, much of the content on these services is available for a limited period of time (often 30 days) and the interfaces routinely include the original date of broadcast and/or indicate which programmes are new to the service. Although these online TV services are not limited by the same temporal constraints as linear television, temporality remains an important structuring device.[15]

It is this link to the linear logics of broadcast television that has led some to argue that subscription online TV services from online natives such as Netflix – and, by extension, the subscription portals examined by Lotz (2016) – should be distinguished from the on-demand services of TV natives such as BBC iPlayer and ITV Hub. For example, Mareike Jenner (2016, pp.261–2) argues that 'Netflix is simply not TV' because it offers a limited range of genres (without the news, game shows, sports events and live programmes associated with television) and is 'largely disconnected from the technological or branding infrastructure associated with television.' This is in contradistinction to the interfaces of the online TV services of TV natives like the BBC that, Jenner argues, tend to utilise the brand identities of channels as their organising logic (ibid.). Yet Jenner rather underplays the extent to which Netflix remains wedded in specific ways to the logics and industrial practices of the television industry. Beyond the arguments made in Chapters 3 and 4 concerning the ways in which Netflix works with TV natives (whether with cable and satellite companies to enable delivery of its service through their set-top boxes or relying on TV natives for much of its content), Netflix's interface integrates elements of the linear and the nonlinear in ways not dissimilar to the online TV services of TV natives. Although Netflix has a model of releasing all of the episodes of new shows in one go, it also includes series that are released weekly to match US broadcast patterns. Christian Stiegler (2016, p.243) gives the example of AMC's *Better Call Saul* (2015–), which is released weekly on Netflix in Germany shortly after each episode is broadcast in the US. Furthermore, Chuck Tryon argues that even when releasing an entire season's worth of episodes, Netflix can be understood as emulating the experience of liveness and immediacy associated with linear television 'by promoting the idea that viewers will be left out if they don't watch new seasons as soon as they are available' (2015, p.107). The integration of linear logics into nonlinear services is also apparent in the ways in which online TV interfaces utilise links to broadcast schedules. For example, Rakuten's Viki indicates in its interface when a series is being broadcast for the first time in its country of origin and displays the dates of original transmission. Here the link to the broadcast schedule works as a legitimating device that indicates the currency of the content on offer and encourages immediate viewing.

Netflix also uses its interface to encourage immediate viewing. Although it offers a large catalogue of content and has sought to acquire exclusive rights (see Chapter 4), most of its rights (at the time of writing in 2018), particularly for acquired content, are for a limited time period, with content regularly appearing and disappearing from the site (Stewart 2016, p.698). One consequence of this is that despite the appearance of a lack of temporal constraints, Netflix's interface works hard to construct a sense of immediacy around its content. Netflix uses its interface to promote new works, indicating when new episodes are available and promoting newly released content. Furthermore, Netflix releases its new content on a Friday (just in time for weekend binge viewing), mirroring the ways in which broadcasters schedule content according to the temporal rhythms of everyday life. For example, Figure 5.3 of Netflix's interface was taken on 27 July 2018 and shows how Netflix was using its interface to promote its original movie, *Extinction*, which was released on the same day, as well as to indicate where new episodes were available for Netflix original and 'trending' shows. Far from being removed from the temporal structures that shape broadcasting, Netflix's prioritisation of more recently released content, use of temporal scheduling and mirroring of broadcast weekly release patterns point to the ways in which the service combines the logics of linear and nonlinear television.[16] Despite the rhetoric that online TV services have the potential to free viewers from the constraints of the linear schedule, the immediacy characteristic of linear broadcasting emerges as both a structuring and a legitimating force in online TV interfaces.

Over and above this, as we have seen, online TV services adopt strategies such as autoplay that are designed to encourage continuous viewing and minimise interactivity. Rather than understanding online TV services as nonlinear, therefore, we can better understand them as integrating aspects of linear and nonlinear logics (see Table 5.3).

In drawing attention to the integration of linear and nonlinear logics in online TV services my intention is not to argue that there are no differences between the varied range of online TV services or between broadcasting and online TV. As well as seeking to examine the differences, it is also important to recognise the continuities, because these point to the ways in which new services, from ITV Hub to Netflix, are having to operate in dialogue with and in relation to long-standing cultural forms and practices that have shaped the experience of television for many decades. It is possible, therefore, to identify different ways in which online TV services attempt to combine the linear and nonlinear, which often exist in tension.

TV natives

- Free-to-air, cable, satellite and digital channels, e.g. BBC iPlayer, CBS All Access, All 4. In their VOD services linear channels sit alongside individual programmes within a database that is organised in part according to the structure of the linear schedule.
- Cable/satellite/telecoms services, e.g. Virgin, Sky, Comcast. Users can shift between the flow of linear TV channels and the database of a PVR. The interface often combines the two, with the linear flow continuing in a corner of the screen while the user interacts with the nonlinear database.

Online natives

- Channel streaming services, e.g. YouTube TV, TVPlayer. These services organise the streams of linear television channels into a database, where the flow of a linear channel exists as one option within a database structure.
- Over-the-top SVOD services, e.g. Netflix, Amazon Prime Video. Although not offering live streams of TV channels, these services construct nonlinear databases that are shaped by temporal constraints and adopt release patterns related to an understanding of the everyday practices of their users that are often explicitly or implicitly linked to broadcast schedules. Furthermore, these services endeavour to construct continuous viewing experiences that downplay the interaction and control of the user.

TABLE 5.3 Online TV as an integration of linear and nonlinear logics

Linear	Nonlinear	Online TV
Flow	File	Live streams of channel flow as one option in a database
Schedule	Database	Databases are shaped by the logics of the schedule
Continuous	Fragmented	Strategies such as autoplay encourage continuous viewing
Viewing	Interacting	Interaction facilitates viewing
Capacity constraints	Abundance	Illusion of abundance belies limits to content
Temporal standardisation	Lack of temporal constraints	Temporal constraints as a structuring device
Immediacy	Extended access	Immediacy as a structuring and legitimating force

Rather than characterising online TV as inherently nonlinear, therefore, I am arguing for the need to recognise the ways in which linear and nonlinear logics combine in various ways to shape the experience of online TV. Recognising the intersection of the linear and nonlinear is an important first step in challenging the dominant industry rhetoric that the internet enables us to watch 'what we want to watch … when we want to watch it' (Harrington 2014). In painting a picture of nonlinear television as an experience in which viewers choose content from an vast database not limited by the temporal constraints of linear television, academic discourses about digital and online TV could be perceived as supporting such industry rhetoric by emphasising the aspects of online TV where users have increased agency and choice.[17] However, as we have seen, this rhetoric belies the ways in which online TV services combine the linear and nonlinear. More importantly, it also obfuscates the ways in which online TV services offer highly structured experiences to viewers with interfaces designed to create an illusion of abundance and control that masks the limits of the content and interaction on offer.

Conclusion

As interfaces become a more quotidian aspect of contemporary media experience, it is easy to underestimate the role that they play in our mediated encounters. Yet to do so would be to overlook how interfaces not only structure the experience of online TV services, but also emerge as mechanisms by which the industry attempts to control the delivery of online TV. Interfaces are the visible manifestation of the protocols that aim to structure users' encounters with computers. As features of software that convert the language of binary code into a visual and textual form that can be easily understood and engaged with, interfaces present online TV as a cultural form and technology to its users, thus constructing online TV as a particular kind of service and experience. This chapter has argued that contemporary online TV interfaces have three related functions. First, they create an illusion of abundance and plenty that obscures the limits of the content on offer. Second, they minimise interactivity while creating an illusion of user agency. Third, they focus user behaviour on viewing-related activities over other activities. Where industry rhetoric argues that online TV services provide users with greater control and agency, an analysis of online TV interfaces reveals some of the ways in which the industry attempts to control and limit the experience of television in a media environment that enables greater user participation and interaction.

In challenging the industry rhetoric of ubiquitous access and user agency, it is important to recognise the ways in which online TV services combine linear and nonlinear logics. Online TV services may be structured as fragmented databases unhampered by the temporal constraints of the linear schedule. Yet, at the same time, they deploy strategies like autoplay to encourage continuous viewing and continue to be shaped by the logics and temporality of broadcast schedules. Examining the integration of linear and nonlinear logics in online TV interfaces reveals the continuities (as well as the differences) between online TV and the long-standing cultural forms and practices that have shaped the experience of television for decades. It also demonstrates the ways in which TV and online natives are bound, in specific ways, to historical practices and expectations associated with linear television, while simultaneously transforming them for the internet era.

Interfaces, however, are just the visible frames of online TV services. Underneath this surface, data and algorithms play a powerful role in shaping the content that appears within online TV interfaces. The next chapter asks how data and algorithms are used by the online TV industry and the extent to which this differs from historical industry practices. Building on the arguments developed in this chapter, it examines how data and algorithms might be understood to construct the experience of online TV and whether this offers greater opportunities for user agency and control.

Notes

1 This sense of tactile immediacy is further enhanced through touch screen devices.
2 Furthermore, as we shall go on to see, the level of manipulation enabled by online TV interfaces is minimal, particularly when compared with the interfaces of desktop computing.
3 Such arguments do not, however, account for interactive services available through digital forms of linear television, such as red button services in the UK that enable viewers to select from additional streams of broadcast content through their television remote (see Bennett 2008).
4 One notable exception to this in the examples looked at for this book was Amazon Prime Video, where searches can be filtered according to the categories available for search across the Amazon retail site.
5 Chapter 6 will examine the role of data and algorithms in shaping how content is selected to be prioritised in online TV interfaces.
6 This is not to argue that in the broadcast era viewers did not engage in communication with broadcasters and programmers through mechanisms such as letters and phone calls.

However, it is to argue that the technology of television in the broadcast era was not principally developed to facilitate two-way communication.

7 Renaming might be restricted according to the permissions under which the file was saved and/or opened.

8 Netflix claims that 70 percent of viewing of its service is on connected television sets rather than phones, tablets or PCs (Kafka 2018).

9 For example, my brother has a desktop computer attached to his living room television screen, alongside a personal video recorder (PVR) and an Amazon Fire TV Stick, and uses a wireless keyboard and mouse to interact with the computer, alongside his various remote controls. There are also apps that turn smartphones into television remote controls.

10 Some interfaces will take viewers to a programme page from which they select a specific episode to view, which then plays in full screen.

11 In addition, some services will autoplay trailers for programmes as soon as they are selected.

12 This point returns us to the arguments made in Chapter 2 about the differences between open and closed services. Open services, such as Twitter, Facebook and YouTube, have come under significant scrutiny since 2016 for the inadequacy of their content moderation systems, leading to calls for them to exercise greater editorial control over the content posted on their sites or to be subject to greater regulation (Gibbs 2018). Online TV services circumvent such difficulties by operating as closed services and limiting user interaction.

13 Many thanks to Filippo Gilardi for sharing these examples with me.

14 To be fair, much of the scholarship on the development of nonlinear television precedes the widespread integration of linear television channels into online TV services.

15 Writing in the Danish context, Hanne Bruun also notes strong links between the commercial broadcaster TV 2's linear and nonlinear services, arguing that 'an understanding of the interplay between flow and SVOD scheduling is slowly emerging and is able to support both platforms' (2018, p.149).

16 Beyond the examples of Netflix and Viki other subscription VOD services also adopt temporally specific release schedules. For example, Mubi introduces subscribers to a new film each day, which is then available to view for 30 days.

17 Tryon (2015) also argues that academic work needs to be careful not to buy into the promotional discourses of new services, such as Netflix, that attempt to position themselves as 'better' than broadcast television.

Bibliography

Bennett, J., 2008. 'Your Window-on-the-World': The Emergence of Red-Button Interactive Television in the UK. *Convergence: The International Journal of Research into New Media Technologies*, 14(2), pp.161–182.

Bennett, J., 2011. Introduction: Television as Digital Media. In J. Bennett & N. Strange, eds. *Television as Digital Media*. Durham, NC and London: Duke University Press, pp.1–27.

Bruun, H., 2016. The Prism of Change: 'Continuity' in Public Service Television in the Digital Era. *Nordicom Review*, 37(2), pp.33–49.

Bruun, H., 2018. Producing the On-Air Schedule in Danish Public Service Television in the Digital Era. *Critical Studies in Television: The International Journal of Television Studies*, 13 (2), pp.137–152.

Chamberlain, D., 2010. Television Interfaces. *Journal of Popular Film and Television*, 38(2), pp.84–88.

Chamberlain, D., 2011. Scripted Spaces: Television Interfaces and the Non-Places of Asynchronous Entertainment. In J. Bennett & N. Strange, eds. *Television as Digital Media*. Durham, NC and London: Duke University Press, pp.230–254.

Curtin, M. & Li, Y., 2018. iQiyi: China's Internet Tigers Take Television. In D. Johnson, ed. *From Networks to Netflix: A Guide to Changing Channels*. New York and London: Routledge, pp.343–354.

Doyle, G., 2016. Resistance of Channels: Television Distribution in the Multiplatform Era. *Telematics and Informatics*, 33(2), pp.693–702.

Ellis, J., 2000. *Seeing Things: Television in the Age of Uncertainty*, London and New York: I.B. Tauris.

European Commission, 2014. *Promotion of European Works in Practice*. Available at: https://ec.europa.eu/digital-single-market/en/news/promotion-european-works-practice.

Fontaine, G. & Grece, C., 2016. *Origin of Films and TV Content in VOD Catalogues in the EU & Visibility of Films on VOD Services*, Strasbourg: European Audiovisual Observatory. Available at: http://www.obs.coe.int/documents/205595/264623/2016+-+Origin+of+films+and+TV+content+%28C.+Grece+-+G.+Fontaine%29.pdf/94cab491-3cf2-4a76-986c-07065f950c99.

Gibbs, S., 2018. EU Gives Facebook and Google Three Months to Tackle Extremist Content. *The Guardian*, 1 Mar. Available at: https://www.theguardian.com/technology/2018/mar/01/eu-facebook-google-youtube-twitter-extremist-content [Accessed August 14, 2018].

Gilardi, F. et al., 2017. Chinese Digital Platforms across National and Global Markets, Audiences, and Regulatory Environments. In Platforms in the Creative, Cultural and Heritage Industries Symposium. University of Nottingham.

Gillan, J., 2011. *Television and New Media: Must-Click TV*, New York: Routledge.

Gitelman, L., 2008. *Always Already New: Media, History, and the Data of Culture*, Cambridge, MA and London: MIT Press.

Grainge, P., 2011. Introduction: Ephemeral Media. In P. Grainge, ed. *Ephemeral Media: Transitory Screen Culture from Television to YouTube*. London: Palgrave Macmillan, pp. 1–22.

Grainge, P. & Johnson, C., 2015. *Promotional Screen Industries*, London and New York: Routledge.

Gray, J., 2010. *Show Sold Separately: Promos, Spoilers, and Other Media Paratexts*, New York: New York University Press.

Harrington, K., 2014. Changing the Way We Watch TV. *Forbes*, 6 Mar. Available at: https://www.forbes.com/sites/kevinharrington/2014/03/06/changing-the-way-we-watch-tv/#5117dd455eeb [Accessed August 14, 2018].

Helberger, N., Kleinen-von Königslöw, K. & van der Noll, R., 2015. Regulating the New Information Intermediaries as Gatekeepers of Information Diversity. *Info*, 17(6), pp.50–71.

Holt, J. & Sanson, K. eds., 2014. *Connected Viewing: Selling, Streaming, and Sharing Media in the Digital Era*, New York: Routledge.

Jenner, M., 2016. Is this TVIV? On Netflix, TVIII and Binge-Watching. *New Media & Society*, 18(2), pp.257–273.

Johnson, C., 2012. *Branding Television*, London: Routledge.

Johnson, C., 2013. The Continuity of 'Continuity': Flow and the Changing Experience of Watching Broadcast Television. *Key Words: A Journal of Cultural Materialism*, 11, pp.23–39.

Johnson, C., 2017. Beyond Catch-Up: VoD Interfaces, ITV Hub and the Repositioning of Television Online. *Critical Studies in Television: The International Journal of Television Studies*, 12(2), pp.121–138.

Johnson, S., 1997. *Interface Culture: How New Technology Transforms the Way We Create and Communicate*, New York: Harper Edge.

Kafka, P., 2018. You Can Watch Netflix on Any Screen You Want, but You're Probably Watching It on a TV. *Recode*, 7 Mar. Available at: https://www.recode.net/2018/3/7/17094610/netflix-70-percent-tv-viewing-statistics [Accessed August 14, 2018].

Kelly, J.P., 2011. Beyond the Broadcast Text: New Economies and Temporalities of Online TV. In P. Grainge, ed. *Ephemeral Media: Transitory Screen Culture from Television to YouTube*. London: Palgrave Macmillan, pp.122–137.

Kim, P. & Sawhney, H., 2002. A Machine-Like New Medium: Theoretical Examination of Interactive TV. *Media, Culture & Society*, 24(2), pp.217–233.

Lotz, A.D., 2016. *Portals: A Treatise on Internet-Distributed Television*, Ann Arbor, MI: Maize Books.

Mittell, J., 2011. TiVoing Childhood: Time Shifting a Generation's Concept of Television. In M. Kackman et al., eds. *Flow TV: Television in the Age of Media Convergence*. New York and London: Routledge, pp.46–54.

Murdoch, R., Tuma, Y.D. & Vernocchi, M., 2013. The Eyes Have It: Guess Who Controls the Future of TV. *Outlook: The Journal of High-Performance Business*, 1, pp.1–8. Available at: https://www.accenture.com/gb-en/insight-outlook-eyes-have-it-who-controls-future-of-television-media.

Nielsen, 2016. Remote Control: VOD Puts Global Consumers in the Viewing Driver's Seat. *Nielsen Insights*, 16 Mar. Available at: http://www.nielsen.com/eu/en/insights/news/2016/remote-control-vod-puts-global-consumers-in-the-viewing-drivers-seat.html [Accessed July 16, 2018].

Ofcom, 2013. *The Communications Market Report 2013*, London: Ofcom. Available at: https://www.ofcom.org.uk/research-and-data/multi-sector-research/cmr/cmr13.

Ofcom, 2016. *The Communications Market Report 2016*, London: Ofcom. Available at: https://www.ofcom.org.uk/research-and-data/multi-sector-research/cmr/cmr16.

Plummer, L., 2017. This is How Netflix's Top-Secret Recommendation System Works. *Wired*, 22 Aug. Available at: https://www.wired.co.uk/article/how-do-netflixs-algorithms-work-machine-learning-helps-to-predict-what-viewers-will-like [Accessed August 14, 2018].

Red Bee Media, 2012a. *Second Screen Series Paper 1: Setting the Scene*, London.

Red Bee Media, 2012b. *Second Screen Series Paper 2: Dual Screen Consumers*, London.

Red Bee Media, 2012c. *Second Screen Series Paper 3: The Commercial Response*, London.

Scarlata, A. & Lobato, R., 2017. Australian Content in SVOD Catalogs: Availability and Discoverability. Submission to the *Australian and Children's Screen Content Review*, (September), pp.1–18.

Sørensen, I.E., 2016. The Revival of Live TV: Liveness in a Multiplatform Context. *Media, Culture & Society*, 38(3), pp.381–399.

Stewart, M., 2016. The Myth of Televisual Ubiquity. *Television & New Media*, 17(8), pp.691–705.

Stiegler, C., 2016. Invading Europe: Netflix's Expansion to the European Market and the Example of Germany. In K. McDonald & D. Smith-Rowsey, eds. *The Netflix Effect: Technology and Entertainment in the 21st Century*. New York: Bloomsbury, pp.235–246.

Tryon, C., 2015. TV Got Better: Netflix's Original Programming Strategies and Binge Viewing. *Media Industries Journal*, 2(2), pp.104–116. Available at: https://quod.lib.umich.edu/m/mij/15031809.0002.206/–tv-got-better-netflixs-original-programming-strategies?rgn=main;view=fulltext.

van Dijck, J., 2013. *The Culture of Connectivity: A Critical History of Social Media*, Oxford and New York: Oxford University Press.

Vonderau, P., 2014. The Politics of Content Aggregation. *Television & New Media*, 16(8), pp.717–733.

Webster, J.G., 2014. *The Marketplace of Attention: How Audiences Take Shape in a Digital Age*, Cambridge, MA and London: MIT Press.

Williams, R., 1990. *Television: Technology and Cultural Form* 2nd ed., London: Routledge.

6

ONLINE TV DATA AND ALGORITHMS

RECAP

- Chapter 1 outlined a conceptual framework for analysing television as a medium. It argued that television can be understood as being made up of five components: technological infrastructures and devices, and cultural services, content and frames.
- Since the late 2000s, the penetration of fast broadband speeds, tablets, smartphones and internet-connected televisions has heralded a new 'internet era' in which television and the internet are increasingly interconnected.
- The internet era has created the conditions for the emergence of online TV, defined in Chapter 2 as *services that facilitate the viewing of editorially selected audiovisual content through internet-connected devices and infrastructure.*
- Chapter 3 examined the industry responsible for providing online TV services. It argued that the industry can be divided into three different categories of company according to business origins:

  1 *TV natives*, that have extended an existing TV service into the internet ecosystem (e.g. BBC, Disney, Sky).
  2 *Online natives*, that have originated online services for the internet ecosystem (e.g. Netflix, Amazon, Apple).
  3 *Content natives*, that have extended a content-based business in another field into an online TV service (e.g. Globe Player, Arsenal Player).

- Central to the provision of online TV services is:

  a The acquisition of content, through origination or licensing.

  b   Editorial control over the user's viewing experience, through infra-
       structure, data and algorithms.

- Chapter 5 argued that interfaces are a central frame in online TV services
  that create an illusion of content abundance and user agency that belies
  the ways in which the experience of online TV is highly structured.

Introduction

Netflix claims that more than 80 percent of the shows watched on its online TV
service are discovered through algorithmic recommendation (Plummer 2017), what
the company refers to as its 'secret sauce' (Godwin 2017). For Elena Shalneva, as
the following quote suggests, Netflix's recommendations are so accurate that she
feels as though the algorithm knows her better than her friends.

> Two years ago, someone suggested that I watch a show. To be precise, they
> did not suggest, they insisted – indeed, demanded – sending me message after
> message which said: this TV drama is for you, watch it, you won't regret it.
> The drama was *The Bridge*, and it was indeed for me: I have since watched *The
> Bridge* three times, and I will probably do it again. And the 'friend' that sug-
> gested it was Netflix, whose algorithm seemed to know me better than any of
> my human friends.
>
> (Shalneva 2017, p.32)

However not all of Netflix's users feel the same way. Brian Hernandez (2015),
writing for the Netflix fan site *What's on Netflix*, claimed that 'One of the complaints
we often hear from our users is they actually spend more time [on Netflix] looking
for content rather than watching it.' In February 2015, *What's on Netflix* offered a
solution to this problem, revealing the 'Netflix ID Bible': thousands of genre categories that Netflix uses to classify and sort its content (ibid.). The website even provided a URL that enabled users to browse and search through these categories in
ways that were not possible through Netflix's own interface. The hack was subsequently picked up in the online and national press, and touted as a way of enabling
viewers to bypass Netflix's sophisticated recommendation algorithm and unearth
content otherwise hidden in the depths of its catalogue (see for example, Beck 2016;
Parsons 2017; Ravenscraft 2016; Titcomb 2018). In many respects the hack returned
some level of control to users, enabling them to operate outside the terrain of
algorithmically created suggestions and circumvent restrictions placed by Netflix on
how users could navigate through its collection of content.

The discourses surrounding the Netflix ID Bible speak to a number of issues
surrounding the use of algorithms and data in online TV services. First, they
demonstrate the role that algorithms can play in determining which content is most
visible in online TV services. Netflix's recommendation algorithm determines what

content appears most prominently within each user's account. It also informs how that content is presented within the service's interface, from the categories it is placed under to the images selected to represent each TV programme and film. Second, algorithms operate in online TV services in ways that viewers cannot always see or control. The Netflix ID Bible was particularly newsworthy because it made visible a crucial set of metadata usually hidden from Netflix's users that shapes how the service works. Gaining access to this metadata gave users greater ability to control the choices that they made about what to watch. Third, the press around the Netflix ID Bible demonstrated that Netflix's recommendation algorithm operates in ways that can appear to be both inhibiting and helpful. On the one hand, recommendation algorithms can seem to know us better than our friends. On the other hand, they can seem to obscure the hidden depths of a service's catalogue and limit the kinds of content people watch. Ultimately, the debates generated by the revelation of the Netflix ID Bible raise the question of how, and with what consequences, the use of data and algorithms by online TV services shapes our encounters with audiovisual culture online.

Most of the academic literature concerning the impact of data and algorithms in the media focuses on social media and/or news and journalism (see, for example, Bucher 2012; Koene et al. 2017; Plantin et al. 2018). Data and algorithms in online TV services demand as much serious attention. The role of data and algorithms is of particular significance in determining how we understand the power of television as a medium in the internet era. Chapter 5 has already argued that online TV interfaces can be understood as frames that structure the experience of online TV services in ways that attempt to limit user agency while creating the illusion of control. Data and algorithms can be understood as the invisible frames that sit behind the visible surface of online TV interfaces and play an equally important part in shaping the experience of online TV.

Drawing on literature from software, media and television studies, this chapter begins by unpacking what 'data' means, particularly in the context of online TV. In doing so, it explores the new forms of data that emerge in the internet era and the challenges that they present to the **market information regime** through which the business of television operates. Where the television industry has traditionally adopted a market information regime based on ratings, online TV services introduce the possibility of new audience measures based on access to detailed and nuanced data about user behaviour. This has the potential to upset established practices that inform the very workings of the television industry. The chapter then goes on to examine the algorithms used to process and manage the variety and quantity of data made possible in the internet age. It interrogates what algorithms are and how they operate, focusing on the collaborative filtering algorithms used by the online TV industry to generate recommendations. Through this analysis it identifies five features that characterise online TV algorithms.

The final section of the chapter examines how big data and algorithms are used by the online TV industry to influence decisions about what content to produce/ purchase, to understand audience behaviour and to shape the audience experience.

In examining this question, the chapter outlines the key aspects of the use of data and algorithms in online TV services that are distinct from earlier periods in television's history. In doing so, it explores the ways in which online TV algorithms have the potential to upset traditional power hierarchies in the television industry by reducing the editorial control of gatekeepers, such as commissioners and schedulers, and placing user behaviour at the heart of the industry, with content, advertising and scheduling decisions driven by algorithms that depend on user input. The chapter concludes by examining the extent to which the user input upon which many online TV algorithms depend can be understood to provide users with greater agency over their experience of online TV services. Digitalisation has been understood to transform television from a push to a pull medium. In the broadcast era television viewing was controlled by the scheduling of television channels, with programmes 'pushed' to the viewer by broadcasters. Since the emergence of the VCR in the 1980s, new technologies have given viewers greater control over their experience of television, enabling them to 'pull' the programmes that they want to watch (Johnson 2012, pp.42–3). The chapter asks whether algorithms enhance or undermine television's development as a pull medium.

Data and online TV

A defining feature of the internet ecosystem within which online TV services operate is the presence of 'big data.' Contemporary digital media systems are managed by servers that enable user behaviour to be tracked and recorded in minute detail, resulting in 'big' datasets that can be utilised by the industry (Webster 2014, p.81). The online TV industry uses two broad forms of data generated within digital media systems: internal and external. **Internal data** is that which is produced within an online TV service and typically consists of:

1. User profile data, which is made up of information provided by the user when setting up an account and/or data generated as a by-product of using the service, including data produced through search, browsing or voice recognition (such as Amazon's Alexa).
2. Linkages, which includes data related to the connections made between content and between content and users as people search and browse through online catalogues.
3. Metadata, which consists of data produced by the service itself in order to classify its content (such as the genre categories that make up Netflix's ID Bible) as well as data attributed to content through users' engagement with it.[1]

The internal data within online TV services is voluntarily created by the user (such as when setting up a user profile), involuntarily created by users as a by-product of interactions within the service itself and actively created by the industry (through attributing metadata to content).

Netflix, for example, describes its use of data through the metaphor of a three-legged stool. One leg of the stool consists of the data generated voluntarily and involuntarily by Netflix users. Todd Yellin (Vice President of Product Innovation, Netflix) describes this data as providing information on 'what people watch, what they watch after, what they watch before, what they watched a year ago, what they've watched recently and what time of day' (cited in Plummer 2017).[2] It is notable that Yellin refers predominantly to involuntarily created data. The second leg of the stool refers to the metadata tags created by in-house and freelance Netflix staff employed to 'watch every minute of every show on Netflix and tag it. The tags they use range massively from how cerebral the piece is, to whether it has an ensemble cast, is set in space, or stars a corrupt cop' (Plummer 2017). It is these tags that form the basis of the ever-changing Netflix genre categories that constitute the Netflix ID Bible.[3] The third leg of the stool refers to the machine learning algorithms that are required to analyse the vast amounts of data generated and transform it into actionable metrics.[4] Beyond Netflix, most online TV services make some use of metadata, user data and algorithms. However, exactly what data is generated can vary from service to service. Requiring users to sign in to a service significantly increases the ability to generate user profile data as it allows behaviour to be attributed to a specific user. The quality of the metadata can also vary from service to service. Many TV natives, that have extended an existing TV service online, have had to improve the metadata attached to their content because it was originally generated for internal archives oriented towards production rather than for externally facing services for audiences (Wolk 2015, p.103).

External data refers to that data generated within websites and social media services outside of an online TV service. It includes data related to the content and to the current or potential audiences of online TV services. David Beer and Roger Burrows argue that online engagement with popular culture, through sharing, blogging, tweeting and so on, is generating new forms of social data gathered into different kinds of 'data archives.' Online TV services themselves can be understood as 'transactional archives' that 'contain materials that can be searched and purchased, viewed or streamed from the source' (Beer & Burrows 2013, p.52). However, Beer and Burrows identify three other overlapping forms of archive where social data about popular culture is generated. 'Archives of the everyday' (ibid., p.54) consist of rich data about people's everyday lives, from status updates on Facebook to home videos posted to YouTube. 'Viewpoint or opinion archives' (ibid., pp.54–5) provide data on people's views of products and services, exemplified by micro-blogging sites like Twitter, but also services that generate user reviews, such as the Internet Movie Database (IMDb). Finally, 'Crowdsourcing archives,' such as Wikipedia, provide data on the construction of knowledge online (ibid., pp.55–6). These new forms of popular culture archive provide useful sources of data for online TV services. Such external sources can offer:

1. Data about the ordinary lives of viewers gathered from archives of the everyday.
2. Data about how people respond to and interact with television shows, movies, stars and online TV services gathered from viewpoint/opinion and crowd-sourcing archives that provide insight into people's values and tastes.

Much of this data can be accessed by online TV services for free; this is particularly the case for data generated within the YouTube channels and social media pages set up by online TV services. However, online TV services can also pay media agencies and specialist digital agencies to gather, analyse and interpret the vast array of data generated online about both their content and their current and potential audiences. Where internal data provides online TV services with granular information about user behaviour, external data can provide an insight into viewers' attachment to and valuation of content and services. Rich data generated through archives of the everyday can also be cross-referenced with internal data to paint a more detailed picture of user profiles and behaviours that can inform content decisions (including commissioning, renewing and licensing content), nuance targeted advertising and improve recommendation algorithms.

These new forms of internal and external data present challenges to the market information regime in which the television industry operates. Market information regimes are the 'socially constructed mechanisms via which marketplace participants assess their performance and the performance of their competitors,' functioning as 'the agreed upon lens through which marketplace participants perceive their world' (Kosterich & Napoli 2016, p.255). An agreed market information regime enables all participants within a marketplace to evaluate their own performance and that of their competitors, as well as to analyse consumer trends (ibid.). The term 'market information regime,' therefore, refers to the informational basis upon which a market operates. Since the mid-1950s the television industry has operated on the basis of a market information regime centred on the measurement of people's exposure to programmes. Specifically, this market information regime has been based on ratings generated through the reported viewing behaviours of a sample of the TV audience (Nelson & Webster 2016, p.10). Adam Arvidsson and Tiziano Bonini argue that this exposure model fits Dallas Smythe's (1981) theory of the audience commodity, in which the audience becomes valuable by being situated in front of the television screen 'so it could be relied on to reproduce a particular consumption norm with calculable predictability' (Arvidsson & Bonini 2015, p.159). The exposure model extracts value from the activity of audiences by transforming viewers into audience commodities that can be sold to advertisers (ibid., p.160). Ratings work to render the potential of audiences to pay attention to and interpret messages predictable so that this data can be sold to advertisers and also used to inform production decisions.

The exposure model of market information under which the television industry has operated since its early years is threatened by digitalisation and the emergence of big data. The expansion of sites (devices, services and channels) through which viewers can watch television undermines the methods used to measure exposure.

Traditional sampling methods adopted by the major television audience measurement companies, such as Nielsen in the US and the UK's Broadcasters' Audience Research Board (BARB), are often inadequate in capturing audiences for niche channels and services with small viewer numbers (Napoli 2010, pp.5–7).[5] Furthermore, as audience viewing behaviour becomes more cross-media and mobile it can be harder to situate and capture, undermining the ability for ratings to make claims to be a reliable and accurate measure of market information for the online TV industry.

The exposure model is further undermined by the emergence of new measures of audience behaviour. Internal data generated within online TV services makes it possible to measure the actual viewing behaviour of all users of that service, providing a more accurate and nuanced understanding of media use than traditional ratings based on small samples and dependant on participants accurately recording their own behaviour. Meanwhile, external data, such as social media metrics, offer different ways of measuring and valuing television audiences, beyond just the time viewers spend watching a particular programme. Combined, these internal and external measures not only challenge the accuracy of an exposure model based on ratings, but also offer alternative ways of valuing audience behaviour. Internal measures can provide data on when someone stops watching, how many episodes of a particular show they watch, how long they spend browsing the catalogue and their viewing journeys within a particular online TV service. For some industry stakeholders such data offers a better reflection of viewer engagement than traditional ratings.

External data, particularly social media analytics, enable the measurement of what Arvidsson and Bonini refer to as the 'noisiness of audience members as they move about in the media landscape' (2015, p.163). Data gathered through 'web scraping' can capture the conversations posted on a wide range of social media sites related to specific programmes, stars, services and so on. Rather than measuring the activity of watching a particular programme, such data can be used to measure 'collective passions' (ibid., p.159). For Arvidsson and Bonini this represents a new way of conceptualising the value of the audience in terms of 'its ability to form a public, that is, a temporary association of strangers held together by a common passion and importantly by a common commitment to particular values or a particular ethos' (ibid., p.167). Here, content is valued not for the number of viewers it attracts but for its ability to engage viewers who form passionate communities online. Such passions can be measured and utilised to predict demand, offering a different means from the exposure model of rendering audience behaviour predictable.

However, for these new internal and external measures to replace the exposure model as the market information regime for the television industry they need to be accepted across the market. Despite the emergence of numerous start-ups in the area of social television analytics (Kosterich & Napoli 2016, p.261), the impact of big data on the television industry's market information regime will depend on the responses of the major audience measurement companies that are currently relied upon to generate market-wide data. The response of Nielsen, the dominant ratings provider in the US and across more than 100 countries globally, provides an indication of the ways in which new audience measures may become integrated into (rather than disrupting) the existing exposure model. According to M.J. Robinson (2017, p.63), Nielsen was relatively slow to alter its traditional audience measurement regime based on measuring linear viewing on television sets from a sample of viewers. In 2016 Nielsen responded to the rise of online TV by launching 'Total Audience Measurement,' a multiplatform measurement tool that purported to measure television viewing across all sites – from linear television to DVR, video on demand (VOD), connected devices (such as Roku and Amazon Fire TV Stick), mobile, desktop and tablet. The system worked by combining data gathered from Nielsen's sample of 40,000 US households with data gathered from a software development kit (SDK) that media owners could install on their apps and players. Once installed the SDK can identify the device ID and collect data whenever a service is used on that device. Nielsen aggregates the devices' IDs and passes them to Facebook, which has around 180 million device IDs based on its own user data. Facebook uses a blind match to attach anonymised demographic data from its own device IDs to Nielsen's data and then returns the combined data to Nielsen, which is calibrated against Nielsen's panel data to remove any anomalies (Lynch 2015).[6] Nielsen also measures internet use through the installation of ratings software on the computers of its panel members. This software can record every link that is clicked on, how long users remain on a particular site, whether they click on advertisements and so on.

As well as developing tools designed to capture television viewing across devices and services, Nielsen has also purchased a leading social media measurement company, SocialGuide, and partnered with Twitter in 2013 to create the Nielsen Twitter TV Rating to measure the number of people tweeting about television programmes and the audience of people who view those tweets. These social media metrics are incorporated into Nielsen's traditional exposure measures (Kosterich & Napoli 2016, p.264; Nielsen 2013). Allie Kosterich and Philip Napoli argue that,

> Nielsen's efforts to diversify into social TV analytics (which would be a logical defensive posture in the face of a potential disruption to/decline of its legacy market information regime) have clearly been accompanied by a discursive effort to explicitly position social TV analytics as supplementary to traditional Nielsen ratings.
>
> (2016, p.265)

The major global media measurement companies that control the market information regime for television, such as Nielsen and BARB, have managed the threat of new metrics derived from social media and online TV by incorporating these new forms of user behaviour data into the traditional exposure model used by the television industry (Nelson & Webster 2016; Robinson 2017).

However, systems such as Nielsen's and BARB's depend on the participation of online TV service providers. Those online TV service providers operating advertising-funded services may benefit from giving Nielsen access to their user data through the installation of Nielsen's SDK. However, for non-advertising funded subscription services, such as Netflix and Amazon, there is limited benefit in participating in a market information regime based on exposure because their business model is premised on generating subscriptions directly from viewers rather than from the sale of advertising time. Subscription services such as Netflix frequently keep their internal data private, often only sharing high-level viewing data (Lotz 2016, p.56; Curtin et al. 2014, p.176). Media measurement companies have attempted to circumvent this. For example, BARB is developing a system of audio watermarking whereby rights' owners provide a copy of their programme assets to BARB's partner, Kantar Media. The programmes are added to an audio reference library which can be used to determine which programmes have been watched by BARB's panel members on any service. However, this will only ever offer an incomplete picture of audience behaviour on subscription services such as Netflix and Amazon, providing content owners with information about when their programmes are viewed on such services, but not offering the more nuanced data about viewing behaviour that the owners of online TV services are able to gather about their users.

The competitive advantage that detailed internal data on viewer behaviour offers to online TV service providers would suggest that we are, therefore, likely to witness the development of a threefold use of data across the online TV industry. First, there will be high-level data generated by major media measurement companies, such as Nielsen and BARB, that incorporate social media metrics into a broader market information regime centred on exposure. Second, there will be external data provided by specialist firms aimed at providing detailed market information to individual companies focused on specific themes or areas. Third, there will be detailed internal data generated within individual online TV services that provides those organisations with valuable insight into their audience behaviours. Although the broader market information regime may well remain intact, the existence of multiple kinds of measurement data will ensure that a level of volatility will characterise the market information regime for the television industry. This is perhaps unsurprising given that there are multiple players operating with different business models that demand varying forms of information within a market in which data can provide a significant competitive advantage.

However, although access to and use of data has the potential to offer the owners of online TV services greater ability to know and understand their audience, it is not without its limits. James Webster (2014, p.86) argues that all media measures are biased because at some point a decision is made about what to measure and how to measure it. The vast amount of data that can be collected through digital media systems might minimise some of the problems of sampling that have informed previous information regimes in the television industry; but a decision still needs to be made about what information to gather, from which sites and in relation to which behaviours. Furthermore, external data generated from social media services and websites cannot be understood as a representative assessment of an audience's response to a programme because it only captures behaviour enacted on those services from users who are inclined to interact online. In an example of the potential bias of such data, research undertaken by technology magazine *Wired* revealed that the Internet Movie Database's overwhelmingly male contributor base strongly favoured films and TV shows with masculine themes and male leads in their rankings (Bridge 2017). There is also the danger of potential misinterpretation of data, in that it might not be possible to capture the reasons why a person has liked a post or comment on a social media site such as Facebook or Twitter (Wolk 2015, p.138).

Internal data also has its limits. Although internal data that captures detailed user behaviour may appear to offer significant insight into what content people like, viewing a programme is not necessarily the same as liking it. As Webster writes, 'use isn't always a well-informed expression of our personal preferences' (2014, p.88). Such 'behaviour biases' (ibid.) are further shaped by the interfaces and algorithms of online TV services that structure user experience. Although the value of online data is premised on the idea that it offers seemingly authentic insight into users' behaviours and tastes, it is gathered on services where people's interactions are highly structured and managed (van Dijck 2013, p.162). This is particularly the case in online TV services that function as transactional archives focused on providing content for consumption by users, where each transaction (and, therefore, each piece of data gathered about user behaviour) is shaped by the structure of the service itself. As Beer and Burrows argue,

> Transactions, as we might call them, are not then a linear process, rather they are a product of recursive data flows shaping encounters and consumer choices (even where the recommendations are ignored or overlooked). The transactional archive is a site of circulation of cultural information instantiated in performative consumer activity.
>
> (2013, p.60)

As such, the data gathered about user behaviour in online TV services cannot be divorced from the structures of the services themselves. Rather, the structure of the service and the user behaviour on that service are bound in a recursive loop in which user behaviour is shaped by the service, but also contributes to the ways in which the service organises and presents content to users. To understand how this recursive loop operates we need to examine the algorithms used to operationalise the user behaviour data gathered within online TV services.

Algorithms and online TV

So far we have examined the ways in which the convergence of television and the internet has increased the scale and range of internal and external data in the online TV industry in ways that introduce volatility into the market information regime that structures the television industry. However, it is not possible to understand fully the impact of data on the online TV industry without examining the role of algorithms. Algorithms are computational processes that define a series of steps or instructions in order to produce a desired outcome (Just & Latzer 2017, p.239; Kitchin 2017, p.16; van Dijck 2013, p.30; Webster 2014, p.84). Data and algorithms are inextricably linked because algorithms provide the mechanisms through which the sheer volume of big data generated online can be analysed and made operational. In this way algorithms give data 'purpose and direction' (Beer 2017, p.3). Algorithms are also a fundamental component of software, providing the 'sets of defined steps structured to process instructions/data to produce an output' (Kitchin 2017, p.14). As such, algorithms can be understood as the engines that run the software applications through which we experience the internet. This has led to the emergence of what Blake Hallinan and Ted Striphas refer to as '"algorithmic culture": provisionally, the use of computational processes to sort, classify, and hierarchise people, places, objects, and ideas, and also the habits of thought, conduct, and expression that arise in relationship to those processes' (2016, p.119). For example, the algorithms that run the search engines that lie behind many contemporary websites perform the function of sorting and classifying culture, shaping which results are prioritised and, therefore, considered more valuable. Striphas (2015, p.396) refers to an example in which a change to Amazon's algorithm designed to filter 'adult' material out of search results on its retail site led to numerous gay and lesbian titles, as well as books related to reproductive and sexual health, effectively disappearing from its site. Algorithms, therefore, have the potential to affect how culture is presented and valued within society.

Online TV services are symptomatic of the spread of algorithmic culture into the television industry, operated through software or software-enabled devices that transform television from a medium of broadcasting into what Tarleton Gillespie terms an 'algorithm machine – designed to store and read data, apply mathematical procedures to it in a controlled fashion, and offer new information as the output' (2014, p.167). The kinds of algorithms used by the television industry are principally designed to order large datasets and predict demand. This section will argue that they can be understood to have the following characteristics:

1. They are the result of human actors, created within a specific social-cultural context and for a particular purpose.
2. They render the multidimensionality of human behaviour into manageable data.
3. They can operate with little or no human intervention.
4. They can identify patterns in data that were not previously visible.
5. They are recursive and ontogenetic – always in a state of becoming – making it difficult to understand why an algorithm makes a particular prediction.

The first two of these five characteristics could be understood to apply equally to historical uses of data in the television industry. The industry has always used mechanisms such as sampling and data modelling to render the complexity of audience behaviour into manageable data in order to fulfil specific business requirements, such as informing commissioning decisions or selling advertising. However, as we shall go on to see, in online TV, algorithms take on a more central and determining role both in analysing and interpreting the increased volume and variety of data and in running the software that shapes the services through which user data is generated, gathered and implemented.

Through the activity of processing and presenting information, algorithms can be understood as delegates, what Steven Johnson refers to as 'agents' that perform for the user, but at a price – namely, giving the computer processing unit the authority to make decisions on your behalf (1997, p.180). Once programmed, algorithms can operate with little or no human intervention, leading to concerns about the propensity for algorithms to exert power over human behaviour and society (Beer 2017, p.3). As performative agents, algorithms have been understood to exert control over user behaviour online. For example, Rob Kitchin describes how

> Algorithms are used to seduce, coerce, discipline, regulate and control: to guide and reshape how people, animals and objects interact with and pass through various systems. This is the same for systems designed to empower, entertain and enlighten, as they are also predicated on defined rule-sets about how a system behaves at any one time and situation.
>
> (2017, p.19)

Algorithms, therefore, shape online TV services and the protocols that structure user behaviour within those services. There are many types of algorithm, but a brief analysis of collaborative filtering, used by many online TV services to generate recommendations, provides a useful insight into the ways in which algorithms operate as what Natascha Just and Michael Latzer refer to as 'governance mechanisms, as instruments used to exert power and as increasingly autonomous actors with power to further political and economic interests on the individual but also on the public/collective level' (2017, p.245).

Collaborative filtering algorithms operate by tracking and recording the behaviour of individual users and comparing it with others who display similar behaviours (Webster 2014, p.86) in order to identify patterns of media use. Based on the 'transferability of taste,' collaborative filtering 'assumes that people who have some interests in common will also share other interests' (Johnson 1997, p.196). Collaborative filtering algorithms are a form of machine learning, which can be understood as 'ways of transforming, constructing or imposing some kind of shape on data and using that shape to discover, decide, classify, rank, cluster, recommend, label or predict what is happening or what will happen' (Mackenzie 2015, p.432). The aim of collaborative filtering is to order and to analyse data in order to generate recommendations. These recommendations function on the basis that user preferences can be predicted based on an analysis of previous user behaviour and comparison with other users – if you watched *Game of Thrones* (HBO 2011–) you are going to want to watch *Stranger Things* (Netflix 2016–). Essentially concerned with classifying things, collaborative filtering algorithms are able to process tens of thousands of variables and sample sizes of millions or billions, and tend to improve with the input of greater volumes and varieties of data (Mackenzie 2015, p.434).

However, as with the work of all algorithms, collaborative filtering is not a neutral process. Kitchin argues that while computer scientists and technology companies tend to present the work of algorithmic coding as 'technical, benign and commonsensical' (2017, p.17), the coding of algorithms involves translating a task or problem into a structured formula with an appropriate rule set, and then translating this rule set into a source code that, when compiled, will perform the task or solve the problem. In relation to collaborative filtering this involves composing an error metric that enables the algorithm to deal with behaviour that seems deviant or outside of the norm (Johnson 1997, pp.203–4; Hallinan & Striphas 2016, p.128). For example, Netflix has revealed two high-profile examples of 'deviant' data that differed significantly from the norm within its service: a user who rated 17,000 movies using Netflix's now defunct five-star ratings system and gave consistently lower ratings than most other users; and the movie *Napoleon Dynamite* (2004), which either seemed to be rated very high or very low by viewers. Hallinan and Striphas argue that the information theory standpoint on such atypical data is to treat it as corrupt or statistically insignificant. Information theory 'is not interested in the status of a single user or title but instead in a pattern or system capable of dealing with substantial groups of fungible users and objects' (2016, p.122). In this sense, collaborative filtering can be programmed to moderate elements of the cultural field that seem atypical or outstanding so that they make sense relative to other more typical examples.

The treatment of atypical behaviour in the programming of collaborative filtering algorithms draws attention to the ways in which algorithmic thinking understands human behaviour as nodes in technological networks, rather than social ones. This is exemplified by the use of 'singular value decomposition' (SVD), which is a technique developed by mathematicians in linear algebra to simplify datasets (Hallinan & Striphas 2016). SVD is a mathematical process that works by placing data into a matrix and reducing it to its constituent parts. In doing so, SVD can be used to identify dependencies between different data points and to remove redundant data. For example, within an online TV service, SVD could be used to analyse the relationships between hundreds or thousands of different datasets about user behaviour in order to identify which relationships are significant (e.g. people who watch action movies also watch gross-out comedies) and which relationships are not significant (e.g. age is not a significant factor determining consumption of comedies). SVD, therefore, enables the online TV service to identify, for example, that genre might be a strong predictor of user behaviour but that geographic location of the user might not be. Rather than relying on users to tell the service in advance what they want, collaborative filtering and SVD work from the bottom up, monitoring and aggregating data generated through user behaviour in order to predict users' tastes, preferences and desires. These algorithms can identify novel patterns within the data, creating new 'congregations of taste' (Johnson 1997, p.197) that are not stable, but change as the algorithm receives new data based on ongoing user behaviour. Netflix, for example, claims that it has identified 2,000 global taste communities based on collaborative filtering of viewing behaviour across international services (Laporte 2017). Challenging assumptions that a user's geographic location determines what they want to watch, Netflix's algorithm has enabled the service to identify new patterns of behaviour that are informing its business practices. In this sense, SVD can identify patterns in human behaviour that might pull against traditional classificatory norms used to measure media audiences (Hallinan & Striphas 2016, p.124).

However, the process by which SVD functions is based on simplifying the complexity of human behaviour. SVD and other statistical, logistic and calculative practices that are used in machine learning operate on the assumption that a function (defined in the mathematical sense as 'a mapping that transforms one set of variables into another') underlines the predictive relationship between input (user behaviour) and output (recommendations) (Mackenzie 2015, p.435). Algorithmic programming assumes, therefore, that human behaviour can be reduced to a mathematical process and operates by removing data that deviates from the norm and approximating the relationship between different points of data. As Hallinan and Striphas state, 'SVD does not arrive at definitive solutions but rather statements of fit that closely approximate relationships amongst salient data points' (2016, p.124). In doing so, algorithms necessarily simplify the multi-dimensional nature of human behaviour to render it into manageable data (Webster 2014, p.143).

As this description of collaborative filtering demonstrates, we need to be wary of understanding algorithms as technological apparatuses that are separate from human interventions and social structures. All algorithms are programmed by human actors and are created for a specific purpose (Kitchin 2017, p.18; Morris 2015, p.452). As Beer writes, 'Algorithms are inevitably modelled on visions of the social world, and with outcomes in mind, outcomes influenced by commercial or other interests and agendas' (2017, p.4). Typically, this involves disparate inputs from a large number of people, making it difficult for one person to understand an algorithm in its entirety (Napoli 2014, p.344). Beyond their initial design, algorithms cannot escape social context because they are woven into everyday practices that are modelled back into algorithmic design in a recursive process (Napoli 2014, p.346). This is particularly the case with machine learning algorithms (such as collaborative filtering) that are designed to alter their outcomes in response to the data received such that the algorithm is constantly changing as it is put to use. Just and Latzer describe this as an ongoing process of co-evolution that has no beginning or end:

> developers design software, software shapes software (self-learning systems), software changes and is changed by users, users form and are formed by societies, societies influence developers and users via institutional imprinting, by social, economic, political, and regulatory forces. Altogether, from an institutional perspective, technologies like algorithms are both instruments and outcome of governance ...; they are part and result of a co-evolutionary process.
>
> (2017, p.244)

Because the work of algorithms is highly contextual and constantly altered through use, described by Kitchin as 'ontogenetic ... always in a state of becoming' (2017, p.18), they are particularly difficult to pin down.

Algorithms in online TV, therefore, can be understood as mathematical processes programmed by human agents to analyse vast datasets in order to render the multidimensionality of human behaviour manageable. As we have seen, algorithms play an important role in putting the large datasets generated within online TV services to work in making the behaviour of users more predictable. Algorithms are able to identify patterns within user data that were not previously visible and to make recommendations that can shape user behaviour online. Although created by people, once programmed algorithms can undertake their work with little human intervention. The recursive and ontogenetic characteristics of algorithms can make it difficult to understand why an algorithm produces a specific prediction or recommendation. Having unpacked what data and algorithms are in the context of online TV, the next section goes on to examine in more detail the different ways in which the online TV industry is making use of data and algorithms and what the consequences of this might be for understanding online TV.

The uses of data and algorithms by online TV services

The online TV industry has incorporated data and algorithms into its existing practice of using data to inform content decisions, advertising sales and user experiences. Algorithmic prediction based on the monitoring of actual user behaviour within an online TV service offers the possibility of more accurate measurements of viewer behaviour than traditional ratings models based on samples of recorded data and can be used to inform content production and acquisition decisions (Napoli 2014: 348–9).[7] Netflix has been the most prominent online TV service in proclaiming its use of algorithms and data to inform the programming it commissions, licenses and renews, as well as shaping how content is released (Hallinan & Striphas 2016, p.128) (see Chapter 4). TV natives that have extended an existing TV service online have a disadvantage in this regard in that they can't monitor all of their viewer behaviour in the same way.[8] However, some TV natives have started using social media data in deciding which programmes to renew (Kosterich & Napoli 2016, p.263).

The use of these different forms of internal and external data to inform content decisions has the potential to alter how content is valued within the online TV industry. For example, Allie Kosterich's comparison of hit shows as measured by traditional ratings and by social media metrics revealed significant differences both in terms of the 'types of programs that succeed and the sources from which these successes originate' (2016, p.55). Kosterich concludes that if programme makers increasingly rely on social media analytics to inform content decisions then the output of the TV industry might change in ways that could enhance the diversity of programme types and the people and companies that make them (ibid., pp.55–6). Meanwhile, because online TV services have increased storage capacity they are able to value content in a number of different ways, rather than adopting a singular measure (such as absolute ratings), and this could lead to increased diversity of content (see Chapter 4). For example, Ted Sarandos (Chief Content Officer, Netflix) has claimed that Netflix uses algorithmic analysis of user behaviour to determine what programming is valued by important niche groups of subscribers, which shapes what they will pay for specific content (cited in Curtin et al. 2014, p.176). Whether through the analysis and use of internal or external data, therefore, algorithms have the potential to determine what kinds of content and viewers count as valuable within the online TV industry (Hallinan & Striphas 2016, p.129).

However, we should be wary of over-emphasising the role of algorithms in commissioning content within online TV services. As discussed in Chapter 4, industry accounts of the role of algorithmic prediction in shaping content decisions need to be tempered against the continued reliance on creative personnel to mitigate the risks of original production. Furthermore, amidst criticism that Netflix's reliance on 'data rather than brain power … has delivered shows that are generally more conservative and less risqué or intellectually challenging' (Smith 2017; see also Heritage 2017), a number of television providers have actively emphasised the human element in their content decisions.[9] For example, in 2016, UK public service broadcaster Channel 4 launched Walter Presents, a curated collection of international television series hand-picked by producer Walter Iuzzolino and offered on demand as a core part of its online TV service All 4. Other TV natives, such as NBC Universal and the BBC, have been keen to stress the value of the editorial expertise of their staff in commissioning and curating content online (Grainge & Johnson 2018, pp.33–4; Landau 2016, p.48; Maheshwari 2017). Here human curation is valued over algorithmic recommendations, with Kieran Clifton (Controller of Digital Strategy, BBC) claiming that the BBC can 'compete with new OTT services because we have people with editorial judgement. My view is, people plus data beats data, and people plus data beats people' (cited in Grainge & Johnson 2018, pp.33–4).

Beyond content decisions, the use of algorithms and data in the sale of advertising also has an impact on the value regimes within the online TV industry. Although some scholars have argued that the affordances of online TV are leading to the decline of advertising as a funding model for television in favour of subscription-based services (see for example Lotz 2016), there are benefits to the ad-funded television industry from the shift to online TV. In particular, streaming services make it possible to use predictive and real-time data to offer advertising that is highly targeted, personalised and non-skippable. The ability to monitor real-time user behaviour online and to correlate this with records of shopping activity not only enables more targeted and individualised advertising, it also makes it possible to more accurately monitor the success of ad campaigns in reaching consumers and driving sales (McGuigan 2015, pp.204–5; van Dijck 2013, p.161). Rather than selling advertising slots based on predicted ratings data, the online media ecosystem enables the sale of ad-space online to be automated through programmatic advertising. Here media inventory is purchased, often through a real-time bidding system, automatically by computers that analyse vast amounts of data to decide which slots to buy and how much to pay for them in order to deliver the advertising to the specified target viewer (Rogers 2017). The automation of the ad-buying process may remove prejudices that shape media buying and increase the value of certain kinds of media content.

However, programmatic advertising depends on servers being able to access and monitor the sites on which the advertising will be placed. For services offered through IPTV, such as set-top boxes, incompatible hardware and software infrastructure presents a significant barrier that would need to be overcome before advertising sales could be fully automated across the industry (McGuigan 2015).[10] Over and above this, algorithmically driven advertising sales also raise problems of transparency and accountability.[11] In the wake of scandals in 2017 that saw adverts for major brands placed alongside extremist content on YouTube, Simon Duke (2017: p.10) claimed of programmatic advertising that,

> Fraud is rife. It is thought that half of online ads are viewed by networks of hacked devices programmed to generate fake clicks. A number of FTSE 100 marketing chiefs have told me of their irritation with Google and Facebook, which have been reluctant to share data on where their ads have been placed and who has viewed them. Their complaint is that Silicon Valley's ad-buying algorithms are, in effect, a big black box. Advertisers have been invited to take it on trust that the Valley giants will do the right thing with their ad dollars. Compared to the shadowy alleys of the internet, the circulation and viewing figures delivered by publishers and broadcasters are a model of transparency.

Some broadcasters, such as NBC Universal, have developed their own software to enable advertisers to purchase targeted ad slots against specific data spots within their portfolio of channels and services. However, for media buyers this leads to the creation of an advertising marketplace in which 'network groups are using different data sets, algorithms and technology, which means buyers can't compare one to another or target audiences across the TV landscape' (Poggi 2017, p.88). Therefore, although big data and algorithms offer the promise of increased accuracy and effectiveness in advertising, the market for television ad-sales remains fragmented and volatile.

Beyond content creation and advertising sales, algorithms designed to predict demand also increasingly manage decisions about how content is delivered to viewers. Where schedulers have historically used data to inform the time and channel upon which to transmit programmes in order to maximise and retain viewers, in the online TV industry recommendation algorithms increasingly undertake this role. Webster argues that recommendation engines 'impose a comfortable discipline on our choices, making our encounters with media a bit more orderly and rational' (2014, p.144; see also Napoli 2014, p.345). Recommendation engines play a significant role in shaping what content is made visible to viewers and considered valuable by the television industry. Natali Helberger et al. argue that, theoretically, recommendation algorithms could be programmed to make content from smaller producers more findable (2015, p.58). Certainly, the Netflix ID Bible points to the ways in which algorithms might draw out new ways of organising and categorising both content and viewers in ways that might differ from the traditional value regimes of the television industry. Algorithms also have the potential to restore the notion of serendipitous discovery, exposing viewers to content in ways that might cultivate new preferences (Wolk 2015, p.138; Webster 2014, p.141).

Algorithms designed to help people find and select content to view function not only within online TV services but also beyond them, such as in Google searches, targeted advertising for television programmes and films, and through apps like JustWatch that aggregate information across a number of different online TV services. In an internet ecosystem where access to marketing messages, reviews and even word of mouth recommendations by friends are increasingly performed online through services operated by software, algorithms play a powerful role in determining which forms of media become visible within culture. There is the potential for significant volatility here, in that certain forms of culture may be very visible to some users but invisible to others. Across the internet ecosystem a range of different services are using algorithms to address the need that users have for 'navigational aids to find their shows and discover new ones' (Mikos 2016, p.160) in a media landscape where the sheer volume of content and number of online TV services can lead to 'choice fatigue' and 'oversearch' (Vonderau 2014, p.726).

In many ways, then, data and algorithms could be understood to be performing an editorial function in the online TV industry (Doyle 2015, p.57). Data and algorithms are being used to inform decisions about what content gets produced, licensed and renewed (traditionally the preserve of commissioners), what content and which viewers are commercially valuable to advertisers (traditionally determined by media buyers) and what content viewers see (traditionally shaped by schedulers). Writing in relation to Facebook, Taina Bucher (2012) draws attention to the ways in which algorithms control what is made visible, and argues that Facebook functions to reward interactions on its service that increase user visibility, such as liking posts. In online TV services algorithms also function to control visibility, but the visibility of content rather than of users. However, although online TV services do not reward interaction with increased user visibility in the same way as Facebook, recommendation algorithms are programmed to adapt according to user behaviour such that increased use of the service should be rewarded with more accurate recommendations. Here, then, the consequence of interaction is a change in the content that is made visible to the user. In this sense, recommendation algorithms function as one way of encouraging increased use of and loyalty to the online TV service.

Furthermore, this role that user behaviour plays in shaping recommendation algorithms points to a crucial difference between the editorial function of broadcast, cable/satellite and digital television and online TV. Helberger et al. argue that in search engines and social networking sites, 'unlike traditional editorial content, the actual output (e.g. search results) very much depends on the interaction with and input from the users' (2015, p.63). This makes it difficult to maintain a one-directional conceptualisation of editorial control online (ibid., pp.62–3). Although online TV services typically offer far fewer opportunities for user interaction than in social media sites (see Chapter 5), this argument equally applies in that the recommendation (and therefore what content is made visible) depends on input from the user generated through their use of the service itself. However, although not one-directional, these inputs are themselves shaped by the affordances and algorithms of the service itself, making it difficult 'to disentangle the effects of agency and structure' (Webster 2014, p.106).

There are, therefore, three crucial differences between the uses of data in broadcast, cable/satellite and digital television and in online TV:

1. Algorithmic analysis of large datasets generated from actual user behaviour enables novel patterns of viewing, taste cultures and genre categories to be identified that were not previously visible and that enable content and viewers to be valued in new ways.
2. Algorithms enable the automation of processes, such as ad-buying and scheduling, that were previously informed by data but ultimately determined through human decision-making. In doing so, algorithms take on an editorial function and have the potential to determine what and how content is made visible to viewers.
3. These automated algorithmic processes differ from traditional editorial practices in that they depend on input from the viewer. However, because this input derives from use of the service itself, it is necessarily shaped by the affordances of the service. Thus, although editorial control in online TV services is more multidirectional than in traditional media, the industry still retains greater editorial control than the viewer because it is the service that programmes the algorithms and designs the interfaces through which user input occurs.

One of the difficulties in analysing the role of algorithms in online TV services, however, is the extent to which they are hidden from scrutiny. There are two aspects at work here. Algorithms are often are 'black-boxed,' deliberately hidden from users, regulators and competitors as commercially sensitive agents (Hallinan & Striphas 2016, p.118; Kitchin 2017, p.15; van Dijck & Poell 2013, p.167). Given that most online TV services, as well as the platforms that dominate the online TV ecosystem within which they operate (such as Google and Facebook), are operated as private rather than public corporations, this leads to what Striphas refers to as 'the privatisation of cultural decision-making' (2015, p.407). In many ways, this represents a continuation of the traditional workings of the media industries where commercial organisations have dominated the global market since the 1990s. However, the increased use of computer-mediated communications in everyday life does mean that the power of private corporations to shape culture through algorithms has extended more readily into quotidian social interactions. Over and above this, even if the algorithms that drive the online TV ecosystem were opened up to scrutiny the ontogenetic and recursive nature of recommendation algorithms would make it difficult to assess why an algorithm had performed a specific action (such as recommending x programme to y user) or behaved in a certain way (such as placing x advert in y media space). As Just and Latzer argue,

> A high degree of complexity in the cooperation between algorithmic agents and humans results in low transparency (not only for users, as in the mass media, but also for producers), controllability, and predictability compared to reality construction by traditional mass media.
>
> (2017, p.253)

Although it is not always possible to easily understand why an algorithm has generated a particular recommendation or prediction, this does not mean that algorithms are completely beyond regulatory scrutiny. All algorithms are programmed to behave in specific ways, which means that it is possible to scrutinise the factors predetermined by their creators that shape the behaviour of any particular algorithmic system. Ansgar Koene and Lillian Edwards (2017) describe this as the difference between understanding why an algorithm produced a specific result (which is difficult to determine) and how an algorithm works (which can be determined with access to the code, data and parameter settings). For example, it is possible to interrogate the optimisation criteria that are used to adapt the behaviour of a machine-learning algorithm. Optimisation criteria are designed to minimise the number of times that an algorithm puts the wrong label on the items it has to classify. In the case of online TV services, a 'wrong label' refers to a recommendation that is deemed unsuccessful according to the service, which might be measured in terms of recommendations not selected, selected but only partially viewed or viewed and rated poorly. Online TV services also utilise algorithms to cluster data by grouping similar items. Here, again, the factor determining the way in which the algorithm measures similarity can be audited. An understanding of the optimisation criteria and similarity measures, along with information about the error metric used to deal with atypical and unusual data, would, therefore, enable scrutiny of the factors that inform how algorithms shape exposure to culture in online TV services.[12]

Analysis of the criteria governing some of the dominant services that use recommendation algorithms has led to accusations of popularity and personalisation bias, both of which undercut the potential for algorithms to increase the diversity of content produced and viewed. Popularity bias refers to the ways in which algorithms can be programmed to favour popular sites, that is those that generate the most hits or the most favourable ratings (Webster 2014, p.90). For example, one of the criteria used in Netflix's algorithm when recommending content is the rating given to that content by other users, particularly where there is similarity in their viewing (and rating) behaviour. Here Netflix's algorithm is programmed to favour popular content when deciding what content to recommend. Personalisation bias refers to the ways in which recommendation algorithms are programmed to offer content similar to that which the viewer has already watched. Critics of personalisation bias have raised concerns that by offering recommendations based on previous online behaviour, online services will create highly individuated viewing environments in which people are no longer confronted with 'attitude-discrepant information' (Helberger et al. 2015, p.56). Just and Latzer caution that

> this may lead to situations where people only access information that confirms their own opinion or communicate with like-minded people, with potentially negative democratic consequences for societies, such as endangering two pre-conditions for democratic systems: unplanned encounters and shared experience.
>
> (2017, p.249)

There remains significant debate about the extent to which popularity or personalisation bias is at work in online TV services and the broader media ecosystem in which they operate (see, for example, Webster 2014). It may be that the effects of popularity and personalisation bias cancel themselves out, leading to a situation where viewers encounter certain forms of shared culture made visible through popularity bias, alongside a narrower selection of highly personalised recommended content. Or popularity bias might operate as a subset of personalisation bias in which viewers are aggregated into taste cultures each of which encounters a similar diet of popular content within that niche community. Regardless, the existence of popularity and personalisation bias points to the ways in which algorithms in online TV services can exert significant power over the content that people encounter, despite (or more accurately because of) the role of human input. What I mean by this is that just because algorithms depend on human input (through making use of a service) this does not mean that users have agency over the service (or the algorithm). Such agency would only emerge if users had the ability to determine the criteria that informed how the algorithm worked to shape their media experience.

In the introduction to this chapter, I asked whether algorithms enhance or undermine the perceived development of television from a 'push' to a 'pull' medium. In the broadcast era television content was organised into a linear schedule and 'pushed' to viewers who had little ability to control their viewing experience. Since the development of the VCR, new technologies have increased the ability for viewers to 'pull' the content that they want to watch. Online TV services appear on the surface to be the epitome of 'pull' television, offering highly personalised experiences in which viewers can choose what programming they want to watch. However, an analysis of the role of algorithms in online TV services challenges a conceptualisation of online TV as a pull medium. Although viewers can choose what content to watch within online TV services, they do so in an environment in which the choices available are highly structured by algorithms (and interfaces) over which they have little or no control. As such, online TV services have far more in common with the push media of traditional broadcasting (where the service exerts significant control over the users' media experience) than might be immediately apparent.

Conclusion

This chapter has argued that the internet ecosystem provides online TV services with access to a significant volume and variety of new forms of internal and external data. The nuanced measures of audience viewing behaviour within online TV services, alongside new forms of external data such as social media metrics, undermine the television industry's market information regime by challenging the accuracy of traditional ratings and offering alternative ways of valuing audiences and content. The major media measurement companies, such as Nielsen, have sought to incorporate the new forms of market data into the television industry's traditional exposure model. At the same time, however, proprietary internal and external data that is not shared across the industry has come to play an increasingly important role in the operations of online TV services. This introduces greater volatility into the market information regime for the online TV industry.

The greater volume and variety of data available to online TV services has also led to the online TV industry being increasingly shaped by algorithmic culture, which informs content decisions, advertising sales and the construction of the user experience. Although algorithms operate in conjunction with other social and industrial processes, the increased use of algorithmic processes to predict demand is having an impact on how content is valued by the television industry. This has the potential to increase diversity of and exposure to content. However, it is difficult to measure the effects of this because algorithms are hidden from scrutiny and are ontogenetic and recursive in nature, making it hard to separate agency and structure. Furthermore, although algorithms are shaped by the behaviour of users, this does not mean that users have greater agency within online TV services. Rather, examination of the use of algorithms and big data by the online TV industry suggests that far from operating as pull media, in which users have significant control over their media experience, online TV services are better understood as akin to the traditional push media of broadcasting in which the service exerts significant control over the user's media experience. Combined, the increased use of proprietary data and the lack of transparency in the use of online TV algorithms should raise concerns about the extent to which users, regulators and competitors are able to scrutinise the effects of data and algorithms within online TV services.

Notes

1 These categories of data are borrowed from David Beer and Roger Burrows, who identify user profile data, linkages and metadata as component features of the popular cultural archives generated through online interactions. Beer and Burrows also include a fourth category, 'play,' which is defined as the ways in which users generate data 'as they have fun and as they find and consume stuff' (2013, p.51). Within the relatively structured spaces of online TV services (see Chapter 5) there is less space for play, although where services enable rating, commenting and sharing this might be understood as a form of data generated through play.

2 Eva-Patricia Fernández-Manzano, Elena Neiro and Judith Clares-Gavilán (2016, p.572) describe eight kinds of data gathered by Netflix from its subscribers as they use its service: viewed/discarded content type; playback characteristics (pausing, rewinding etc.); playback intensity (number of hours streamed); user ratings; access device; paths taken by the user (searches, where on the service the content was located); location/time/day of access; and playback quality (e.g. effect of transmission speed and content storage rate).

3 Philip Napoli (2016, p.1) claims that Netflix segments its content offerings into over 75,000 'microgenres' on the basis of these content characteristics (see also Fernández-Manzano et al. 2016, p.573).

4 Netflix uses a range of algorithms to process its data. See Fernández-Manzano et al. (2016, pp.573–4) for a description of Netflix's algorithms.

5 Allie Kosterich and Philip Napoli point to some estimates that 20 percent of all television viewing in the US in the mid-2010s went unmeasured (2016, p.260).

6 UK media measurement company BARB launched a similar audience measurement system in September 2018 which produces programme viewing figures for TV sets, tablets, PCs and smartphones (BARB 2018).

7 Algorithms are also being used in some instances to create content. At the time of writing, this is largely the domain of text-based media, such as journalism and social media content (Napoli 2014, p.348). However, there are examples of algorithmically produced videos on YouTube. Most high profile are videos targeted at children through the use of metadata that are designed in response to the recommendation engines of services like YouTube so that they appear high up in search results and, therefore, attract advertising (Bridle 2017). In many instances the production of these videos is automated through assemblages of stock animations, sound tracks and key words (ibid.). For online TV services whose value is premised on the quality of the editorially selected content that they provide, algorithmic content creation is not likely to be a significant disruptive force.

8 It is likely that this disadvantage will erode over time as more linear television is delivered over internet-connected devices – whether through internet protocol television (IPTV) or over-the-top (OTT) – and the industry invests in software that enables the monitoring of user behaviour on set-top boxes.

9 Without access to Netflix's own data it is not possible to assess whether the programmes criticised in these press accounts, such as *Gypsy* (Netflix, 2017) and *Friends from College* (Netflix, 2017–), were successful in achieving Netflix's own production goals, such as appealing to specific niche audiences. However, analysis of English-language newspaper articles published in 2017 related to algorithms and television did evidence a critical backlash against algorithmic recommendations within the popular press.

10 Lee McGuigan (2015) examines the abortive attempts amongst a consortium of US cable companies to develop a standardised programming interface to enable the delivery of interactive and programmatic advertising through set-top boxes. The project was beset with difficulties because of the conflicting interests of the collaborating partners and the challenge the service presented to entrenched practices of media buying.

11 Burt Helm (2017) provides a fascinating account of the experience of a start-up using Facebook's algorithmically driven advertising service. The entrepreneurs were able to track in real time the outcome of the algorithm as it placed their adverts in different spots for varying prices. They were also able to see which adverts led to sales. However, it was not possible to know why the algorithm placed certain adverts in certain slots and to assess whether this was because of how the algorithm was programmed, how people responded to the ad or because of the nature of the ad creative itself.

12 I am very grateful to Ansgar Koene for his detailed explanation of the 'black box' problem of algorithms, how they operate in online TV services and the ways in which they may be opened up to regulatory scrutiny.

Bibliography

Arvidsson, A. & Bonini, T., 2015. Valuing Audience Passions: From Smythe to Tarde. *European Journal of Cultural Studies*, 18(2), pp.158–173.

BARB, 2018. BARB Launches Multiple-Screen Audience Reporting. *barb.co.uk*. Available at: https://www.barb.co.uk/news/barb-launches-multiple-screen-audience-reporting/ [Accessed October 11, 2018].

Beck, K., 2016. Netflix Has Tons of Hidden Categories: Here's How to See Them. *Mashable UK*, 11 Jan. Available at: https://mashable.com/2016/01/11/netflix-search-codes/?europe=true#i3uWGRlt95qH [Accessed August 14, 2018].

Beer, D., 2017. The Social Power of Algorithms. *Information, Communication & Society*, 20(1), pp.1–13.

Beer, D. & Burrows, R., 2013. Popular Culture, Digital Archives and the New Social Life of Data. *Theory Culture and Society*, 30(4), pp.47–71.

Bridge, M., 2017. Rotten Tomato and IMDb: Film Rankings Skewed by Mostly Male Voters. *The Times*, 31 Oct. Available at: https://www.thetimes.co.uk/article/rotten-tomato-and-imdb-film-rankings-skewed-by-mostly-male-voters-zznpfv20z [Accessed August 14, 2018].

Bridle, J., 2017. Something is Wrong on the Internet. *Medium*, 6 Nov. Available at: https://medium.com/@jamesbridle/something-is-wrong-on-the-internet-c39c471271d2 [Accessed August 14, 2018].

Bucher, T., 2012. Want to Be on the Top? Algorithmic Power and the Threat of Invisibility on Facebook. *New Media & Society*, 14(7), pp.1164–1180.

Curtin, M., Holt, J. & Sanson, K. eds., 2014. *Distribution Revolution: Conversations about the Digital Future of Film and Television*, Berkeley: University of California Press.

Doyle, G., 2015. Multi-Platform Media and the Miracle of the Loaves and Fishes. *Journal of Media Business Studies*, 12(1), pp.49–65.

Duke, S., 2017. Is the Ad Party over for the Online Giants? *Sunday Times*, 6 Aug., p.10. Available at: https://www.thetimes.co.uk/article/is-the-ad-party-over-for-the-online-giants-hs7xl2wpq [Accessed August 14, 2018].

Fernández-Manzano, E.-P., Neira, E. & Clares-Gavilán, J., 2016. Data Management in Audiovisual Business: Netflix as a Case Study. *El Profesional de la Información*, 25(4), pp.568–576.

Gillespie, T., 2014. The Relevance of Algorithms. In T. Gillespie, P.J. Boczkowski & K.A. Foot, eds. *Media Technologies: Essays on Communication, Materiality and Society*. Cambridge, MA and London: MIT Press, pp. 167–193.

Godwin, R., 2017. Stream If You Want to Go Faster: How TV Became a Billion Dollar Business. *Evening Standard*, 9 Nov. Available at: https://www.standard.co.uk/lifestyle/esmagazine/apple-tv-original-content-netflix-tv-hulu-a3677626.html [Accessed August 14, 2018].

Grainge, P. & Johnson, C., 2018. From Catch-Up TV to Online TV: Digital Broadcasting and the Case of BBC iPlayer. *Screen*, 59(1), pp.21–40.

Hallinan, B. & Striphas, T., 2016. Recommended for You: The Netflix Prize and the Production of Algorithmic Culture. *New Media & Society*, 18(1), pp.117–137.

Helberger, N., Kleinen-von Königslöw, K. & van der Noll, R., 2015. Regulating the New Information Intermediaries as Gatekeepers of Information Diversity. *Info*, 17(6), pp.50–71.

Helm, B., 2017. The Ads That Know Everything: How Facebook's Oracular Algorithm Determines the Fate of Start-Ups. *New York Times*, 5 Nov., p.41.

Heritage, S., 2017. What Happened, Netflix? You Were King of the Hill – Now You're Circling the Drain. *The Guardian*, 14 Jul. Available at: https://www.theguardian.com/tv-and-radio/2017/jul/14/what-happened-netflix-you-were-king-of-the-hill-now-youre-circling-the-drain [Accessed August 14, 2018].

Hernandez, B., 2015. The Netflix ID Bible – Every Category on Netflix. *What's On Netflix*, 15 Feb.

Johnson, C., 2012. *Branding Television*, London: Routledge.

Johnson, S., 1997. *Interface Culture: How New Technology Transforms the Way We Create and Communicate*, New York: Harper Edge.

Just, N. & Latzer, M., 2017. Governance by Algorithms: Reality Construction by Algorithmic Selection on the Internet. *Media, Culture & Society*, 39(2), pp.238–258.

Kitchin, R., 2017. Thinking Critically about and Researching Algorithms. *Information, Communication & Society*, 20(1), pp.14–29.

Koene, A. & Edwards, L., 2017. Are Algorithms Really a Black Box? In University of Strathclyde (Scotland) Algorithms Workshop. University of Strathclyde. Available at: https://www.slideshare.net/AnsgarKoene/are-algorithms-really-a-black-box.

Koene, A., Perez Vallejos, E., Webb, H., Patel, M., Ceppi, S., Jirotka, M. & McAuley, D., 2017. Editorial Responsibilities Arising from Personalization Algorithms. *ORBIT Journal*, 1(1). Available at: https://www.orbit-rri.org/ojs/index.php/orbit/article/view/26.

Kosterich, A., 2016. Reconfiguring the 'Hits': The New Portrait of Television Program Success in an Era of Big Data. *International Journal on Media Management*, 18(1), pp.43–58.

Kosterich, A. & Napoli, P.M., 2016. Reconfiguring the Audience Commodity. *Television & New Media*, 17(3), pp.254–271.

Landau, N., 2016. *TV Outside the Box: Trailblazing in the Digital Television Revolution*, New York: Focal Press.

Laporte, N., 2017. Netflix Offers a Rare Look Inside Its Strategy for Global Domination. *Fast Company*, 23 Oct. Available at: https://www.fastcompany.com/40484686/netflix-offers-a-rare-look-inside-its-strategy-for-global-domination [Accessed June 11, 2018].

Lotz, A.D., 2016. *Portals: A Treatise on Internet-Distributed Television*, Ann Arbor, MI: Maize Books.

Lynch, J., 2015. A First Look at Nielsen's Total Audience Measurement and How It Will Change the Industry. *Adweek*, 20 Oct. Available at: https://www.adweek.com/tv-video/first-look-nielsen-s-total-audience-measurement-and-how-it-will-change-industry-167661/ [Accessed August 14, 2018].

McGuigan, L., 2015. Direct Marketing and the Productive Capacity of Commercial Television: T-Commerce, Advanced Advertising, and the Audience Product. *Television & New Media*, 16(2), pp.196–214.

Mackenzie, A., 2015. The Production of Prediction: What Does Machine Learning Want? *European Journal of Cultural Studies*, 18(4–5), pp.429–445.

Maheshwari, S., 2017. Networks Offer Taste of Future, and Marketers Want More. *New York Times*, 22 May, p.1.

Mikos, L., 2016. Digital Media Platforms and the Use of TV Content: Binge Watching and Video-on-Demand in Germany. *Media and Communication*, 4(3), pp.154–161.

Morris, J.W., 2015. Curation by Code: Infomediaries and the Data Mining of Taste. *European Journal of Cultural Studies*, 18(45), pp.446–463.

Napoli, P.M., 2010. *Audience Evolution: New Technologies and the Transformation of Media Audiences*, New York: Columbia University Press.

Napoli, P.M., 2014. Automated Media: An Institutional Theory Perspective on Algorithmic Media Production and Consumption. *Communication Theory*, 24(3), pp.340–360.

Napoli, P.M., 2016. Special Issue Introduction: Big Data and Media Management. *International Journal on Media Management*, 18(1), pp.1–7.

Nelson, J.L. & Webster, J.G., 2016. Audience Currencies in the Age of Big Data. *International Journal on Media Management*, 18(1), pp.9–24.

Nielsen, 2013. Nielsen Launches 'Nielsen Twitter TV Ratings.' *Nielsen Press Room*, 7 Oct. Available at: http://www.nielsen.com/us/en/press-room/2013/nielsen-launches-nielsen-twitter-tv-ratings.html [Accessed August 14, 2018].

Parsons, J., 2017. Netflix Tips and Tricks: How to Get the Most out of the Streaming Service this Christmas. *The Mirror*, 27 Dec. Available at: https://www.mirror.co.uk/tech/netflix-tips-tricks-christmas-tv-9530695 [Accessed August 14, 2018].

Plantin, J.C., Lagoze, C., Edwards, P. N. & Sandvig, C., 2018. Infrastructure Studies Meet Platform Studies in the Age of Google and Facebook. *New Media and Society*, 20(1), pp.293–310.

Plummer, L., 2017. This is How Netflix's Top-Secret Recommendation System Works. *Wired*, 22 Aug. Available at: https://www.wired.co.uk/article/how-do-netflixs-algorithms-work-ma chine-learning-helps-to-predict-what-viewers-will-like [Accessed August 14, 2018].

Poggi, J., 2017. NBCU Seeks $1 Billion in Data-Driven Ad Sales. *AdAge*, 2 Mar. Available at: http://adage.com/article/special-report-tv-upfront/nbcu-commits-1-billion-ad-deals-move-nielsen-guarantees/308142/ [Accessed August 14, 2018].

Ravenscraft, E., 2016. These Secret Netflix Codes Can Reveal Tons of Hidden Categories. *Life Hacker*, 1 Sept. Available at: https://lifehacker.com/these-secret-netflix-codes-ca n-reveal-tons-of-hidden-ca-1752004157 [Accessed July 24, 2018].

Robinson, M.J., 2017. *Television on Demand: Curatorial Culture and the Transformation of TV*, New York and London: Bloomsbury.

Rogers, C., 2017. What is Programmatic? A Beginner's Guide. *Marketing Week*, 27 Mar. Available at: https://www.marketingweek.com/2017/03/27/programmatic-advertising/ [Accessed August 14, 2018].

Shalneva, E., 2017. My Best Friend the Algorithm is a Better Human Than You Are. *City A.M.*, 24 Feb., p.32.

Smith, T., 2017. Data vs Daenerys. *Sunday Times (South Africa)*, 30 Jul.

Striphas, T., 2015. Algorithmic Culture. *European Journal of Culture Studies*, 18(4–5), pp.395–412.

Titcomb, J., 2018. Netflix Movie Codes: The Secret Numbers That Unlock 1000s of Hidden Films and TV Shows. *The Telegraph*, 16 Jul. Available at: https://www.telegraph. co.uk/on-demand/0/netflix-codes-secret-numbers-unlock-1000s-hidden-film s-tv-shows/ [Accessed August 14, 2018].

van Dijck, J., 2013. *The Culture of Connectivity: A Critical History of Social Media*, Oxford and New York: Oxford University Press.

van Dijck, J. & Poell, T., 2013. Understanding Social Media Logic. *Media and Communica- tion*, 1(1), pp.2–14.

Vonderau, P., 2014. The Politics of Content Aggregation. *Television & New Media*, 16(8), pp.717–733.

Webster, J.G., 2014. *The Marketplace of Attention: How Audiences Take Shape in a Digital Age*, Cambridge, MA and London: MIT Press.

Wolk, A., 2015. *Over the Top: How the Internet is (Slowly but Surely) Changing the Television Industry*, CreateSpace Independent Publishing Platform.

CONCLUSION

The volatility of online TV

I was a child of the 'television generation,' growing up in the UK in the 1970s when television was a ubiquitous, but ephemeral, medium. My childhood experiences of television would bear little resemblance to those of a child growing up in the internet era. As a kid I had to choose from three linear channels of programming; if I missed a programme when it was broadcast it was not possible to watch it again, and with only one television set in the house I wasn't always the one who got to choose what to watch. In 2018, in many countries around the world, television has entered an internet era in which children (and adults) can watch television on a wide range of viewing devices through online TV services that offer large catalogues of content and the ability to select, pause, rewind and re-watch programmes at will in and outside of the home. These changes are made possible by the growth in access to high-speed broadband and 4G, and increased ownership of smartphones, tablets and internet-connected television sets. Although not global, where these conditions are apparent they form the basis of an internet era in which the internet simultaneously competes with and transforms television as a medium.

As discussed in Chapter 1 of this book, the internet era has expanded television at the level of technology and cultural form, increasing the complexity of TV as a medium. Once a medium of broadcasting, television can now be experienced in multiple ways – downloaded on a smartphone on the bus home, streamed onto a television set through a digital media player such as Roku, watched live through an online TV service on a tablet. Trying to make sense of television in the internet era can be likened to the task of unravelling a tangled ball of wool. All the strands seem to be intricately interconnected, but in ways that are not clear or visible, and it can be difficult to know where to begin. The aim of this book has been to offer some conceptual models that provide a clearer language with which to analyse the changes that are taking place to television in the internet era. These conceptual models should not be approached as rigid categorisations, but rather as tools that are designed to be played with, adapted and challenged. This is particularly important because, as this concluding chapter will argue, the internet era can be understood as a period of particular volatility for television. This makes it difficult to provide rigid definitions of online TV and demands a more flexible approach. The conceptual models developed in this book should be seen, therefore, not as immutable characteristics of online TV but as frameworks and tools that can help us think through the changes that are taking place to television within the tangled mess of the contemporary media ecosystem.

One consequence of the complexity and instability of the contemporary media landscape is that it can make it difficult to understand how and by whom power is enacted. In providing tools to analyse online TV, this book brings into focus the power dynamics of the online TV industry. In doing so, it has revealed the strategies and sites through which the online TV industry attempts to control access to culture. This concluding chapter explores how the conceptual frameworks developed in this book enable us to navigate the volatility of television in the internet era to reveal the power dynamics operating within the contemporary media ecosystem.

The volatility of television in the internet era manifests itself in a variety of ways: definitions of television are unstable; the internet ecosystem within which online TV services sit is fluid and fast-changing; the industry that produces online TV services is characterised by a range of competing business models; the attributes of online TV services are transient and subject to change; and the concept of television as 'service' is redefined. There are five approaches that this book has taken to navigate this volatility:

1. It has put forward a framework for examining change to television over time.
2. It has offered a definition of online TV.
3. It has provided two approaches to categorising the online TV industry.
4. It has explored ways of analysing the transient and ontogenetic forms of online TV interfaces and algorithms.
5. It has developed a conceptual model of television as 'service.'

A significant challenge faced by any contemporary study of television is the definitional instability of the word 'television.' In the internet era normative definitions of television have been undermined such that it is no longer possible to assume that we are all working from the same understanding of what the word 'television' means. Should YouTube channels that show episodes of classic TV shows count as television? What about news websites that accompany their written reports with short videos? This book has adopted a twofold approach to this problem. First, in Chapter 1, it argued that television as a medium can be understood to be composed of five elements: technological infrastructures and devices (viewing and add-on), and cultural services, frames and content. These five elements are shaped by (and can help to shape) contextual factors, such as organisational, regulatory and funding structures, as well as user experiences. Identification of these elements provides a framework and consistent language with which to talk about television and how it has changed over time. It allows comparison of contemporary television with television in earlier periods, bringing to the fore both the continuities and changes as television has converged with the internet.[1]

Second, in Chapter 2, this book developed a definition of online TV as *services that facilitate the viewing of editorially selected audiovisual content through internet-connected devices and infrastructure*. This definition is designed to draw attention to the differences between the wide range of services and sites that provide access to video and television-related content online. Online TV services offer access to editorially selected audiovisual content, which differentiates them from online video services like You-Tube that provide open platforms through which users can upload content. At the same time, the emphasis within online TV services on providing viewing experiences distinguishes them from sites that use video as a supplement to other forms of activity, such as news websites and pages dedicated to television programmes that privilege reading over viewing. As well as drawing attention to the differences between the wide range of contemporary online services that offer access to audiovisual content, this definition of online TV also reveals the continuities (as well as the changes) as television has developed from a broadcast to an internet-connected medium. It speaks to the ways in which contemporary online TV services share many of the characteristics of television from the broadcast, cable/satellite and digital eras. This is important because although the internet era has led to the expansion of television as a technology and a cultural form, these changes have been additive rather than substitutive; older forms of television, such as linear channels, continue to coexist and are integrated with newer forms of online TV. The definition of online TV developed within this book, therefore, enables examination of the ways in which entrenched understandings of television as a medium continue to influence the development of online TV, just as much as the internet challenges and changes television.

This definition of online TV, however, is not set in stone. As online TV develops we may see new services being launched that push at the distinctions made between online TV and online video within this book. My aim in Chapter 2, therefore, was not to provide a fixed and immutable definition of online TV. Rather, my intention has been to get us thinking about the attributes that differentiate the kinds of TV and audiovisual services that circulate online in the internet era – from how open or closed they are, to how they source their content, to the kinds of activities that they encourage from their users. These characteristics can be used in future studies to examine how and why online TV shifts and develops in particular ways.

The volatility of the internet era extends beyond the definitional instability of television to the industry that provides online TV services. The challenge of writing about online TV from an industrial perspective is twofold: this is a highly varied industry, and also one characterised by rapid change. There is no single type of business offering online TV services: the online TV industry is made up of a diverse range of companies with contrasting business models. Chapter 3 addressed this problem by offering two different (yet not incompatible) approaches to segmenting the online TV industry. The first approach focused on business origins and identified three kinds of organisation offering online TV services: *TV natives* that have extended an existing television service online; *online natives* that have originated online services for the internet ecosystem; and *content natives* that have extended a content-based business from another field into an online TV service. The benefit of this approach is that it draws attention to the different dependencies and competencies at work within the online TV industry. TV natives are embedded in TV industry ways of working and bound by the demands of their existing and ongoing television businesses. Online natives have expertise in originating services for an online environment. Content natives lack competencies in the provision of television and online services, and rely on the appeal of their content to niche communities of viewers.

However, this approach overlooks crucial differences between the companies categorised as online and TV natives. To address this, Chapter 3 offered an alternative approach based on categorising the industry according to core business focus rather than business origins. This approach revealed two kinds of organisation: *content businesses* and *technology businesses*. Content businesses are focused on the production, acquisition and delivery of content to viewers. Technology businesses provide the technological infrastructures and/or devices that are required to access online TV services. Approaching the industry through this lens drew into relief the ways in which different segments of the industry exert control over their competitors. However, it also demonstrated the dynamic and interdependent relationships between different segments of the online TV industry.

As with Chapter 2, the conceptual categories outlined in Chapter 3 should be understood as analytical tools rather than rigid descriptions of the industry. The online TV industry is characterised by rapid change. Digitalisation has lowered barriers to entry into certain aspects of the industry, including add-on devices, services and content. This has contributed to a media landscape characterised by accelerated and seemingly endless innovation. As a consequence, the strategies and business models of the companies that provide online TV services are subject to frequent revision. Over time the categories of TV, online and content natives, and of technology and content businesses, may no longer be adequate to describe the different kinds of organisation providing online TV services. In addition, these categories might not map easily onto the online TV industry in other countries. However, analysing the online TV industry according to business origins and business focus is an approach designed to accommodate the volatility of the online TV industry in that it can be easily adapted to other contexts and used to examine changes to the industry over time.

Combining analysis of business origins and business focus is particularly helpful in revealing the controlling points within the online TV industry through which competitive advantage is exerted. For example, Chapter 3 used these categories to map out the dominant points of competition and co-dependence in order to identify four core battlefields in the online TV industry: technology, content/rights, interfaces and data/algorithms. This is important because one danger is that the volatility of the internet era can function to mask the ways in which power is enacted within and through the online TV industry. When a media landscape appears so confusing and difficult to get a purchase on, it can be hard to see where and how power is enacted. In particular, this book has held up for scrutiny the industry and media rhetoric that online TV brings with it an abundance of content and increased control for users. Across the book, I have examined the ways in which technology, content/rights, interfaces and data/algorithms are used to constrain user agency and access even while creating an illusion of content ubiquity and user control. This is not to argue that these services determine how people use them in practice. Resistance is possible, and there are plenty of examples of it being exercised, such as the use of virtual private networks (VPNs) to circumvent geoblocking. However, while Michael Strangelove (2015, pp.11–5) emphasises the increased potential for users to challenge industry control, as online TV becomes more mainstream it is important to pay attention to the strategies and mechanisms used by the industry that aim to exert control, particularly as these are often disguised within a broader industry and media rhetoric of increased user agency.

Beyond definitional challenges, online TV services themselves can be understood as inherently volatile. Services can be launched with great fanfare, only to be dropped a few years later after failing to meet business expectations or due to a change in organisational strategy. Furthermore, the experience of using online TV services themselves can be highly variable. Online TV services can be frequently updated, with new iterations bringing novel features and removing old ones. The experience of using online TV services can also vary according to technology, often due to the costs involved in creating multiple versions of a service to run across the full range of available devices. Over and above this, many online TV services are highly personalised, using algorithms to adapt the content and interface on the basis of previous user behaviour. As a consequence, my experience of a particular online TV service will be different from yours.

This service variability makes the task of analysing the cultural form of online TV services a particular challenge. However, Chapters 5 and 6 demonstrated that it is possible to identify the broader protocols underlying online TV interfaces and algorithms. Doing so reveals the ways in which online TV services tend to create an illusion of content abundance and user agency while offering highly structured experiences that have much in common with traditional conceptualisations of television as a 'push' medium. Despite the industry rhetoric that the internet era brings greater control to the consumer, this analysis suggested that online TV services are seeking to adopt strategies that minimise the threat that a more geographically expansive, networked and participative internet ecosystem presents to traditional television business models. Interfaces and algorithms are a central, yet often overlooked, site upon which this battle is being enacted.

Beyond these specific battlegrounds, however, we can understand the broader industry rhetoric of increased user agency as being ideologically aligned with a shift in the ways in which television as a 'service' is understood. Central to this book has been the conceptualisation of online TV as a service that functions as the entry point for viewers to audiovisual content. The term service has a long and significant history in relation to television, carrying strong connotations of the histories of public service broadcasting in which television (and radio before it) was established to serve the needs of national publics understood and addressed as citizens. The concept of the online TV service is a far cry from this understanding of television as a public service, and speaks to a broader shift away from the idea of television as a public utility that should serve the nation to a neoliberal conceptualisation of television as a service that helps or does work for the individual viewer. Briefly tracing this change in meaning around the concept of television as service demonstrates how online TV is imbricated within broader neoliberal ideologies of individualised choice.

There are two broad definitions of service that can be applied to television:

- Public need: a system or organisation that is responsible for providing a particular thing/activity that people need – for example, the postal service, the National Health Service (NHS).
- Help/work: the act of helping or doing work for someone, the act of dealing with customers or clients; supplementary activities that are for the advantage of customers – for example, customer service, voluntary service.

Across much of the world, when television was introduced nationally it was positioned specifically within the definition of a public need. Although most apparent within countries with public service broadcasting – where television was developed as a public utility along with radio, water, electricity and gas – even in commercial systems, such as that in the USA, television was understood to act in the public interest. This concept of television as a public need was tied to the infrastructure of broadcasting where it was not possible to pay for television at the point of reception. With an aerial and a television set, programmes could flow unbidden into households; and this technological characteristic of television played an important role in shaping discourses about television as a powerful utility with the potential for significant social and cultural impact (Hendy 2013). Governments positioned broadcast television as a public need because it had the potential power to transform the lives and minds of those who watched it.

With cable, satellite and, later, digital television came the possibility of being able to pay for television at the point of reception. This new technological infrastructure burgeoned over the 1980s and 1990s largely within commercial hands during a broader political and economic period characterised by the rise of neoliberalism and deregulation. The provision of cable, satellite and digital television, funded largely by subscription, brought the second definition of service as help/work more significantly into play. Cable and satellite television providers, for example, needed to offer customer service to deal with consumers who wanted to buy, cancel, upgrade or complain about their cable or satellite provision. In addition, cable and satellite (and later digital) television also introduced systems that did work for viewers. Electronic programme guides (EPGs) helped subscribers navigate the increased number of channels, and personal video recorders (PVRs) helped customers not to miss the programmes that they liked by automating recording and offering reminders.

In relation to television, therefore, we might identify two parallel definitions of service. First, television can be understood as a service that fulfils a public need. This definition refers to the entire system responsible for providing television as a service to the public. The second definition describes the systems, processes and people that help enhance the TV viewing experience. This concept of the television service as help/work became more prominent from the cable/satellite era onwards in part because viewers gained choice over how television was delivered; viewers could opt to subscribe to cable or satellite services or not, and could choose between different kinds of cable/satellite packages as well as amongst an increased number of television channels. Service, in this sense of helping customers, became a key distinguishing factor in the commercial market for television. Viewers could choose a cable/satellite package on the basis of the programmes or channels it offered, but also on the basis of the attributes of its service (the features of the set-top box, the quality of the customer service and so on).

The emergence of online TV services in the internet era can be understood as an extension of this concept of service as help/work that came to the fore in the cable/satellite era. Online TV services are premised on the offer of providing easy access to the content that we want to watch, and include tools designed to do work for users, such as recommendation engines that offer personalised lists of content to choose from. The industry rhetoric that online TV services help us watch what we want, when and how we want (see, for example, Harrington 2014) is the epitome of the ways in which enlightenment notions of public service television operated in the interests of citizens, nations and democracy have been replaced by commercial, neoliberal notions of user choice. Online TV represents, therefore, a shift in which the idea of television as service has been transformed from an over-arching system constructed for the public good to a personalised product designed to fulfil individual demands for user choice.

This is not to argue that online TV services can never operate as public services. The ways in which individual online TV services function to help or do work for the user could be reconceptualised through the lens of the public interest. This would involve bringing the concept of the public into the design and philosophy of online TV services. Rather than thinking of online TV as serving the needs of individuals, we could approach it as serving the needs of the public more broadly. For example, personalisation might function less to provide recommendations based on previous user behaviour, and more to structure viewing experiences designed to serve the public need for an informed, educated and cultured citizenry. Interfaces could be designed to encourage greater diversity of media consumption and to offer opportunities for users to feed back and communicate with industry. A truly 'public service' online TV service would help or do work for the individual only insofar as it supported a broader remit to serve the public.

However, for online TV to truly operate in the interests of the public, we need to approach the television service as a whole system operated in the public interest, not just as individual services. Doing so would require extending the requirement to operate in the public interest across all online TV services, not just those funded by public money or with specific public service remits. Furthermore, as television converges with the internet, any attempt to meaningfully support the development of television as a public service needs to recognise that online TV services sit within a broader fluid and interconnected internet ecosystem. Doing so requires us to think about how the values and protections at the heart of the public service mission might be extended across the whole system of the internet, so that we might have media spaces for searching, communicating, sharing and watching that are designed to serve the needs of the public as citizens.

In the current political climate, it is difficult to image much appetite for such wide-reaching regulatory intervention into the media landscape, and I hold out little hope that I will see such changes in my lifetime. In the meantime, as students, scholars and users of contemporary television, it is important that we pay particular attention to the ways in which the industry attempts to exert control over our encounters with audiovisual culture online. By taking the television 'service' as a focus of analysis, this book has directed attention specifically to the ways in which the industry attempts to structure the experience of television through control of technologies, content/rights, interfaces and data/algorithms. As we follow the volatile developments of television over the subsequent months, years and decades, it is my hope that the concepts and frameworks established across this book provide other scholars with tools with which to trace the varied, dynamic and volatile ways in which power is enacted as online TV expands and develops around the world.

Note

1 This model of television as a medium could also be used to facilitate international comparisons.

Bibliography

Harrington, K., 2014. Changing the Way We Watch TV. *Forbes*, 6 Mar. Available at: https://www.forbes.com/sites/kevinharrington/2014/03/06/changing-the-way-we-wa tch-tv/#5117dd455eeb [Accessed August 14, 2018].

Hendy, D., 2013. *Public Service Broadcasting*, Basingstoke: Palgrave Macmillan.

Strangelove, M., 2015. *Post-TV: Piracy, Cord-Cutting, and the Future of Television*, Toronto: University of Toronto Press.

GLOSSARY

Add-on devices devices that attach to a viewing device to enable extra features and/or functionality.

Algorithms computational processes that define a series of steps or instructions in order to produce a desired outcome.

Binge viewing the practice of watching several episodes of a television series in one sitting.

Content businesses online TV providers that focus primarily on the production, acquisition and delivery of content to viewers.

Content delivery network (CDN) a geographically distributed network of servers that work together to provide fast delivery of internet content.

Content natives online TV providers that have extended a content-based business in another field into an online TV service.

Cost plus the industry practice of paying producers up front for the full production costs required to make a programme, plus a production fee.

Deficit financing the industry practice of paying production companies less than the costs required to make a programme, but giving them some or all of the secondary rights.

Digital rights management (DRM) the technological means by which access to copyrighted material is controlled.

External data data generated within websites and social media sites that is related, but external, to an online TV service.

Frames the cultural form that organises television content and services, shaping how they are experienced – for example, the electronic programme guide or interface.

Graphical user interface (GUI) a human–computer interface that utilises graphical elements (such as icons and menus).

Interfaces   features of software that function to convert the language of binary code, through which computers operate, into the textual language of images, words and sounds that humans can easily understand.

Internal data   data generated within an online TV service.

Internet era   the period roughly from the late-2000s in which the penetration of fast broadband speeds, tablets, smartphones and internet-connected televisions created the conditions for the emergence of online TV.

Internet protocol television (IPTV)   television content and services delivered on a private, dedicated internet protocol network managed by a service provider, usually one of the telecoms, cable and/or satellite providers offering combined internet and television services.

Internet service provider (ISP)   a company that provides customers with access to the internet.

Linear television   television programmes organised into a schedule within a television channel in which one piece of content flows seamlessly into the next.

Market information regime   the industry-wide agreed and accepted informational basis upon which a market operates.

Metadata   data that provides information about other data, such as descriptions that classify content within an online TV database.

Multichannel networks (MCNs)   companies that own or affiliate with multiple channels on online video services like YouTube to facilitate audience development, collaborations, digital rights management and monetisation.

Nonlinear television   television programmes organised into a database in which users can select what to watch from a menu of content.

Online natives   online TV providers that have originated online services for the internet ecosystem.

Online TV   services that facilitate the viewing of editorially selected audiovisual content through internet-connected devices and infrastructure.

Over-the-top (OTT)   television content and services delivered via an internet browser or application over the public internet.

Platforms   flexible infrastructures that operate an intermediary function through the aggregation of a range of services for multiple users that are designed to be extended and elaborated by third parties.

Products   one or a set of content, services and/or technologies that meet a defined user need and are united by a clear brand.

Protocols   sets of rules that govern how users can behave when using an online service.

Technological infrastructure   the technologies required to deliver television signals to viewers (e.g. aerials, cables, satellites).

Technology businesses   online TV providers that are responsible for the provision of the technological infrastructures and/or devices required to access online TV services.

Television content   the audiovisual programmes, adverts and interstitials delivered through television services.

Television service   the entry point for viewers to television content.

TV natives   online TV providers that have extended an existing TV service online.

Viewing devices   devices through which audiovisual television content can be viewed.

INDEX

Page numbers in **bold** refer to figures. Page numbers in *italic* refer to tables.